Victims of Environmental Harm

In recent years, the increasing focus on climate change and environmental degradation has prompted unprecedented attention on the criminal liability of individuals, organizations and even states for polluting activities. These developments have given rise to a new area of criminological study, often called 'green criminology'. Yet in all the theorizing that has taken place in this area, there is still a marked absence of specific focus on those actually suffering harm as a result of environmental degradation. This book represents a unique attempt to substantively conceptualize and examine the place of such 'environmental victims' in criminal justice systems both nationally and internationally.

Grounded in a comparative approach and drawing on critical criminological arguments, this volume examines many of the areas traditionally considered by victimologists and relates these areas to victims of environmental crime and, more widely, environmental harm. These include victims' rights, compensation, treatment by criminal justice systems, and participation in that process. The book approaches the issue of 'environmental victimization' from a 'social harms' perspective (as opposed to a 'criminal harms' one), thus problematizing the definitions of environmental crime found within most jurisdictions. *Victims of Environmental Harm* concludes by mapping out the contours of potential further research into a developing green victimology and how this agenda might inform criminal justice reform and policy-making at national and global levels.

This book will be of interest to researchers across a number of disciplines including criminology, international law, victimology, socio-legal studies and physical sciences, as well as to professionals involved in policy-making processes.

Matthew Hall obtained a PhD from the University of Sheffield in 2007, having previously graduated from Sheffield's MA in International Criminology Programme. He is now senior lecturer in Law and Criminal Justice at Sheffield, where he teaches many aspects of criminology, as well as criminal law and the law of evidence. He is an editor for the *International Review of Victimology*.

Routledge Frontiers of Criminal Justice

1 **Sex Offenders: Punish, Help, Change or Control?**
Theory, policy and practice explored
Edited by Jo Brayford, Francis Cowe and John Deering

2 **Building Justice in Post-Transition Europe**
Processes of criminalisation within Central and Eastern European societies
Edited by Kay Goodall, Margaret Malloch and Bill Munro

3 **Technocrime, Policing and Surveillance**
Edited by Stéphane Leman-Langlois

4 **Youth Justice in Context**
Community, compliance and young people
Mairead Seymour

5 **Women, Punishment and Social Justice**
Human rights and penal practices
Margaret Malloch and Gill McIvor

6 **Handbook of Policing, Ethics and Professional Standards**
Edited by Allyson MacVean, Peter Spindler and Charlotte Solf

7 **Contrasts in Punishment**
An explanation of Anglophone excess and Nordic exceptionalism
John Pratt and Anna Eriksson

8 **Victims of Environmental Harm**
Rights, recognition and redress under national and international law
Matthew Hall

9 **Doing Probation Work**
Identity in a criminal justice occupation
Rob C. Mawby and Anne Worrall

Victims of Environmental Harm

Rights, recognition and redress under national and international law

Matthew Hall

Routledge
Taylor & Francis Group
LONDON AND NEW YORK

First published 2013
by Routledge
2 Park Square, Milton Park, Abingdon, Oxon OX14 4RN

Simultaneously published in the USA and Canada
by Routledge
711 Third Avenue, New York, NY 10017

Routledge is an imprint of the Taylor & Francis Group, an informa business

British Library Cataloguing in Publication Data
A catalogue record for this book is available from the British Library

Library of Congress Cataloging-in-Publication Data
Hall, Matthew (Criminologist)
Victims of environmental harm: rights, recognition and redress under national and international law/Matthew Hall.
pages cm. – (Routledge frontiers of criminal justice)
Includes bibliographical references and index.
1. Offenses against the environment. 2. Victims of crimes–Legal status, laws, etc. 3. Reparation (Criminal justice) 4. Liability for environmental damages I. Title.
K5278.H35 2013
344.04'6–dc23

2012033403

ISBN: 978-0-415-67700-4 (hbk)
ISBN: 978-0-203-08344-4 (ebk)

Typeset in Times New Roman
by Wearset Ltd, Boldon, Tyne and Wear

MIX
Paper from responsible sources
FSC www.fsc.org FSC® C004839

Printed and bound in Great Britain by
TJ International Ltd, Padstow, Cornwall

For Kate

Contents

Foreword

The field of 'green criminology' has grown remarkably in recent years and will no doubt continue to expand rapidly as environmental conditions deteriorate. Climate change, in particular, is set to fundamentally transform the present world. The impact of global warming is already being felt, and rises in the Earth's temperature will continue to generate increasingly profound shifts in weather conditions and climatic events. The devastation wrought by Superstorm Sandy along the eastern seaboard of the United States in October 2012 was not simply a once-in-a-generation phenomenon; it marks part of the beginning of regular chaotic events, the predicted result of anthropogenic contributions to greenhouse gas emissions.

Meanwhile, the demise of plant and animal species, both through legal and illegal means, the growth in human population, and the shrinking of natural resources (such as drinking water) and non-renewable resources (such as oil and gas), all add up to enormous pressures on the environment generally. With biodiversity under threat, global resilience to the impacts of climate change is being reduced. Yet the commodification of nature ensures that economic value is, ironically, best realised in conditions of advancing scarcity. Environmental degradation and destruction is, for some, profitable.

Simultaneously, the global pursuit of the Western consumer lifestyle daily adds to the pollution of air, water and land. Factories belch out smoke, as do cars, buses and trucks designed to transport people and goods. Illegal transfer of electronic waste is fast becoming one of the biggest environmental crimes, while vast areas of the planet continue to suffer deforestation in the global scramble for new mega-mines, for coal-seam gas, for GMO crops and for pastures for cattle and sheep. Changing land uses are creating new toxic towns; new forms of recycling of ships and electronic products are producing contaminated communities. And the planet continues to heat up.

The study of environmental crime and harm has been the core focus of green criminology for more than two decades. Who is doing what, where, and how have been the key questions of those working in this area. The main focus has been on offenders and perpetrators of harm, and on detailing specific instances of environmental vandalism. The pursuit of social and ecological justice has informed much of this work, yet aside from that literature specifically linked to and stemming from the Environmental Justice movements, little has expressly been written about environmental victims.

This is now set to change. As our collective knowledge of global environmental harm increases, there is an appreciation that those who suffer from environmental victimisation deserve sustained analysis and strategic interventions in their own right. As Matthew Hall demonstrates in this book, however, this is not a straightforward task. Environmental victimisation is, indeed, an extremely complicated and multifaceted issue. The complexity is much further compounded if we include the non-human in addition to the human as victim.

As with 'ordinary' victims within criminal justice, there are persistent issues of recognition, acknowledgement, participation, redress, compensation and restoration that pertain to matters of justice for victims of environmental crime. Unpacking the myriad issues that obtain in such cases is a key task of the present work by Hall. Insights are needed, for example, into the impacts of environmental harm on human victims, including the inequalities in these impacts among diverse population groups. It is vital to gain a picture of how such harms are or could be dealt with within existing criminal laws, and of the potential for human rights law to offer protection and newly conceptualised rights in relation to the environment. What is to be done with and for victims and survivors of environmental harm takes us into the realms of restitution, compensation and restoration, and is likewise in need of illumination.

Dealing with issues pertaining to environmental victims takes the reader into murky legal waters, abstract theoretical matters and substantive areas of application. Offenders are victims, and victims are offenders. The state is perpetrator of harm, and giver of solace and recompense. The Janus nature of criminalisation and victimisation means that there are often more than two sides to specific questions. It is for this reason that calls for a 'green victimology' include assertions of the importance of a critical, holistic approach to the subject matter. Not all is as it seems.

Yet the need for recognition and redress is substantial and urgent, and demands action in the here and now. The intertwining of academic and activist projects are thus crucial to the further development of green victimology.

This book provides a broad conceptual canvas upon which dedicated discussion and debate about the victims of environmental harm take place. It is the first book of its kind. While providing a sophisticated and careful analysis of existing laws and policy applications in this area, it constantly affirms the need for further refinement and continued development of the criminological imagination. Accordingly, it provides the platform for analysis of what is, what could be, and what should be when it comes to the situation of victims of environmental harm. In this regard, it is intended to provoke and stimulate as much as to establish conceptual precision and summarise existing institutional responses. This, too, is what makes the book foundational for those of us interested in the study of environmental harm and in actively supporting those most affected by the processes and institutions that are destroying life as we know it.

Analysis of who or what is being harmed ultimately leads to consideration of environmental victims. This, in turn, highlights the need for a green victimology. In this respect, Matthew Hall has provided a path-breaking initiative that will help to guide research and action in this area for many years to come.

Rob White
University of Tasmania, Australia

Acknowledgements

I owe a large debt to numerous individuals who helped make the following volume a reality. I would particularly like to thank my colleagues from the University of Sheffield Centre for Criminological Research, and from the University of Sheffield School of Law, for innumerable discussions, consultations and brainstorming sessions on every aspect of this project. Dr Richard Collins and Dr Russell Buchan in particular have always been on hand to help this criminologist understand and appreciate the subtleties of international law and its scholarship. I would also like to thank Professor Stephen Farrall for his important advice and insights into numerous aspects of criminological theory and research and how they might apply to climate change and environmental degradation more widely. My thanks also to Professor Rob White of the University of Tasmania for his invaluable advice at the early stages of this project and for penning the foreword to this volume: which of course is to say nothing of his enormous contributions to the development of green criminology as a whole.

A special mention must be made here of Professor Duncan French of the University of Lincoln School of Law. Professor French was the international environmental lawyer who initially asked me what, if anything, criminology had to say about environmental victims. It is hoped that this volume will go some way to providing an initial, if somewhat belated, answer.

Finally, I would like to thank my wife Claire, my son Edward and my daughter Kate, whose support and love – as ever – are reflected on every page of this volume.

Any errors or omissions remain my own.

Abbreviations

BBC	British Broadcasting Corporation
CERCLA	Comprehensive Environmental Response, Compensation, and Liability Act, 1980 (USA)
CIViTAS	Institute for the Study of Civil Society (UK)
CNTV	Chinese Network Television
CVRA	Crime Victims' Rights Act 2004 (USA)
ECHR	European Convention on Human Rights
ECtHR	European Court of Human Rights
FCCC	United Nations Framework Convention on Climate Change
FTA	Freight Transport Association (UK)
ICC	International Criminal Court
ILC	International Law Commission
IPCC	Intergovernmental Panel on Climate Change
NGO	Non-governmental organization
RSPCA	The Royal Society for the Prevention of Cruelty to Animals (UK)
TSDF	Treatment, storage and disposal facilities
UNECE	United Nations Economic Commission for Europe
UNEP	United Nations Environment Programme
UNHRC	United Nations Human Rights Committee
WHO	World Health Organization

1 Victims, environmental harm and international law

1.1 Introduction and goals of this book

In the twenty-first century, criminal victimization has become a major area of academic debate and policy movement across most of the developed world. One of the most significant consequences of this has been the light that has been shed on the needs and suffering of a multitude of victims who were previously all but invisible in the eyes of both criminal justice systems and the public at large. Such victims include those affected by domestic violence; child and other vulnerable victims; the friends and family of murder victims; and both male and female victims of rape.[1] Recognition of the problems faced by these distinct groups, both within and beyond criminal justice processes, has undoubtedly led to significant improvements in their treatment and support in many jurisdictions (Hall, 2010). Yet the victimological literature increasingly recognizes that other groups have to some extent been left behind the main vanguard of this 'victims' movement'. Among these still neglected groups are those victimized by actions of the state, corporate victims, the corporate and individual victims of white collar crime, and those harmed by the effects of environmental degradation perpetrated or brought about by individuals, corporations and states. It is with this last group, which I will refer to as 'environmental victims', that this volume is primarily concerned.[2]

In recent years, the enduring problem of environmental pollution and climate change[3] has become an accepted reality for most scholars and practitioners working in both the physical and social sciences.[4] The progress made in our understanding of the causes of environmental degradations of all kinds has presented a number of challenges for lawyers in particular, as questions are increasingly raised concerning the responsibility of individuals, corporations and states for environmental harms. Given the transboundary nature of the issue, international law has also been obliged to adapt itself rapidly to meet these new challenges, with the development of international environmental law.[5] Surprisingly, however, there has been almost no attempt by commentators to combine an analysis of these developments in the domestic and international legal orders with some of the relatively well-established lines of critical criminological and victimological enquiry.

In light of the above observations, the present volume addresses the issue of environmental victimization: representing the first broad-scale attempt to apply ideas and concepts developed by victimologists over the last 30 years to this relatively new field. The book will also explore the question of who are the victims of such environmental harms and how such victimization is often unequally distributed among the world's populations (see White, 2008a). The resulting analysis will be grounded in the author's long-term interest in the legal position and rights of victims of crime and other social harms (Hall, 2009, 2010) coupled with the growing field of green criminology (Edwards *et al.*, 1996) and the development of international environmental law.

In combining these areas of analysis, and thereby approaching the issue of environmental crime and environmental victimization from an interdisciplinary and comparative perspective, this volume will offer fresh insight into the important questions raised by such victimization. In particular, because international (environmental) law has tended to exclude consideration of the individual in favour of the state, the approach taken by this volume will offer a rare, *unified* consideration of both structure and agency as they relate to such matters. Given the growing interest from governments and international organizations in the harms caused by environmental pollution (spurred on by the developing evidence of the full impact of environmental degradation of all kinds), such an analysis is long overdue, and should prove an important contribution to the on-going policy debate now occurring in all jurisdictions on how they can adapt their justice systems (and other forms of conflict redress) to address these matters. To this end, this volume will present a theoretical framework for understanding and approaching the issue of environmental victimization through criminal (and other) justice mechanisms.

With the above aims in mind, the principal research questions to be addressed in this volume are these:

1 Can criminal justice play an effective role at the national and international levels in providing official recognition, support and redress for victims of environmental harm?

This necessitates two secondary questions:

2 What are the limitations to current provisions for official recognition, support and redress for victims of environmental harm[6] through criminal justice, both within individual jurisdictions domestically and at the international level?
3 What does an interdisciplinary approach (encompassing socio-legal analysis, criminology, victimology and international law) teach us about how to effectively address these limitations?

The principal contention of this book is that closer collaboration between international legal scholars, criminologists interested in green issues generally, and those interested in victimization specifically, has the potential to markedly advance our understanding of a wide range of under-researched issues, including: the support needs of those affected by environmental harms; the state's responsibility for the adverse impacts of climate change; and the mechanisms of redress and compensation available to those suffering the impacts of man-made environmental disasters at the national and international level.

To clarify the intended scope of this volume, two points need to be made from the outset. First, as mentioned above, this book is primarily concerned with the victims of *man-made* environmental disasters as opposed to the 'casualties' (Williams, 1996) of natural catastrophes. Of course, the distinction between what is 'natural' and what is 'man-made' may be at the heart of any dispute over the obligations of the state or other parties to provide compensation, restitution and support to victims. An analysis and comparison of the state's responsibility in both cases forms an important component of Chapter 5. The second preliminary point is that this volume is chiefly concerned with the *human* victims of man-made environmental degradation. This is not however to deny or dismiss the wealth of arguments in the literature that such an anthropocentric approach ignores the complex relationship between humans, animals and the biosphere (Lynch and Stretesky, 2003), together with wider notions of ecological justice (White, 2008a), and these issues will not be excluded from my overall analysis. Indeed, White (2011) has also found it necessary to confine his most recent chapter dedicated to victims of environmental harm to human victims, as a way of situating his discussion within a conception of environmental rights (as an extension of human social rights), and also in the context of an argument[7] that environmental victimization, like other forms of victimization, is an active social process. The present volume draws on a similar theoretical approach but, unlike White, factors in a more legalistic analysis of the position of environmental victims at the national and international levels. At the same time, however, I fully acknowledge (along with White) that a book of this length can inevitably offer discussion of only one part of a far wider problem.

Three further terms require explanation before proceeding further. First, as I have already noted, individuals or groups harmed by the effects of environmental degradation perpetrated or brought about by individuals, corporations and states will be referred to as 'environmental victims' in this volume. It is important to note that this term is deliberately wider than 'victims of environmental crime'. It will be seen later in this chapter that the question of whether any given environmental victimization is officially criminalized within a given jurisdiction (or internationally) will be an important theme for this volume as a whole.

Second, throughout the course of this book I will often draw contrasts between both environmental victims and victims of environmental crime on the one hand with 'traditional victims' on the other. 'Traditional victims' here refers broadly to all classifications of victims of crime which have received extended attention by criminologists and victimologists, and by policy-makers, in most developed jurisdictions (see Goodey, 2005). These include those usually covered on crime surveys (victims of acquisitive and violent crime, the latter comprising both 'public' violence and domestic violence) and victims of sexual crimes. I am also including within this category secondary victims ('survivors') of homicide. The term is not used in a prescriptive sense, and will usually be used to draw comparisons between the availability of services, support and redress mechanisms for other kids of victims and the relative absence of such facilities for environmental victims.

Finally, this volume will use the term 'environmental degradation'. This has been variously defined (see Lonergan, 1998), but is used here in the same sense as the UN's International Strategy for Disaster Reduction (2007): 'the reduction of the capacity of the environment to meet social and ecological objectives and needs' (unpaginated). Note that this definition includes the effects of climate change more broadly. In light of the above definition of 'environmental victims', in practice this volume will often be discussing environmental degradation brought about by human actions or inactions, albeit of course the question of culpability will often be key to any associated legal debates.

The remainder of this chapter has two key purposes. First, it will set out the academic and conceptual background informing the above research questions. Second, the chapter will highlight at various points the potential contribution of an interdisciplinary approach (advocated by this volume) to these issues, both as a means of taking forward this established literature and, perhaps more importantly, of converting the *theory* into something *practical* that can be utilized by legal practitioners and policy-makers. It seems logical to begin this discussion with an introduction to a number of the key literatures that will be drawn upon, starting with the developing field of 'green criminology' and moving on to the growth of the victims' movement; cultural victimology; 'green victimology'; and the role of the state in environmental harms.

1.1.1 Green criminology?

'Green criminology' is defined by White (2008a) as 'basically refer[ing] to the study of environmental harm, environmental laws and environmental regulation by criminologists' (p. 8). Although the term 'environmental criminology' is sometimes used interchangeably with 'green criminology',[8] the former label has more traditionally been associated with the study of crime patterns as they relate to particular locations. For this reason the terms 'green criminology' and 'green victimology' are generally employed throughout this volume. Indeed, on the question of terminology Ruggiero and South (2010) have argued:

> [F]or all that it invites criticism as lacking precision and possibly being open to interpretation as aligned with a 'green political party' position, the term 'Green Criminology' has become the most familiar and suggestive term, and also serves well as the most comprehensive conceptual umbrella.
>
> (p. 247)

As hinted by this extract, the use of such terminology is still contentious in some quarters. On this point, Lynch and Stretesky (2003) have refined the use of the term 'green' in this context to include environmentally damaging outcomes brought about by actions that are not necessarily illegal[9] or in contravention of regulatory frameworks, or even at odds with public morals. As noted by Skinnider (2011):

> [M]any environmental disruptions are actually legal and take place with the consent of society. Classifying what is an environmental crime involves a complex balancing of communities' interest in jobs and income with ecosystem maintenance, biodiversity and sustainability.
>
> (p. 2)

Or, as Gibbs *et al.* (2010) have put it:

> A grey area emerges for environmental risks that are not currently subject to regulation or criminal enforcement but where further understanding of the risk may lead stakeholders to argue for regulation and/or criminalization.
>
> (p. 133)

Halsey (2004), in criticizing Lynch and Stretesky (2003), has argued that the label 'green criminology' is in fact too simplistic to adequately reflect the complexities of the issues at hand:

> Indeed, I want to suggest that the term 'green' should be jettisoned from criminological discourse, primarily because it does not adequately capture the inter-subjective, inter-generational, or inter-ecosystemic costs which combine to produce scenarios of harm.
>
> (p. 247)

For Lynch (1990) 'green criminology' was a product of the coming together of at least three movements. First, 'ecofeminists' (as Lynch understands this label) from the mid-1970s began arguing that the effects of environmental degradation fall disproportionately on women compared to men[10] (Griffin, 1978; Nash, 1989). Lynch attributes the second foundation of green criminology to growing discussions of what has come to be known as 'environmental racism'. This is the suggestion that the impact of environmental degradation falls disproportionately on some races (Collin, 1994). Finally, Lynch draws on what he calls 'red/green alliances', by which he means forms of ecological socialisms, the adherents of which sought to emphasize the inequalities of wealth and power in society which lead to increased environmental degradation while also ensuring it is the poor and socially excluded who bear the brunt of its negative effects (Pepper, 1993).

What is significant about Lynch's conception of the growth of green criminology for the purposes of the present volume is that all three of his pillars are essentially commentaries on the *victims* of environmental degradation. Particular discussion of the unequal impact of environmental victimization (by socio-economic status, nationality and race as well as by gender) is presented in Chapter 2. Given the absence of debates focusing on environmental victims in the modern literature, it is notable that such discussions were in fact at the heart of green criminology in its earliest forms.

Gibbs *et al.* (2010) provide an excellent overview of the various classifications and definitions of green criminology, starting with the 'legalistic' understanding of environmental crimes as violations of criminal laws[11] designed to protect the health and safety of people, the environment or both (p. 126). The legalistic position is contrasted to the socio-legal approach, which acknowledges that the differences between 'crime', 'deviance', 'civil wrongs' and 'regulatory violations' are all socially constructed. Both perspectives are contrasted to the concept of 'environmental justice', which is discussed in greater detail below and is generally distinguished by being less anthropocentric. The final classification drawn upon by Gibbs *et al.* is the notion of 'biocentric' or 'deep green' perspectives, which construe environmental crime as 'any human activity that disrupts a biotic system' (p. 127).

One of the key contentions of Gibbs *et al.* (2010) is that '[g]reen criminology needs an interdisciplinary framework' (p. 129).[12] As noted above, the present volume is very much a response to such concerns. For these authors, the difficulty with much of the existing literature in this field is that it is value-laden and presupposes set conclusions to environmental problems (criminalization, regulation etc.). Their 'conservation criminology' is research-based and draws on three specified disciplines: criminal justice and criminology; risk and decision analysis; and natural resource conservation and management. The advantages and key principles of this approach are worth reproducing here:

> The explicitly stated need to integrate perspectives – within and across disciplines – forces the inclusion of multiple stakeholders, theories, methods and interventions rather than focusing exclusively on any one. Theoretical integration forces theoretical elaboration as insights regarding the strengths and weaknesses of current perspectives are shared across disciplines. As a result, the integration of disciplines increases knowledge of the relationship among and between factors that shape human interactions with the environment and choices to influence sustainability of resources. Conservation criminology also calls for scholars to avoid a priori assumptions about the causes and solutions to environmental risks, attempting to avoid an overly anthropogenic or ecocentric definition of the problem or of potential interventions. In addition, conservation criminology calls for scholars to be dynamic and adaptive. Scholarship should evolve as technical assessments are updated, public perceptions and regulatory interventions to address environmental risk change and new issues emerge. Finally, conservation criminology encourages scholars to be guided by principles of inductive reasoning.
>
> (p. 139)

The present volume is intended to reflect many of the epistemological values expressed in the above statement. It could be argued that, by incorporating a specific focus on international *law* (which Gibbs *et al.* do not), this work inherently assumes that such *law* is the key to the dilemmas presented by environmental harm. In fact, an important goal of this project is to expose areas where law of any kind may indeed be *insufficient* to tackle such issues. The argument that, ultimately, the criminalization of environmental harms is unlikely to achieve a great deal is made by Mares (2010), who advocates an alternative civilizing or 'shaming' approach[13] consistent with developments in wider criminology around the notion of 'restorative justice' (Bottoms, 2003):

> Rather than relying on strict criminalization of behaviors harming our carrying capacity,[14] I would suggest that we emphasize both collective and individual responsibility for our actions and that we underline their negative impact by employing a shaming approach (Braithwaite 1989). This would require a cultural shift in thinking about the environment and take the form of a 'civilizing offensive', or 'civilizing spurt'.
>
> (p. 289)

Notwithstanding these views, there are arguably negative implications to completely divorcing social harms of any type from the ambit of law, in that this might represent or lead to a divesting of responsibility by the state. The criminal law is the principal means by which victims of any harm can acquire the recognition we know they desire from official sources (see Miers, 1980). Hall and Shapland (forthcoming) have argued that the concept of 'social harm' runs the risk of a further side-lining of victims by officials (fixated with 'criminal harms') and by those with power in society. This issue will be returned to later in the chapter. At this stage it seems expedient to introduce the development of the 'victims' movement' and of 'victimology' more generally.

1.1.2 The 'victims' movement'

Most discussions centred around the broad concept of 'victimization' begin with some historical introduction to the global spread of activist, academic, and policy interest in this issue across jurisdictions, which is often described collectively as the 'victims' movement'. It is clear, however, that what different groups mean by 'victims', and their respective views about which types of victimization merit particular attention, differ markedly. Thus labelling this as a 'movement' at all is to some extent misleading,[15] in that it suggests a clarity and consistency of purpose that was (and is) often not present, certainly not among jurisdictions and often not within them.[16] For example, Pointing and Maguire (1988) discuss how the victims' movement in the US was originally driven by a host of 'strange bedfellows' concerned with different aspects of victimization in its broadest sense. These ranged from feminists[17] and mental health practitioners, to survivors of war and atrocities such as the Nazi concentration camps (Young, 1997) and victims of the apartheid regime in South Africa (Garkawe, 2004). Notwithstanding such complexities, it is important in the context of the present study to examine the background to these developments in an effort to explain why victims of *environmental harm* appear to have been overlooked throughout much of this history.

Reviews of the development of the victims' movement are almost as diverse in scope and aims as the movement itself (see Maguire, 1991; Kirchhoff, 1994; Jackson, 2003). In view of this, any attempt to summarize these developments should be approached with caution and with due regard to Kearon and Godfrey's (2007) warning against the academic tendency to 'force social phenomena into false chronologies' (p. 30). With such warning labels firmly in place, I have previously conceptualized the development of the movement in terms of three distinct waves (Hall, 2009). The first of these waves was characterized by a growth of academic interest in victims. The second saw the development of victim assistance organizations in many jurisdictions, while the third corresponds to the acceptance of victims as the topic of mainstream policy-making and legal reform in the criminal justice systems of such jurisdictions.

This set of 'third-wave' developments is demonstrated by the publication of service standards for victims of crime in many jurisdictions and, in most cases, the enactment of primary legislation. Of course, these stages did not develop in any jurisdiction in a neatly chronological fashion. In reality there has been much overlap and continuing development on all three fronts up until the time of writing, which will almost certainly continue beyond it. Moreover, any discussion of policy-making in this area must be read with reference to the specific point made by Rock (1986, 1990, 1998) in a number of contexts that reforms presented as 'victim policies' may derive from quite different political agendas and serve other ends.[18] Perhaps one of the most telling observations, made by Furedi (1998), is that victimization is an issue which is able to galvanize support from both sides of the political spectrum:

> Unlike traditional conservative contributors, who treated individuals as victims of evil, feminist and leftist writers portrayed them as victims of a system of patriarchy. But although there were differences in the interpretation of aspects of the problem, there was a shared assumption that people are victims. It was this unexpected ideological convergence between left and right around the celebration of the victim, which has given this cult so much influence in British society.
>
> (p. 83)

As such, it is perhaps this bridging of political divides that ultimately best explains the pervasiveness of the victim issue for policy-makers in so many jurisdictions in recent years.

The term 'victimology'[19] as an academic label is usually attributed to Frederick Wertham (1949) or sometimes to Benjamin Mendelsohn (Kirchhoff, 1994). Rather than entering into an exaggerated debate concerning victimology's status as an individual 'discipline' in its own right,[20] this volume adopts the term simply as a convenient and well-used descriptor for specialist investigations, usually by criminologists and sociologists, into criminal and (more rarely) non-criminal victimizations. Early victimologists largely focused on the 'precipitation question', whereby criminal victimization was attributed to the choices and lifestyle of victims themselves. This perspective dominated academic discussion of victimization up until the late 1950s and early 1960s (von Hentig, 1948; Mendelsohn, 1956; Wolfgang, 1958; Amir, 1971; Fattah, 1992). Schneider (1991) argues that at this point, victimology was set off in two directions: as a discipline concerned with human rights, and also as a sub-discipline of criminology concerned specifically with victims of *crime*.

Indeed, like the victims' movement itself, victimology as a sub-discipline has been far from unified. The 1970s saw further disputes between victimologists who focused on the provision of services to crime victims, and those who were interested in broader, research-driven victimology (van Dijk, 1988). Conflict also arose between 'positivist victimology', which employs scientific methods (such as victimization surveys) to examine criminal victimization specifically, and 'general victimology', which encompasses wider victimizations, including war and, of particular relevance to the present study, natural disasters (Cressey, 1986; Spalek, 2006). Walklate (1994, 2007a) and Young (1997) have each highlighted the continuing tensions between various groups of victimologists. In addition, from its outset victimology has shared a common trait with the study of environmental derogation in that its activist and academic branches have frequently overlapped. Speaking of Gloria Egbuji, the Nigerian lawyer and campaigner for victims' rights, Jan van Dijk (1998), himself a major figure in the proliferation of victimology across Europe,[21] notes: 'Like many of us, our Nigerian colleague resists [being] qualified as either researcher or activist. Most of us are happy to wear both hats' (p. 2).

Despite the initial divergence of foci and aspirations among victimologists, as the view gradually developed that victims of crime were being neglected in many criminal justice systems throughout the world, the study of crime victims took centre stage (Maguire, 1991). A major facilitator of this process was the Dutch academic Nils Christie (1977), who argued that the criminal justice systems of many countries, having become over-professionalized, effectively 'stole' conflicts from their 'rightful owners', meaning victims and offenders.[22] Over the next 20 years, numerous research projects concerning victims' marginalized role within the criminal justice process would reinforce the prominence of victims of *crime* as the key concern for most commentators (Shapland *et al*., 1985).

Although the field of zemiology has continued to address victimization through social harms beyond crime and the traditional confines of criminology (Hillyard, 2006), much of victimology (and criminology) continues to be centred on notions of victimization espoused by official sources, often through the criminal law. It is important to note that this focus is not based on any inherent limitations of criminology[23] as a discipline or of the theories it promotes. As noted by Matthews and Kauzlarich (2007):

> Most criminological methods and theories can be applied to behaviors independent of whether those behaviors are officially defined as crimes. In short, criminological theory attempts to explain behavior – and that behavior may or may not be criminal, but is likely deviant in some way.
>
> (p. 53)

For McBarnet (1983), it is victimolog*ists* themselves (rather than victimolog*y* or criminolog*y*) who are partly to blame for this state of affairs. By concentrating their attention predominantly on traditional notions of victimhood (with particular emphasis on rape victims) the author argues that researchers in the field have somewhat played into the hands of governments wishing to derive political capital from victims, and from punitive criminal justice responses:

> Indeed, *politically,* victimology has contributed to the strengthening of the state's role. It has set itself up as engaging not just in academic debate but in 'affirmative action for the victims of crime', and, like traditional criminology before it, its too-ready acceptance of official definitions of criminal and victim have reinforced rather than questioned the status quo.
>
> (p. 302, emphasis in original)

These views take on an added dimension when applied to the issue of environmental harm, because such discussion may often relate to harms perpetrated (or at least endorsed) by the state itself, or even to state crime. Elias (1983, 1986) and Rock (1990) go further to argue that society's narrow conception of victimization is brought about by selective definitions of crime, construed for political purposes, and in the case of environmental degradation, we might add *economic* purposes. For Garland (2001), this is because the traditional measure of criminal justice effectiveness, the system's ability to control crime, has become redundant at a time of falling public confidence in these systems. In the face of the growing public concern that little can actually be done about crime, Garland argues that governments deny their failure by turning to ever more punitive policies, such as mandatory minimum sentences and 'three strikes' legislation. Victims, so goes the argument, are used by governments to justify such measures by reference to their 'need' to be protected and have their voices heard. Such ideas may oversimplify the complex interaction of social processes that lead to activities being labelled as 'deviant', but the point remains very significant in the context of the present discussion, which is grounded on the marked absence of environmental victims from the academic and (as will be discussed in Chapters 3 and 4) policy agendas.

Such arguments have led to the development of 'critical victimology' and its expanded notions of victimhood beyond simple, criminal classifications (Hough, 1986; Dignan, 2004). In many ways those suffering environmental harm fall squarely within the category of 'real, complex, contradictory and often politically inconvenient victims' (Kearon and Godfrey, 2007: p. 31) with which the critical debate is so concerned. This is particularly so given the reality that not only do environmental harms often derive from entirely *legal* activities, but also there may in fact be very sound economic and/or political justifications for a company or a state to passively allow such activities to continue, or even actively promote them (Walters, 2006). Of course, as noted by Ruggiero and South (2010), such political and economic decisions are heavily influenced by power inequalities, which are another feature of the critical school:

> [T]he high status of those causing the most [environmental] harm who (like other powerful offenders) frequently reject the proposition that criminal definitions should apply to them while constantly striving to persuade legislators that the imposition of norms of conduct on them would be detrimental to all. Powerful actors whose conduct impacts on the environment possess the ready-made rationalisation that a law imposing limits to the harm they cause would implicitly endanger the core values underpinning economic development and therefore be damaging to the collective wellbeing.
>
> (p. 246)

Partly in response to such radical criticisms of the status quo, there has been a marked expansion of official notions of victimhood over the last decade in many jurisdictions,[24] but even when this is taken into account, victims of environmental harm have received very little attention.

1.2 Theoretical perspectives

1.2.1 Cultural victimology

The ever expanding remit of criminology and victimology demanded by the critical school has in more recent years led to the promotion of literature which attempts to analyse how *cultural* factors impact upon our ideas of victimhood and official constructions of victimization (Cole, 2007). This development of so-called cultural victimology begs the question of whether we are to some extent all victims now.

Mythen (2007) warns against the overuse of culture as a ‘magic explanatory bullet through which the experiences of all victims can be deciphered’ (p. 479). As the author correctly points out, the nature of victimization is diverse to the point that any theory that purports to explain it in its entirety must be approached with a high degree of scepticism: ‘whilst macro theories are important tools in the development of Victimology, their generality affords them only partial utility across different contexts and situations’ (p. 479). Nevertheless, Mythen remains confident that the cultural lens is an important tool in modern victimology, and his conclusion is one of cautious optimism as to the capacity of such cultural perspectives to explain the rise of the victim in recent decades.

It should be said that not all commentators are willing to accept an ever-widening expansion of victimhood. Furedi (1998) expresses concern regarding this development on a number of grounds, the most philosophical of which is that it denies individual responsibility and self-determination:

> Recent events in Britain indicate that the cult of vulnerability goes beyond the terms of the existing debate. This cult has emerged as a key element in a moralizing project that touches upon every aspect of social life. Critics of the culture of victimhood often direct their fire at its more mendacious and self-serving manifestations, such as the predictable demand for compensation or the evasion of responsibility for the outcome of individual action. There is, however a more profound issue at stake. The celebration of the victim identity represents an important statement about the human condition. It regards human action with suspicion. It presupposes that human beings can do very little to influence their destiny. They are the objects rather than the subjects of their destiny. Consequently the human experience is defined by not by what people do but what has happened to them.
>
> (p. 80)

Regarding the first part of Furedi's argument, reports from England and Wales highlight the problem of false claims being made to the UK Criminal Injuries Compensation Authority (Verkaik, 2001). The 'compensation factor' has also been the subject of discussions in the UK by the House of Commons Select Committee on Home Affairs (2002), along with associated concerns of prompting false allegations. To give another example, the assertion of false or frivolous claims similarly marred the operation of the World Trade Center Victims Compensation Fund in the US after the terrorist attacks on New York and the Pentagon in 2001 (Mullenix, 2004).[25]

More specifically for present purposes, Furedi (1998) questions the authority now apparently being afforded to victims, as 'moral custodians', to influence policy debates:

> Other victims, notably Mrs. Frances Lawrence, whose teacher husband was murdered outside his school, were also elevated into 'expert' moral custodians for the rest of society. So far no leading politician has dared to ask the question of 'why should a tragic bereavement confer the right to dictate public policy?'.
>
> (1998: p. 84)

Importantly, Furedi's discussion again goes beyond the traditional boundaries of victimological or criminological thought to encompass wider societal developments. The question could thus be justifiably raised as to why victims of *environmental harm* should be allowed to exert any disproportionate influence over political, economic and industrial decisions that carry an environmental impact. At the more radical end of the spectrum, the Institute for the Study of Civil Society (CIViTAS), a right-wing think tank in the UK, has drawn on similar themes to suggest that the ever-widening cultural ambit of victim status[26] affords a degree of influence to such groups that is incompatible with liberal democracy (Green, 2006). While this argument must be judged in the context of its specific political perspective, it does demonstrate the application of the victim label beyond traditional notions of crime.

This book is in part a response to the challenges posed by the critical school in its application of concepts usually reserved for 'traditional' forms of officially recognized (criminal) victimization to environmental harm, as well as a practical attempt to fill perceived gaps in knowledge on the victims of such harm. The book also takes its lead from the cultural view of victimization discussed in the preceding paragraphs. It is hoped that the above overview demonstrates that the time is right for such a discussion as a natural extension of more recent theoretical debates. This is particularly the case given the overriding focus on 'harm' as a central concept in modern literature and policy-making concerning victimization, which the next section will address in more detail. Some commentators believe the extension of victimhood has negative connotations, and one can easily appreciate the concern that ultimately this might lead to excessive litigation, frivolous compensation claims and the promotion of a 'blame culture'. Such warnings have particular resonance in relation to environmental harms, for which there is arguably no single blameworthy party or legal entity. On the other hand, it could be argued that more research into the actual impacts of environmental crime on individuals and their respective needs could guard against the form of 'excessive' claims which Furedi (1998) and others (see Miers, 1997) fear.

1.2.2 Environmental harm, environmental victims

In the above paragraphs, as well as in the research questions for this project, I have made mention of the concept of 'environmental harm'. The concentration in this volume on 'harm' as opposed to 'crimes' is an application of the critical critique discussed above and, more specifically, the 'social harms approach' advocated by Hillyard and Toombs (2003: p. 2). These authors have argued that, in recent years, the progress of both critical criminology and victimology has stalled somewhat from their heyday in the 1960s and 1970s, giving way to an empiricist 'applied science' orientation driven by the political issues of the day. The authors advocate in response to this a return to a criminology based on social harms, and it is in this tradition that the present volume situates itself,[27] albeit the application of such ideas to environmental degradation is highly novel.

Again emphasizing the cultural context of these issues, one prominent commentator in this field has been Hans Boutellier (2000), who argues that, as the process of secularization goes on, common standards of morality decline, but common appreciation and sympathy for those who have suffered harm remains. Boutellier refers to this as the 'victimalization of morality'. Furedi (1998) also makes a similar point in terms of social solidarity in the UK context: 'It is difficult to avoid the conclusion that, with British people feeling so fragmented, the ritual of grieving [for victims] provides one of the few experiences that create a sense of belonging' (p. 82). The conceptualization of victims as those who have suffered harm (as opposed to a more technical, legal or prescriptive definition) has two key implications. First, as an underlying principle it gives scope for a wide cross-section of individuals, communities or organizations to be included within the ambit of victimhood, especially given the inclusion of 'emotional suffering' within such definitions. Second, this understanding of victimhood to some extent allows victims to be self-defined. In other words, such a definition is not, on the face of it, confined to cases where prosecutors in a given state feel there is an arguable case, but merely requires that victims feel they have been harmed in some way.

Focusing on 'harm' rather than crime has, according to Hillyard and Toombs, several advantages. In terms of the present volume, a number of these seem to have particular resonance with the impacts of environmental pollution and climate change. 'Crime', as argued by Hulsman (1986), has no 'ontological reality' and hence 'the criminal law fails to capture the more damaging and pervasive forms of harm' (Hillyard and Toombs, 2003: p. 12). One may debate the degree to which one agrees with the wider implications of such a sweeping statement, but it remains clear that focusing on harm has the potential to include the often legally ambiguous activities which foster environmental damage. Indeed, even when such activities are criminal in the strict legal sense, focusing on harm allows us to account for such activities in cases where whatever mechanisms of justice which are available (at the national, transnational and international levels) fail to adequately prosecute such transgressions. Another salient point made by Hillyard and Toombs is that the social harms approach allows for the consideration of 'mass harms'. Again this chimes well with the problems inherent to man-made environmental degradation, where many thousands of people might be affected. Traditional criminology, on the other hand, has struggled to fully embrace the concept of mass victimization and, with the exception of limited inroads into the fields of state crime and corporate crime, has largely remained focused on the individual. For similar reasons, the authors argue that the social harms approach poses a challenge to individual-based conceptions of crime grounded around notions of risk (Giddens, 1990).[28]

In relation to *environmental* harm, Hillyard and Toomb's approach has much resonance with some of the earliest literature from what has been termed 'the environmental justice movement' (Williams, 1996: p. 200). Environmental justice has been variously defined and is generally acknowledged as a wide concept which emphasizes the involvement of people and communities in decisions which might impact upon their environment: defined broadly to include their cultural norms, values, rules, regulations and behaviours (Bryant, 1995: p. 6; see also Hofrichter, 1993 and Čapek, 1993). One of the main commentators on these issues (and on green criminology in general) is Rob White (2008a) who, in following a more holistic approach, has criticized this understanding of environmental justice as being anthropocentric, ignoring the wider issue of *ecological* justice (acknowledging that humans are just one part of a complex ecosystem) and also *animal* and *species* justice.

White (2008a) also reflects on the concept of harm itself, offering four groups of key 'considerations of environmental harms' (p. 92). The first of these considerations is that of *identifying* the victims of such harm. Although in this volume I am mainly concerned with human victimization, White makes the important point that victims of environmental harm include the biosphere and non-human animals. It follows that a further advantage of applying the social harms approach in this field is that it allows commentators to explore the non-human consequences of environmental degradation beyond the highly anthropocentric concept of 'criminal victimization'.

The second of White's considerations is geographical, encapsulating the fact that environmental harm is often a regional, national, international or even global problem. It is for this reason that the present volume advocates closer collaboration between green criminologists and those studying international law: in an effort to address those forms of harm which national legal systems alone may be ill-equipped to deal with. In a similar vein, White distinguishes geographical considerations from considerations of 'place', by which he means the different types of harm experienced in urban, built-up centres of human habitation, compared with harm caused to natural environments such as oceans, wilderness areas and deserts. Finally, White conceives environmental harm in terms of temporal considerations, meaning that the impact of environmental damage may be short, medium or long-term and may have immediate and/or lasting social impacts. There is a key link here to be made with more mainstream victimology and its growing acceptance that the impacts of harms to individuals (crime) vary considerably over time (as well as between individuals), as do the support needs of those victimized. Even in mainstream victimology there is an absence of longitudinal studies which truly encapsulate the progression of the impacts of individual victimization over time (Shapland and Hall, 2007). Discussion of the temporal development of the impacts of environmental harm will be discussed in Chapter 2.

White's 'considerations' of environmental harm may in one sense be criticized for failing to 'pin down' the concept to specific human or non-human impacts. Certainly Hillyard and Toombs (2003) are more explicit in their definition of social harm in that they conceive it as including physical harm; financial/economic harm; emotional/psychological harm; and consideration of 'cultural safety'. Nevertheless, the counter-argument can be made that to rigidly define 'harm'[29] would in a sense defeat the purpose of the critical exercise, which is to be inclusive rather than exclusive. As such, for White (2008a) it is important for commentators, especially those concerned with green issues, to move beyond *defining* harm and on to *debating* harm, because only the latter can leads to real-life, operational developments:

> Defining harm is ultimately about philosophical frameworks as informed by scientific evidence and traditional knowledges; debating harm is about processes of deliberation in the 'real world' and of conflicts over rights and the making of difficult decisions.
>
> (p. 24)

Of course, such a view presents real difficulties for those seeking to develop *legal* systems for addressing environmental harms, as such a system must ultimately be based on concrete and predictable definitions of victimization. This apparent conflict between predictable legal rules and flexible notions of environmental harm will be a recurring issue throughout this volume, and the tackling of this debate an important outcome of this volume as a whole in Chapter 6.

While assigning a precise definition to environmental harm is problematic (certainly with regard to *legal systems*) and perhaps undesirable, the evidence is increasingly clear that whether such harms are criminalized or not, they are a pervasive and significant problem of the modern world. Globally, for example, it has been estimated that as many as 800,000 premature deaths can be attributed to ambient air pollution, many in the developing world (Croall, 2010; Tombs and Whyte, 2010). In the UK, the Department of Health estimates that 24,000 deaths each year can be attributed to poisoning by various forms of air pollution, a figure which may well be an underestimate (Tombs and Whyte, 2010). Air pollution is now also thought to reduce life expectancy by eight months (Walters, 2010). The implications of environmental harm for issues such as energy security and food security across the globe are equally significant, and will be returned to in Chapter 2, where the impacts of environmental harms on victims are also discussed in greater detail. Having laid out the wider theoretical basis for this book, this chapter will next turn to the existing literature specifically concerned with environmental victimization.

1.2.3 A green victimology?

As noted previously, the application of criminological principles to environmental degradation is a new and emerging specialism, under which various issues have been addressed by scholars from different backgrounds in a piecemeal fashion.[30] Specific focus within this literature on those actually affected by environmental degradation is relatively scarce. The first call for the development of what was then termed 'environmental victimology' came as early as 1996 in an article by Christopher Williams. Williams begins his argument by acknowledging the 'limits of law' in addressing environmental victimization, and notes the 'obvious need for social justices to parallel formal legal processes' (Williams, p. 200), a theme that Hillyard and Toombs would later take up (albeit in more general terms). Nevertheless Williams is keen to develop some form of predictable legal mechanism for dealing with environmental harms; he shares White's opinion that the environmental justice approach is limited, although for different reasons. For Williams, the problems with notions of environmental justice are three-fold. First, he argues that the concept relies too heavily on subjective understandings of victimhood and on self-definition as a victim: 'This may work well in relation to activism, but ultimately the development of justice perspectives, legal or social, requires objective benchmarks' (p. 201). Leading on from this, Williams makes the criticism that the environmental justice movement is overly swayed by activism and lacks the academic objectivity which would put it in a stronger position to effect real change. Finally, Williams is of the view that environmental justice tends to be based around the stereotypes of relations, group identities, gender, class and ethnic structures found in mainstream criminology. In reality, he argues, the social majority, the rich and the powerful may all become environmental victims alongside minority groups, the poor and the weak.[31]

These criticisms prompt Williams to call for a move away from concepts of environmental justice and to embrace victimology as a means of addressing environmental victimizations, which for him is a discipline 'broadly concerned with human rights, abuse of power, and human suffering irrespective of whether the circumstances are within the ambit of law' (p. 202). While the present volume essentially takes forward Williams's suggestion, it can be argued that he has perhaps placed rather a lot of faith in victimologists, given the fragmented state of the 'discipline' described above. At best, Williams's view represents only one form of victimology, grounded in a legal tradition, which relatively few commentators have since taken forward (Jackson, 2003; Doak, 2005; Hall, 2009). It has been noted already that victimologists have often embraced rather than rejected an overlap of activist and academic viewpoints. That said, the victims' movement has also shown signs of maturing to the point of accepting that pure activism is unlikely to foster political change. The most obvious example of this in the UK context is the national charity Victim Support, which over the years has achieved significant government backing principally by sticking strictly to an apolitical philosophy (Rock, 1990). It is true that some victimologists have embraced notions of human rights and abuse of power, the application of which to environmental victims will be discussed in Chapter 4, but it is less clear that victimology can provide the 'objective benchmarks' Williams is searching for when research in this (sub)discipline, like almost any other area of social study, is inevitably tainted by subjective views of the researcher (Sieber, 1998). Consequently, this volume will take a far more interdisciplinary approach than Williams seems to envisage.

Williams's understanding of the notion of environmental victims (discussed in Chapter 2) also stresses the concept of intergenerational justice, which is often cited as a core component of the anthropocentric environmental justice model (Hiskes, 2008). Mares (2010) has also alluded to intergenerational justice in his conceptualization of environmental degradation as compromising the 'carrying capacity' of the Earth (that is, the planet's ability to support a given number of human and non-human life forms):

> The criminological question that arises is whether it is acceptable to artificially and temporarily inflate human carrying capacity in order to support a growing population on finite resources. In other words, in our attempts to shake our dependency on the unpredictable natural circumstances (local crop failures, disease, local climate and so forth) we find ourselves in, we have created dependency relations between humans which have ultimately allowed the existence of so many people at such high levels of consumption that it undermines our ultimate goal of human cooperation: human security.
> (p. 282)

Williams's view also includes omissions, leaving open the possibility that *failure* on the part of the state to sufficiently regulate an activity could lead to it being held responsible for any consequential environmental harms. While Williams is clearly attempting to achieve a measure of certainty with this definition, the understanding of the exact links between harms to the 'chemical, physical, microbiological, or psychosocial environment' may change over time with scientific knowledge, possibly leading to lengthy court cases with a great deal of complex expert evidence. One last point to make about Williams's definition is that he clearly means for it to include the long-term victims of what he calls 'creeping environmental disasters', such as climate change and changes in sea level, as opposed to one-off events such as oil spills or nuclear leaks.

It is extremely telling of the state of the literature in this field that when White compiled a reader on environmental crime in 2009, the only chapter specifically focused on the victims of such crimes was a reprint of Williams's 1996 work. A further edited collection from White (2010) has no specific chapter on victimization at all, although it does contain a chapter from South (2010) who in one section reflects upon the unequal impact of climate change on various groups of (usually poor) victims, and the possibility that some 'environmental rights' are being breached (see Chapter 4). Notably this discussion contradicts Williams's view that the impacts of environmental harm are evenly spread between rich and poor. White (2011) has more recently dedicated a chapter to environmental victims in which he emphasizes the socio-cultural context of understanding and responding to environmental harm: 'Ultimately the construction of [environmental] victimhood is a social process involving dimensions of time and space, behaviours involving acts and omissions, and social features pertaining to powers and collectivities' (p. 122). As further noted by White, this state of affairs in relation to environmental victims reflects 'one of the truisms of victimology that being and becoming a victim is never socially neutral' (2011: p. 111).

At the end of his earlier book, White (2008a) calls for further research to examine environmental 'harm' 'in many contexts and guises, regardless of legal status and existing institutional legitimations' (p. 280). This volume seeks to addresses this prevailing gap in our knowledge by drawing on different sets of literature and investigating the relevant national and international legal frameworks directly. The timing seems right for such an endeavour given that, in the European context, in 2008 the European Commission issued a Directive (2008/99/EC) on the protection of the environment through the criminal law, to be implemented in member states by December 2010. Of particular note is the absence of any reference to the rights of victims in that Directive, notwithstanding previous precedents in the 1998 Council of Europe Convention on the Protection of the Environment through Criminal Law, developments in US law on this issue (2004 Crime Victims' Rights Act), and indeed in the EU's own Stockholm Programme on an Open and Secure Europe.

1.3 The role of the state and of international law

1.3.1 The role of the state

It was noted at the start of this chapter that traditional victimology has largely ignored victimization of individuals or groups as a result of *state* actions or inactions. Indeed, 'state crime' is itself a markedly underdeveloped concept even in mainstream criminology. Green and Ward (2004) characterize state crime as exhibiting two chief components: objective evidence of a violation of human rights, and subjective evidence of one or more relevant social audiences (i.e. civil society) negatively reacting to such actions or negligence. In this volume, both aspects of this definition will be examined in relation to environmental degradation, in Chapters 4 and 2 respectively. Nevertheless, although such theorization of state crime has proved an important driving force to the development of critical criminology, discussed above, Kauzlarich *et al.* (2001) have noted that

> The criminological study of immoral, illegal, and harmful state actions has not developed as fully as would have been expected from the explosion of research in the late 1980s to mid-1990s, which lifted the optimism about criminology's interest in understanding state malfeasance.
>
> (p. 173)

This is perhaps surprising in light of the point made by Matthews and Kauzlarich (2007) that 'the practice of states engaging in illegal and/or harmful behaviour is as old as the concept of the state itself' (p. 43). Furthermore, the authors argue, the neglect of state crime by criminologists is not born from any inability to apply criminological theory to state crime as a concept.

One significant side-effect of the increasing prevalence of 'green' debates among criminologists is the rekindling of ideas and research concerning state crime. Faust and Carlson (2011), for example, have labelled human rights violations in the aftermath of hurricane Katrina's devastation of New Orleans in 2005 as a state crime. Similarly, Lynch *et al.* (2010) have remarked on the complex interaction between state and corporate liability following what they call the 'politicalization of global warming'. White (2008b) has also discussed state crime in relation to the environmental effects of the use of depleted uranium munitions in the Gulf wars.

Clearly, the global nature of environmental derogation, coupled with national factors in its precipitation and in its consequences, requires criminologists to examine the issue at the level of the state, as opposed to restricting itself to issues of corporate or individual crime and harmful behaviours. It is for this reason that such discussion must also to some extent incorporate an analysis of *international* environmental law. Indeed, such an interdisciplinary approach has the potential to markedly advance our understanding of a still under-researched issue: that of a state's responsibility for the adverse impacts of environmental degradation, including climate change, on individuals. Such responsibility might exist both internally, where the actions or inactions of a state lead to harm for its own citizens, and also externally, where such harm occurs outside the state in question. One of the foremost difficulties posed by climate change is that associated harms often occur in one state when the acts or omissions (lawful or otherwise) leading to climate change occur in a separate state. To choose one prominent example, the people of the Maldives are now facing significant risk to their homes, economy and traditional ways of life as a result of sea-level rises apparently brought about by climate change, despite the fact that the country itself is among the lowest contributors to the problem (Pernetta, 2002).

As might be expected from the absence of extensive literature on state crime as a whole, academic focus on *victimization* by the state has been similarly limited. This is all the more surprising because the United Nations General Assembly acknowledged the concept of victimization at the hands of the state as early as 1985 in its Declaration of Basic Principles of Justice for Victims of Crime and Abuse of Power.[32] One of the few exceptions at present is the attempt by Kauzlarich *et al.* (2001) to develop a 'victimology of the state'. The authors' typology effectively categorizes 'state crime' into four classifications. 'Domestic-International Governmental Crime' occurs within a state's geographic jurisdiction against international law or human rights. 'International-International Governmental Crime' occurs outside a state's geographic jurisdiction against international law or human rights. 'Domestic-Domestic Governmental Crime' occurs within a state's geographic jurisdiction against domestic criminal, regulatory, or procedural laws or codes. Finally, 'International-Domestic Governmental Crime' occurs outside a state's geographic jurisdiction against domestic criminal, regulatory, or procedural laws or codes. The authors place environmental derogation under the category of Domestic-Domestic Governmental Crime, although it is possible to take issue with this, given that actions by one state might well lead to environmental derogation in another state, which could constitute International-Domestic Governmental Crime.[33] Specifics aside, the models of Kauzlarich *et al.* models provide a rare insight into the complexities inherent in the notion of being victimized *by a state*, which will be discussed in greater depth in Chapter 3.

1.3.2 Broadening horizons: what international environmental lawyers might learn from victimology and vice-versa

Having established the significance of the *state* in any discussion of environmental victimization, one of the principal goals of this volume is to achieve a truly interdisciplinary analysis of the issue that draws on both the fields of criminology (victimology) and international law. The added value of collaboration between these disciplines lies in the cross-fertilization of structural ideas from the field of international environmental law (concerning the operation of international redress mechanisms, state liability, and human rights) and the more agency-driven ideas which inform much of victimology (focusing on the place of the *individual* within the quantum of harm brought about by environmental damage and climate change).

There is from the outset a fundamental difficulty in trying to apply international law to the harms brought about to individuals by environmental degradation, in that the international legal order is traditionally conceived as one devised by states, for states.[34] This conventional approach leaves little room for the concerns of those *individuals* actually suffering harm within states, whether that harm comes in the form of physical or health-related issues or as the broader loss of traditional ways of life, means of economic sustenance, or territory as a result of environmental degradation. While the recent incorporation of human rights within international law is improving the situation, reference to individuals in the international legal order is still relatively scarce.[35] Consequently, international environmental law generally lacks reference to individual harm, or the agency of individuals affected by that harm.

Agency here is given the conventional sociological meaning as a synonym for undetermined human action (Abercrombie *et al.*, 2006). In traditional sociology, agency is contrasted with structure, which broadly means recurring social processes, institutions and rules which limit the action of individuals and to some extent determines them. Structure therefore generally includes the legal systems put in place by society (Burns and Flam, 1987). This duality informs much of traditional criminology, being the essential basis of debates between the rational-actor and deterministic views of criminality. Of greater significance to the present volume, however, are the more recent debates concerning the interrelationship, and possible interdependence, of these concepts. One of the most influential writers to offer such arguments is Antony Giddens (1984), who champions the concept of a 'duality of structure' (p. 85) whereby the structural properties of social systems are produced and reproduced by social practices (i.e. by human agency). Bourdieu (1990) too proposes a model of closer integration between structure and agency, essentially arguing that individuals become disposed to act in a manner which promotes certain codes of behaviour and their associated social structures. Hence structure becomes embedded within agency over time. More recently, Mouzelis (2008) has commented and expanded upon both Giddens's and Bourdieu's perspectives to incorporate the changing of social structures through agency (not just their production and reproduction as per Giddens) and also for a 'rational, calculative and reflective social actor' (p. 57) endowed with greater freedom of action than Bourdieu recognizes.

The full detail of these debates is beyond the scope of the present volume. The important point is that the previous dualistic conceptions of structure and agency, whereby one or the other is championed as *the* principal driver of social phenomena (including law and legal systems), has been replaced by the understanding that both, variously configured, are necessary to understand society. This returns us to the critique of the traditional international legal order regarding environmental harms and its denial of individual (or indeed group) human agency. At an operational level, many international lawyers defend this position by reference to the supremacy of the state in the international legal order (Alston, 2005).[36] This structural straightjacket has, however, led to a dearth of commentary among international environmental lawyers on the issue of environmental harm *that also encompasses human agency*. If Giddens, Bourdieu and Mouzelis are correct, a full understanding of this issue can never be reached given such limitations.

Here then lies the added value of victimological discussion in this debate, and a key contribution of this volume, because victimologists have long concerned themselves with the (usually criminal) harms perpetrated against individuals. Victimology is also of course concerned with social structures and the place of victims within them, particularly the place of victims within criminal justice systems (Shapland *et al.*, 1985). Nevertheless, one of the key limitations of victimology is its failure to develop a structural and theoretically-informed debate as to how such victims could achieve official recognition by national and international justice agencies (Walklate, 2007b). While there is now a great deal more rhetoric in both academic and policy circles concerning the 'rights' of victims, in fact their formal legal position is usually characterized by a general lack of enforcement structures for their rights at the national and international level, and the theory of victim rights is underdeveloped.[37] Unlike most victimologists, international lawyers are well versed in arguments concerning enforceability, which is often much more contestable in the international arena than in most other areas of legal scholarship (where the basic legal force of an instrument is often a given). Indeed, Thirlway (2010) has described how international lawyers (compared with lawyers in other fields) deal much more regularly with 'secondary rules' which determine the sources and authority of legal and quasi-legal rules. What this means is that international law can furnish victimology with a ready-made vocabulary in which to conceptualize victim-orientated measures, as well as presenting victimologists with another dimension to the transnational and international policy networks connecting such reforms (Hall, 2010).

In sum, international environmental lawyers can benefit from the individual-based and agency-based discussion provided by the victimological literature (incorporating the *people* who, after all, constitute states), whereas victimologists can draw from the structural frameworks developed by international lawyers as a means of furthering official recognition and redress for victims of harms brought about by environmental degradation (and perhaps other harms). Such an approach not only benefits from the best of both academic traditions, but also conforms to modern theoretical notions in social science concerning the links between structure and agency. The remainder of this volume will be devoted to applying this interdisciplinary approach[38] to the key questions raised by environmental victimization and the efforts (or absence thereof) of states and justice systems to address them, in an effort to answer the research questions introduced earlier in this chapter.

1.4 Summary and book structure

Chapter 2 conceptualizes the scope of environmental victimization and its impacts upon those who are victimized. The chapter examines in particular how the impacts of environmental derogation and climate change are distributed among the world's population and begins to explore the kind of support and redress mechanisms they require. The chapter also offers a new conceptualization of those affected by environmental harms: as victims of abuse of power, under the UN 1985 Declaration of Basic Principles of Justice for Victims of Crime and Abuse of Power discussed above. Williams (1996) has argued that the definition of such victims utilized by the 1985 Declaration can serve as a useful starting point for ascribing rights to environmental victims, especially as the 1985 Declaration was intended to encompass victimization by the *state*,[39] making this definition particularly relevant from the perspective of victims of environmental harms.

Chapter 3 looks at substantive legal avenues for recognition of environmental victims in criminal justice systems at the domestic, European and international levels. The chapter then examines state responsibility for environmental derogation and the various avenues of liability put forward by international legal scholars through which states may be deemed responsible for the impacts of environmental harms (especially climate change) on individuals. These include: the UN Framework Convention on Climate Change, its Kyoto Protocol, and the Copenhagen Accord of 2009; the UN Convention on the Law of the Sea; the obligation on states to ensure that activities within their territory do not cause damage beyond the limits of their jurisdiction; the precautionary, polluter-pays, and sustainability principles; the concept of equity between generations; the concept of due diligence; and the notion that the need to minimize the effects of environmental harms give rise to obligations *erga omnes*. For each of these mechanisms, the chapter offers a critique from a victimological perspective, contending that none of them offers much scope for the individual victims of environmental harms to gain redress from states, either their own or that of another. The victimological literature is then utilized to propose a way forward for developing state responsibility in this area.

Chapter 4 discusses in more detail the twin developments in victimology and international environmental law linking the plight of victims with wider human rights. The chapter considers the prospect of individuals gaining redress from states for the impacts of environmental harms (both natural and man-made) through a supposed right to a clean environment, as well as the impact of the 1998 Aarhus Convention.

Chapter 5 examines the possible means by which (human) victims of environmental harm might gain redress, with particular emphasis on receiving awards from their own state and other states. It begins by examining the difficulties faced by traditional redress mechanisms, both nationally and internationally, to adequately address the issue of environmental harm, and draws comparisons with the advent of compensation funds for other harms including violent crime, terrorism and human trafficking. As in other areas of the volume, the victimological literature has much to say: notably here on the subject of compensation and restitution and, perhaps more significantly, the role of no-fault compensation mechanisms. Again, the analysis is informed by the prevailing philosophy that compensatable environmental 'harm' need not necessarily equate with environmental 'crime'. Ultimately the chapter puts forward a new model of combined redress for victims of environmental crime, drawing on both criminal and administrative mechanisms,[40] and argues the merits of this combined approach.

The final chapter summarizes the volume's general argument that victimologists and international lawyers have much to learn from one another, and sets out detailed answers to the two research questions posed at the beginning, with particular emphasis on how policy-makers and legal practitioners could adopt these ideas and take them forward into operational practice. It is further argued that developments in the recognition of victims of environmental harm by international law have to some extent reflected broader trends in the victims' movement as a whole. By borrowing concepts and language from each other, both disciplines can advance in understanding. The chapter makes a first attempt at this by offering a new framework for a 'green victimology', taking Williams's (1996) typology as a starting point but developing it in light of the discussions throughout the volume.

2 Identifying and conceptualizing the victims of environmental harm

The previous chapter outlined a broad definition of environmental victimization and, in particular, set out the 'social harms approach' to be adopted in the majority of this volume. This approach is useful in this context principally because it allows us to problematize the official recognition and labelling of such victimizations. Nevertheless, the social harms approach has one clear disadvantage that, as noted in Chapter 1, is especially problematic for commentators seeking the development of legal (especially criminal) sanctions against those whose actions or inactions result in environmental victimizations. This disadvantage lies in the apparently all-encompassing nature, and near-limitless scope, of such victimizations. It is a difficulty acknowledged by Williams (1996) who, as a consequence, purposely restricts his own proposed definition of 'environmental victims' to those suffering 'injury':

> those of past, present, or future generations who are injured as a consequence of change to the chemical, physical, microbiological, or psychosocial environment, brought about by deliberate or reckless, individual or collective, human act or omission.
>
> (p. 35)

In presenting this definition, Williams argues that to draw on the concept of 'injury'[1] as opposed to the wider notion of 'harm' 'creates a much narrower frame of reference than that used within the environmental justice debate' (p. 205). Williams's justification for this is a pragmatic one: in the context of his overall aim to achieve a workable legal system which incorporates environmental victims, the author makes the point that

> if an aim of a victim conceptualization is to change policy, then governments are more likely to respond in relation to tight, manageable definitions, which may be stretched a little, than to 'catch all' concepts that might appear to carry a host of hidden ramifications.
>
> (p. 205)

Certainly one can appreciate the value of Williams's perspective; nevertheless, the purposeful underestimation of environmental victimization by academics does call to mind the criticism of McBarnet (1983) discussed in Chapter 1 that the academy itself has allowed a situation to proliferate in which a whole host of actual and potential victims are ignored by governments. The social harms approach was never intended to exclude victims from the ambit of legal recourse,[2] but instead represents a *challenge* to established legal systems to find ways of *adapting* themselves to meet such needs. Certainly this is the spirit in which the approach was adopted for the present research. Indeed, in response to such criticisms, one of the underlying goals of this volume is to determine how national and international law can be applied to a wider range of environmental victims, many of whom do in fact suffer 'harm' (a wide concept) rather than 'injury' (a more restrictive one) per se.

2.1 Investigating environmental victimization and its impacts

In the context of the above remarks, the goal of this chapter is to offer a conceptualization of the scope of environmental victimization and its impacts upon those who are victimized: something which is largely absent from both the existing green criminological and victimological literatures. The most systematic review of environmental victims and legal systems now available is that carried out by Skinnider (2011), who argues that 'Victimologists have generally not included victims of environmental crime in their research. Further study is required to get a better understanding of this type of victimization and how it differs from other types of victimization' (p. 25). From the limited information available, Skinnider goes on to extrapolate the following broad characteristics of environmental victims:

- The victims are not always aware of the fact that they have been victimized.
- The victimization is often delayed, with the victim becoming aware of the victimization much later.
- Victims are not sure about who victimized them or who exactly is responsible.
- The victimization is often serious not so much because any individual victim was seriously affected, but because numerous victims were affected by the crime.
- Victimization can often include repeat offences.

Skinnider then goes on to postulate that environmental victims can be classified by a number of different typologies, including: by the type of wrongful act; by the nature of the harm; by the extent of the damages suffered; by the scope of the harm; or by the perpetrator(s) of that harm. The report goes on to give examples of all these differing classifications. The report's purpose is largely descriptive and the summary is grounded in the Canadian perspective; Skinnider does not draw extensively on wider criminological or victimological theory. The present chapter focuses on a typology based on classifications of harm, largely because such an approach is consistent with the social harms perspective outlined previously. Nevertheless, all of these possible means of distinguishing among environmental victims will be considered at various points where they become especially relevant. This chapter will also examine how the impacts of environmental derogation are distributed among the world's population and the significant overlap which appears to exist between 'environmental victims' and 'environmental offenders'. In addition, the definition of 'victims of abuse of power' utilized by the UN General Assembly's 1985 Declaration of Basic Principles of Justice and Abuse of Power will be discussed, and an assessment made as to how well this definition fits with the categories of victimizations discussed previously.

To provide a comprehensive overview of environmental victimization is clearly impossible. This chapter has the more modest aim of presenting a typology of the forms of harm such victims might experience, which will give both academics and policy-makers a starting point from which further developments can be built. It will also form the basis of discussions in subsequent chapters in this volume, notably Chapter 5. This typology splits environmental victimization into health impacts; economic impacts; social and cultural impacts; and impacts on security. In the case of security, this chapter represents the first attempt in the literature to apply lessons learned from victimological studies to the growing debates on what has been termed 'environmental security' by international lawyers and researchers in other fields (Homer-Dixon *et al.*, 2011).

As discussed in Chapter 1, this book adopts a largely anthropogenic approach, which admittedly underplays the full degree of environmental victimization as it extends to the animal and plant kingdoms, as well as to the biosphere. This shortcoming will be particularly evident in the present chapter, but is necessary in the context of the volume's wider aim of examining how national and international criminal justice mechanisms respond to such (human) victims, further to the second research question set out in Chapter 1. One final point to note before commencing this chapter's discussion is that at this stage I am not concerned with issues of causation, but rather with establishing the varied effects environmental degradation and climate change can have on individuals and groups of individuals. In every case, it may be asked whether these effects can be attributed (or partially attributed) to specific bodies, individuals or states. Such questions are left to Chapters 3 and 5. The goal here is merely to demonstrate the types and scale of impact which might (and perhaps should) be subject to criminalization if such a line of culpability were established, if the political will were present and if national and international criminal justice systems were geared up to facilitate this.

2.1.1 Health impacts

Some of the clearest and most immediately worrying impacts of environmental degradation, including climate change, are the health implications for human beings (see McMichael, 2006). Indeed, at first glance the health effects associated with environmental victimization appear to substantially bypass many of the difficulties outlined at the start of this chapter concerning the wide ambit of 'social harm'. This is chiefly because, certainly compared to the more subtle categories of environmental harm to be discussed below, 'health impacts' tend to be relatively obvious (or at least become so over time) and are usually scientifically verifiable.[3] This renders such effects a much better fit with existing legal principles in most jurisdictions around the world, which tend to favour positivistic virtues such as certainty, predictability and objectivity. Such harms are also generally speaking quantifiable,[4] which aligns them well with systems already in place at the national and international levels to compensate parties physically and mentally injured as a result of criminal acts (Miers, 1997; Hall, 2010).[5] This of course is before we enter the realm of *civil* justice, which routinely attributes responsibility for physical and psychological illnesses for the purpose of awarding damages.

From a legal perspective, then, it seems we are in fairly recognisable territory when we consider the health implications of environmental degradation. Of course, any legal system set up to consider or address these issues will be premised on set, usually restrictive, ideas on matters such as 'health' and what it is to 'be healthy' (see Patrick *et al.*, 1973). White (2011) has commented on the 'politics of knowledge' in this context, noting that:

> At the heart of investigations of transnational crime is the question of whose knowledge of 'wrong' is right? … What counts as 'science', what counts as 'evidence', who counts as being a 'scientific expert' and what counts as 'sensible' public policy are all influenced by factors such as economic situation, the scientific tradition within a particular national context, the scientific standards that are used in relation to specific issues, and the style and mode of government.
>
> (pp. 117–118)

This notwithstanding, health impacts are (at least relative to more social or macro impacts) obligingly discrete, and indeed are easily accommodated within Williams's notion of 'injury' discussed above. That said, the scope of such health effects is wide, and indeed continues to widen as the effects of environmental degradation become more obvious and as scientific knowledge develops. The paragraphs below provide only indicative examples, representing the beginning rather than the end state of a growing body of recognized health impacts associated with environmental victimization.

In a seminal criminological piece, Lynch and Stretesky (2001) analysed the question of corporate harm and violence, utilizing evidence from medical literature and related studies that focus on the health consequences associated with toxic waste, pesticide and dioxin exposure. In so doing, they argue that the significant health consequences associated with modern industrial production of toxic waste 'can be thought of as "criminal" in the broadest sense since alternative, nontoxic methods of production are often available' (p. 153). They also make a point, to be taken up in greater detail below, that the health impacts of such dumping are not evenly distributed around the world's population, and in fact tend to fall disproportionately on the already impoverished.

More broadly, the regularity with which we are presented with alarming facts and statistics concerning the impact on human health of almost any form of environmental degradation, pollution, dumping, or climate change reflects the significance of the challenges faced by the world's legal systems. For example, in the UK alone the Department of Health (1998) has estimated that at least 24,000 deaths can be attributed to air pollution each year. Globally, the World Health Organisation (WHO, 2008b) has estimated the same annual figure at around two million premature deaths. Mortality rates of course only represent a very small proportion of all health impacts brought about or contributed to by air pollution. Indeed, the WHO's working group on the Quantification of the Health Effects of Exposure to Air Pollution identified premature deaths as the least numerically significant of a whole continuum of health effects (generally associated with impaired pulmonary function) brought about by air pollution. These included such diverse impacts as cardiovascular hospital admissions, chronic change in physiologic function, and lower birth rates (WHO, 2008b).

Broadening the scope of the discussion beyond air pollution, Patz *et al.* (2000) report that the long-term consequences of climate change as a whole will bring about adverse impacts on public health (in this case in the USA) via a diverse range of consequences which include: heat-related illnesses and deaths; extreme weather events; water- and food-borne disease; and vector- and rodent-borne diseases.[6] Another pertinent example is the legal and illegal dumping of hazardous waste materials, as a by-product of industrialization, where the health implications of such activities are if anything more directly palpable. Ruggiero and South (2010), for example, cite numerous cases of death and illness brought about in areas exposed to hazardous waste materials, including the 'cancer villages' of China, where residents' increased susceptibility to several classifications of tumours has been directly attributed to their exposure to cadmium and mercury released through the recycling of e-waste (electronic waste; Watts, 2010: p. 21).[7] In Italy, Martuzzi *et al.* (2009) have identified a statistically significant increase in cancer mortality and congenital anomalies in Campania, a region subject to intense environmental pressure due to uncontrolled and illegal practices of industrial waste dumping. More recently, the United Nations Environment Programme has reported that the environmental restoration of Ogoniland in Nigeria, following 50 years of oil operations, could prove to be the world's most wide-ranging and long-term oil clean-up exercise ever undertaken. The data for the report included over 5,000 medical records, and the conclusion was that in 'at least 10 Ogoni communities where drinking water is contaminated with high levels of hydrocarbons, public health is seriously threatened' (UNEP, 2011). The Nigerian situation, and in particular how the oil industry has impacted upon the Ogoniland community, has been the subject of repeated legal actions and rulings at the international level, to be discussed in Chapters 3 and 4.

Of course, the above examples do not illustrate the impacts on human health of distinct man-made environmental disaster events such as the Deepwater Horizon oil spill in the Gulf of Mexico in 2010. The human health implications of this event – including both physical and mental health – are now the subject of a rapidly expanding scientific literature (Lee and Blanchard, 2010; Yun *et al.*, 2010). Another prominent example is the negative long-term health impacts of the 1984 Bhopal gas leak in India, including respiratory and neurological disorders, which have been demonstrated by Cullinan *et al.* (1996). These long-term effects are in addition to the estimated 8,000 people who reputedly died in the immediate aftermath of the disaster itself (D'Silva, 2006). The Chernobyl nuclear disaster of 1986 has of course led to very long-term health implications for those affected at the time, and for subsequent generations who have lived in the area. In this case, long-term health impacts identified by the WHO (2006) include a prevalence of leukaemia, thyroid cancer, and increased mortality. Of course, while disasters such as these have received a great deal of media attention and a certain notoriety,[8] the crucial point is that these more visible examples of environmental victimization inevitably represent a tiny minority of all those suffering health complaints as a result of environmental harms.

While the above paragraphs provide only a brief and unsystematic glimpse of some of the health implications of environmentally destructive activities,[9] they serve to illustrate the pervasiveness, complexity and scope of the issue. They also illustrate why those who fall victim to such health effects may well feel aggrieved and choose to seek redress in a criminal court if and when such victimization is attributable to identified parties, organizations or states. Criminal justice systems need to be in a position to respond to such harms.[10] Health impacts also of course have significant knock-on effects that blur the boundaries between these impacts and some of the other categories discussed below. For example, increased sickness brought about by contaminated water in a given locality will lead to higher healthcare costs in that area, and higher health insurance premiums (see International Association for the Study of Insurance Economics, 2009). They may also have social impacts if those affected are unable to participate in the same social and community activities they did before. As with all areas of victimization, it is important to realize that environmental harms do not fall within neat, easily separable categories (such as 'the objectively verifiable' and 'the intangible') but rather flow into each other to create a holistic social problem. The argument can thus be made that as with many other social problems, criminal justice systems have a role to play in their resolution.

2.1.2 Economic impacts

Like many of the consequences of environmental victimization discussed in this chapter, the negative economic impacts of environmental degradation can be felt on both a collective, societal level (for example, higher taxes levied on the population at large to fund national initiatives to combat greenhouse gases) or at a very individual level (for example, individuals facing loss of livelihoods or increased insurance premiums due to changes in the local ecology, weather patterns and so on). The full 'economics of climate change' (Stern, 2007) and other environmental degradation could of course fill a whole book (see Stern, 2009; Helm and Hepburn, 2009); once again, the goal here is rather to give a broad indication of the kind of economic harms which are occurring and which look set to increase in the coming years.

The best estimates that exist of the monetary or fiscal cost of environmentally damaging activities run into the billions. Following on from the increased mortality rates highlighted in the previous section, the WHO recently estimated that deaths caused by air pollution are costing economies within the European Union around €161 billion a year (see BBC, 2007). The United Nations Environmental Programme (Mullier, 2010) estimates the worldwide turnover of green crime at $31 billion annually. In the business world, studies have indicated a likely negative impact of climate change on a wide variety of industries including paper production (Jaggi and Freedman, 2006); the wine industry (Nemani *et al*., 2001); tourism (Berrittella *et al*., 2006) and fishing (Possnert *et al*., 2004). Another example of the broader economic impact of environmental degradation is that of the insurance sector. In 2009 the International Association for the Study of Insurance Economics acknowledged that climate change will inevitably lead to higher costs 'largely due to socio-economic factors such as value concentrations in coastal areas' (International Association for the Study of Insurance Economics, 2009: p. 42).

In some cases, such negative impacts on industry will have significant financial implications at the national level. For example, in one case study Reid *et al.* (2007) conclude that climate change will have a major impact on the Gross Domestic Product (GDP) of Namibia:

> Our results show that the climate change impacts on the total GDP could range between losses of N$500 and 1,000 million if only the agricultural impacts are considered. These figures correspond to about 1.5 per cent and 3.5 per cent of GDP. If production losses within the fishing industry are included, the total losses could be up to N$2,000 million in a worst case scenario, implying 6.5 per cent of the total GDP.
>
> (p. 33)

In all such cases, of course, a threat to any national or local industry is a threat to the livelihoods and, in many cases, ways of (social and economic) life of those involved in those industries. As Lee (2009) has noted in the context of communities polluted by dioxin around the An-shun plant in southern Taiwan:

> The research findings underscore that poverty can be a serious issue for residents in polluted areas. The reasons for unemployment among able-bodied household breadwinners may include pollution-related illness, the loss of markets for local products due to pollution or stigmatization, or the migration of business away from the community.
>
> (p. 27)

While the economic effects of environmental degradation appear to fall disproportionately on poorer countries,[11] people in more developed parts of the world face similar threats to their means of economic sustenance. In one recent report, a fisherman in Louisiana facing reduced shrimp hauls apparently as a result of the 2010 Gulf oil spill was quoted as saying: 'We don't have millions of dollars sitting in the bank where we can go do something else. We live and die on the seafood industry. This is our culture. ... This is how we live.' (Lee, 2011: unpaginated.) It is at this point that the impact becomes not just economic, but social and cultural,[12] again illustrating the holistic nature of the issue highlighted in the last section. Indeed, increased poverty due to economic downturns precipitated by environmental degradation will almost certainly feed back as negative health implications on those impoverished (Murray, 2006). Again the differing 'impacts' of environmental harm prove difficult to separate from one another.

Less directly, increased costs, and therefore increased taxes, may also come about within jurisdictions as a result of the increase in *regulation* of potentially environmentally damaging activities, and certainly the criminalization of such activities. On this point Hall and Farrall (forthcoming) have highlighted how the increase in regulatory processes to tackle environmental crime bring increased costs for the local and national governments charged with enforcing them, which are likely to be passed on to the taxpayer. Indeed, a form of so-called eco-tax is already in operation in Germany and in parts of the US (Jackson, 2000). In the UK, increased taxation on polluting industries was a contentious issue for the Conservative/Liberal Democrat coalition government elected in 2010 (Harvey, 2011).

Increased environmental regulation may also of course place even further cost strains on industries themselves. This has led some to argue that there is a trade-off to be had between employment levels (at national and local levels) and increasing environmental standards and associated regulations or criminalizations (see Stewart, 1993). Such effects have been the source of particular contention in the United States, following the original enactment of the Clean Air Act in 1963 and through its subsequent amendments (Morss, 1996).[13] The impact of environmental regulation on employment levels is however a highly contested issue, with Goodstein (1994) dismissing the alleged trade-off as a 'myth'. There is indeed increasing evidence to support the dismissal of this link, although again much of the research has been confined to the United States. Levinson (1996), for example, offers statistical evidence to the effect that 'interstate differences in environmental regulations do not systematically affect the location choices of most manufacturing plants' (p. 5). More recently, Northeast States for Coordinated Air Use Management[14] (2011) has argued that, far from causing unemployment and economic degradation in the northeast/mid-Atlantic region of the US, the introduction of programs to promote clean transportation fuels will in fact create tens of thousands of jobs each year in the area:

> The results of the analysis suggest that the transition to lower carbon fuels could provide important energy security, climate change, and economic

> benefits in the region. For example, electricity, advanced biofuels, and natural gas are low carbon fuels not yet widely used in the region for transportation. A gradual transition to one or more of these fuels would reduce carbon emissions and those of other harmful pollutants, enhance energy independence and reduce vulnerability to price swings in imported petroleum, and create jobs in the region.
>
> (p. 9)

Furthermore, a review of studies published by The Lancet Series on Climate Change (Watts, 2008) suggests similarly positive outcomes of attempts to address environmental polluting activities when any negative economic impacts are weighed against the benefits to health:

> The threat of climate change has generated a global flood of policy documents, suggested technical fixes, and lifestyle recommendations. One widely held view is that their implementation would, almost without exception, prove socially uncomfortable and economically painful. But as a series of new studies shows, in one domain at least – public health – such a view is ill founded. If properly chosen, action to combat climate change can, of itself, lead to improvements in health. The news is not all bad.
>
> (p. 2)

There has been some counter-argument that those advocating such a positive view of environmental regulation and its effect on industry and employment are also those with more eco-activist credentials (see Vogel, 2003). This on-going debate serves as a good illustration of White's (2011) point, discussed earlier in this chapter, that the 'objective' nature of 'science' and 'knowledge' in this area must always be subject to scrutiny.

Although it is inevitably a complex issue, the above discussion clearly supports the basic proposition that environmental degradation does have and will continue to have significant negative economic impacts on individuals, as well as on states and corporations. From a legal perspective, reducing such victimizations to economic measures is useful, because it allows for more consistent application of redress mechanisms of compensation or restitution. This is a theme that will be returned to in Chapter 5. It is also of course useful from a policy perspective, because it allows judgements to be made regarding the cost-effectiveness of mechanisms intended to reduce environmental degradation and also of systems of regulation or criminalization. In the latter case, we have seen that the balance of evidence now seems to be swinging away from the suggestion that regulation may in fact *increase* victimization in the form of economic hardships, which is a positive development from the perspective of the criminological exercise and the goals of the present volume. Indeed, attempts by collaborations of economists, criminologists and victimologists to express the impacts of more traditional crimes in economic terms have recently gathered pace (Loomes, 2007). Nevertheless, it is also clear that expressing all such impacts in monetary terms is extremely difficult, and indeed there is no clear line between economic and non-economic impacts. Consequently, to focus exclusively on monetary calculations of harm is likely to underestimate the true extent of environmental victimization. This becomes increasingly clear as we move on to examine social and cultural impacts of such victimization.

2.1.3 Social and cultural impacts

Quantifying 'social' or 'cultural' damage to a people or community as a result of environmental harms is of course extremely challenging, although as an exercise it is by no means alien to more mainstream criminology (Dolan and Moore, 2007). As a category of impact, it is also central to the notion of environmental justice, which (as we saw in Chapter 1) includes harm to 'cultural norms, values, rules, regulations and behaviours' (Bryant, 1995: p. 6). Initially it may seem straightforward to dismiss these impacts as 'less tangible' than some of the others discussed above. These are not abstract speculations, however: indeed, loss of one's traditional cultural activities and lifestyle can itself have significant economic and health effects. For example, there are a number of discussions in the literature concerning the people of the Maldives, who are at present facing significant risk to their homes, economy and traditional ways of life as a result of sea-level rises apparently brought about by climate change (Brown *et al.*, 1997; Mörner *et al.*, 2004; Possnert *et al.*, 2004; Domroes, 2001). Of particular relevance here is that these discussions have reflected at length on whether corporate entities or even foreign states might be held responsible (criminally or otherwise) under international law for the damage that has been done to the islanders' traditional fishery culture (Mörner *et al.*, 2004). The further example of shrimp fishing in the Gulf of Mexico has already been discussed. The key point for present purposes is that it is these traditional *cultures* which also provide these environmental victims with the *practical* necessities of living (food, livelihood, etc.), as acknowledged by the 2012 Rio+20 UN Conference on Sustainable Development in its Outcome Document: 'many people, especially the poor, depend directly on ecosystems for their livelihoods, their economic, social and physical well-being, and their cultural heritage' (Para. 30).

The above notwithstanding, the harms brought about by cultural and social damage to a community or an individual extend beyond those that can be followed through to a more tangible impact. In one telling example, Wheatley (1997) has elaborated on the social and cultural impacts of mercury pollution on aboriginal peoples in Canada. The author stresses the holistic view of the environment taken by such communities and notes that the impacts of such harm therefore go well beyond the physical or that which can be expressed (or redressed) in monetary terms:

> Degradation of the environment by western industrial development, including by contaminants such as mercury, is seen by Aboriginal people as lack of respect. The harmonious balance on which Aboriginal people's

> philosophy is based has been disrupted by forces outside their control. The ability to provide for present and future generations, an integral part of this philosophy, is threatened. The knowledge that traditional foods contain mercury may produce a range of social and cultural impacts, apart from any direct health effects.
>
> (p. 88)

Similar observations have been made in the US context, where Brook (1998) has labelled the threat to Native American sovereignty precipitated by the industrial dumping of toxic waste on tribal lands as a form of 'environmental genocide'.

A further dimension to the loss of cultural and social stability brought about by environmental victimization is the far-reaching criminogenic implications, leading to further victimizations. One especially relevant issue, with which the criminal justice agencies of most developed countries are already heavily concerned, is that of human trafficking. The concern with trafficking in the context of the present discussion stems from the expected increase in displaced peoples and forced migrations, as well as a general increase in poverty in the parts of the world which are hardest hit by climate change (Mendelsohn *et al.*, 2006). Indeed, the link between displaced peoples/forced migrations and human trafficking has been expressly drawn by a number of researchers (see Lee, 2007). The United Nations University's Institute for Environment and Human Security (Warner *et al.*, 2008) in particular has demonstrated specific connections between migrations *forced by environmental factors* and a susceptibility of these displaced individuals to human trafficking. Jasparro and Taylor (2008) have also summarized the links between climate change, culture and the threat of human trafficking (as well as the trafficking in illicit drugs, wildlife and arms), arguing that:

> Southeast Asian livelihood and social systems will be pressured, while state and civil society capacity will be strained. This will intensify existing vulnerabilities to non-state security threats and raise the overall level of vulnerability and risk to both human and state security.
>
> (p. 1)

In Europe, too, the expectation of human trafficking is already a high concern for member states (Shelley, 2007). It is submitted that the effects of climate change and other environmental degradation are likely to create a further pull in the direction of stringent collaborative action, with implications for the human rights of those trafficked, many of whom end up working in illegal and poorly regulated sectors of the economy.[15]

In sum, cultural and social impacts brought about by environmental victimization can have very real consequences (some more practical and others less so) and indeed cause harm of a systemic and long-term nature. The question this poses for criminal justice systems across the world is how (or whether) these systems can offer any kind of meaningful redress mechanism for this category of harms. The challenge of doing so turns largely on victims being able to convey the full impacts of this non-monetary damage in a way that courts and legal practitioners will understand and are culturally prepared to take into account; which in turn raises questions of the participation of environmental victims in any justice process. This issue will be discussed in more detail in Chapter 4. Of course, the victims of social and cultural damage brought about by environmental degradation are not just those being affected now, but potentially future generations of peoples. This recalls the notion of intergenerational justice discussed in Chapter 1 and, furthermore, would seem to imply that any mechanism of redress must address the underlying problems causing the degradation and work towards the restoration of the damaged environment as well as the short-term needs of currently identifiable environmental victims. The challenges inherent in achieving this will be discussed in Chapter 5.

2.1.4 Security impacts

In recent years, ideas regarding 'security' have been increasingly linked to environmental concerns in a distinct literature on 'environmental security' (see Hough, 2012). Definitions of environmental security differ, with no overarching understanding yet agreed upon (see Heckler, 2011), but generally the concept tends to link environmental degradation and the associated scarcity of resources with human conflict at individual, group and state levels. Brunnée (1995) conceives it as 'the prevention and management of conflicts precipitated by environmental decline' (p. 1742). Although typically limited to the field of armed conflicts (which naturally result in considerable loss of life and personal injury to human victims), more recent definitions of environmental security tend to include a wider body of threats to the natural environment (Ullman, 1983). For example, in recent years the concept of environmental security has led some commentators to speak of 'environmental terrorism', which Chalecki (2001) defines as 'the unlawful use of force against in situ environmental resources so as to deprive populations of their benefit(s) and/or destroy other property' (p. 3).[16] Schofield (1999) adds to this the use of the environment as a conduit for destruction (such as poisoning the water supply of an urban centre). While this is a contested topic, Schwartz (1998) discusses how the notion of environmental terrorism has gained considerable public, political and academic attention since the early 1990s, even before the terrorist attacks in the United States of September 2001.[17] By 2008, New York City was spending a $12 million grant from the US Environmental Protection Agency on its Water Security Initiative, a pilot program to develop and evaluate a contamination warning system for its drinking-water distribution network. Concerns have also been voiced regarding the possibility of terrorist attacks on oil pipelines in Russia and Central Asia (see Adams, 2003). Schwartz also called for the development of a crime of 'ecocide' to reflect the social condemnation of such deliberate acts of wasteful environmental destruction.[18]

For the purposes of this discussion, the important observation is that, as natural resources become restricted by the various impacts of climate change and wider environmental degradation, this is likely to make such resources increasingly precious to states and therefore increasingly attractive to terrorist groups seeking to achieve symbolic victories. The response of governments is therefore likely to be increased regulation and the rollout of harsher penalties (and new crimes) for environmental terrorists, just as the scope of 'terrorism' itself was expanded in many jurisdictions in the light of the 2001 US terrorist attacks (Mythen and Walklate, 2006).

While the human impacts of threats to environmental security in general are very real (whether they take the form of increased susceptibility to direct or indirect harm through terrorist activity, increased fear, threats to livelihoods, or the need to adapt to stricter regulatory regimes), they are perhaps less immediate or widespread than the dangers posed by the more specific threat to food security. 'Food security' has been defined by the World Food Summit of 1996 as existing 'when all people at all times have access to sufficient, safe, nutritious food to maintain a healthy and active life' (United Nations Food and Agriculture Organization, 2010). The concept is usually understood as including both physical and economic access to food that meets people's dietary needs as well as their food preferences (Pinstrup-Andersen, 2009).

At present much of the literature and policy attention in various countries has focused on the immediate health and humanitarian implications of food security coming under threat; however, the legal and criminogenic implications are also beginning to be assessed. MacLeod *et al.* (2010), for example, have written at length on the introduction of regulative frameworks intended to preserve food security.[19] In China, the National People's Congress Standing Committee has recently introduced criminal sanctions, including heavy fines and prison sentences, to anyone convicted of adding poisonous or harmful ingredients during the production of food (CNTV, 2011).

It has been widely predicted that the impact of climate change on crop levels would lead to a drop in supply and therefore a rise in the price of food, with obvious implications for food security (see Schanbacher, 2010). This effect was confirmed by Lobell *et al.* in May 2011. Of course, a rise in the price of food itself has many criminogenic and victimogenic implications. Lack of food may lead to localized violence and riots about food prices, as demonstrated by the unrest felt across some 20 countries in 2008, when world food prices reached crisis levels (Ivanic and Martin, 2008). In the African context, Takemura (2007) asserts that there is a 'deepening anger and resentment among people at the bottom of society, fostered by a rize in food prices, which could threaten stability in developing countries' (p. 273). The author also asserts:

> The great threat is global warming. The vast Sahara Desert is encroaching slowly but steadily into cropland. One-third of Sub-Saharan Africans live in drought-prone areas. The effects of global warming are serious indeed because food production relies more than 90 per cent on rainwater.
>
> (p. 247)

Indeed, the violence that has been predicted to come as a result of food insecurity may well have already found expression, with some suggesting that food prices helped to trigger the unrest in Tunisia and Egypt in early 2011.[20] Historically, food riots are also not alien to the UK, where they occurred in the eighteenth century (Thompson, 1991), or to the US, where the 1862 'Bread Riots' were precipitated by droughts, leading to a reduction in grain and other basic foodstuffs, exacerbated by the pressures of the civil war (Steinberg, 2008).

Food security is a good example of the often indistinguishable quality of the impacts of climate change and environmentally harmful activities on the wider environment on the one hand, and human victimization on the other. Mares (2010), for example, emphasizes the knock-on effects of soil erosion brought about by changes in temperature and reduced rainfall:

> Annually the world loses about 24 billion tons of topsoil (Montgomery 2007, p. 4). While this sounds and is a lot, public discussion of ecological harm continues to focus mostly on climate change. Nonetheless, soil is critically important to ecosystems and thus humans. Without good soil, plants are less productive and less food can be produced per acre. There is ample historical evidence that some previous civilizations literally ran out of 'dirt' and collapsed (Catton 1993; Diamond 2005; Fagan 2008; Foster 1999).... In short, the exhaustion of soil resources across the globe has great potential to create substantial future human insecurity and harm. Most of the negative effects are likely to be found in poorer, developing nations.
>
> (p. 283)

Environmental degradation therefore undermines security in a number of ways, which have major potential consequences for human beings in terms of their health, safety and continued prosperity. It can also be gleaned from the above that threats to security may prompt increased deviance and criminal activities. It is to this link between victimization and offending or deviant behaviour that I turn in the next section.

2.2 Victims as offenders, offenders as victims

One extremely revealing factor, which is often under-conceptualized in the literature, is the substantial overlap which seems to exist between those prompted to commit criminal offences by environmental pressures and the victims of those pressures. There is a large body of criminological literature indicating that, far from being the ideal, blameless characters that policy-makers, the public and indeed many victimologists tend to associate with 'victims of crime' (see Christie, 1986), real victims (of most kinds) in fact substantially overlap with real criminals, and vice versa (Lauritsen *et al.*, 1991; Farrall and Maltby, 2003). Farrall and Maltby (2003) have argued that this reality in fact prevents any divorcement of 'victimology' from the wider ambit of criminology:

> Because an accurate victimology is desirable (as are accurate crime statistics, weather forecasts and petrol-tank gauges), we, as scholars, need to tackle one of the most common findings of victimology, namely that victims and offenders are often drawn from the same population 'pool'. Because this ultimately means grappling with offending behaviour as much as it does victim behaviour, it begs the following question: Can victimology ever really distinguish itself from criminology? The authors' feelings are that it cannot.
>
> (p. 50)

It is becoming increasingly clear that the same overlap occurs when one considers *environmental* victims. Take for example the potential victims of human trafficking discussed above. Clearly, as is the case with many trafficked individuals, such victims will inevitably find themselves engaged in illegal activities in the 'receiving' country or region, be it prostitution or illegal working. Marmo and La Forgia (2008) comment on how official and unofficial authorities in Australia have a tendency to characterize trafficked women as undesirables, regardless of the circumstances that left them in their present situation and regardless of whether such people are actively engaged in illegal activities:

> In Australia, trafficked women are portrayed and maintained as the 'other', as unbelonging matter of the moral and legal community. Trafficked women are dealt with as an external issue – to the point that their conditions and situation are unable to affect domestic policy objectives. Their status as irregular immigrants is used to re-establish a social and moral order, a social identity of the Australian system, which is disturbed by the unwanted presence of trafficked women.
>
> (p. 174)

It is worth noting that such an attitude is certainly against the spirit (and possibly the letter) of the 2005 UN Protocol to the United Nations Convention against Transnational Organized Crime of 2000, which obliges each State Party 'to take appropriate measures within its means to provide assistance and protection to victims of offences covered by this Convention in particular in cases of threat of retaliation or intimidation'.[21] Yet even non-trafficked immigrants may be treated as criminal, both by the original population of a country or area and by the criminal justice system. Furthermore, it has been demonstrated by Sampson (2008) that the presence of minority groups in an area or country appears to increase the perception of crime and disorder among existing residents, even though crime itself shows little increase. Smith (2007) has commented on how some countries have gone so far as to deploy their military forces in reaction to the flow of displaced human populations, perceiving them as a security threat.

Further examples of the overlap between 'environmental victims' and 'environmental offenders' can be drawn from the above discussion. Food suppliers, for example, who are tempted to adulterate their product in times of reduced harvests and rising costs may be seen as victims of their economic circumstances, as Mandalia (2005) has argued occurred following the 'Sudan 1' red spice-dye scandal of 2005. In this case Croall (2007)[22] has highlighted the reality that 'it was not just unscrupulous suppliers who are to blame, as such practices are ultimately linked to European demand for low prices which "more or less forces" producers – who need Western currencies to survive – to cheat' (p. 226). Indeed, on the issue of food security, those who protest or even riot as a consequence of a lack of food, or high food prices, are arguably only doing so as a result of the harms climate change has visited upon them. Clearly, given such a situation, there is a concern that the poorest people will turn to illegal food markets. As well as being criminal in themselves, such illegal markets will undoubtedly be run by those who will be willing to use threats or actual violence to ensure that they get the prices they want for the goods they sell, and who may also be involved in other allied trades (such as the supply of weapons and drugs and the control of prostitution) which can only prompt still further victimizations.

The same may be true of those entering illegal trade markets as a way of sustaining themselves economically because, for example, the tourist industry in the Mediterranean (see Berrittella *et al.*, 2006) or the Maldives (see Domroes, 2001) is suffocated by rising temperatures and coastal erosion. Even those white-collar criminals who avoid eco-tax and/or defraud insurance brokers have initially been victimized (in economic terms) by reason of having to pay more for their services. Since many people may not wish to pay increased rates of taxation, so rates of tax avoidance may increase as a response. This may be particularly the case given that, as evidenced by public reaction in the UK, so-called green taxes are politically unpopular and have been met with suspicion by the electorate (see Brown, 2008). Thus, in contrast to the social attitudes in favour of prosecuting polluters in criminal courts, those same public attitudes may not consider the avoidance of taxes intended to fund environmental projects, nor over-claiming in response to the environmental levy placed on insurance premiums, as representing 'real' criminality.

Returning to the case of insurance, higher costs of insurance may lead to an erosion of confidence in the insurance sector, and to widespread mis- or over-claiming among consumers. In 2004 Karstedt and Farrall (2006) asked citizens in England and Wales about the extent to which they trusted their insurers to make them a fair offer during a claim; around 20 per cent said that they did not. They also asked people if they had ever been offered less by their insurer than they felt that were entitled to; 27 per cent said that this had happened at least once to them. When asked if they were worried about being left out of pocket on an insurance claim, some 39 per cent said that they were very or fairly worried about this possibility. Five per cent said that they had deliberately cheated on an insurance claim. Such cheating is likely to increase if insurers start to withdraw some coverage from some parts of a country or if they start to raise their premiums based on environmental factors. Insurance may seem like an odd service to highlight in a discussion of victimization-precipitated consequences of climate change and wider environmental degradation. However, for many people who see themselves as 'non-criminal', insurance claims offer one arena in which they might extract (illegal) profit in difficult economic times without feeling that they are offending. As insurers become more discerning over whom or what they are prepared to cover and how much of an excess they are prepared to request, so insurance clients may seek to gain redress via such illicit practices.

In addition to those turning to activities that have for the most part always been criminalized, increased regulation of the environment can expand the official ambit of 'deviance', in a process criminologists often label 'net widening' (McMahon, 1990), to make new offenders out of the victims of ecological change. Here White (2011) draws on the work of Duffy (2010) to give an example of the creation of wildlife reserves in parts of Africa: 'When wildlife reserves are established, local communities can suddenly find that their everyday subsistence activities have been outlawed and they have been redefined as criminals' (p. 113). White backs up this assertion by reference to climate-induced subsistence activities that do further harm to the environment, but become necessary in face of mass displacement of peoples:

> The plight of the displaced and disadvantaged means that often any environmental destruction brought about by their actions (cutting down of forests, fishing in protected areas or in another state's exclusive economic zone) is best remedied by social justice initiatives rather than criminal justice interventions.
>
> (p. 113)

The issue of how environmental regulation may expand the power of the state, bringing those to its attention who previously would not have merited official sanction, will be discussed in more detail in Chapters 5 and 6. Clearly, however, it is worrying that some of those most harshly affected by environmental victimization (social, economic, health or security) might in fact find themselves recast as environmental criminals. White's point also recalls the suggestion made in Chapter 1 of this volume that the law is not necessarily the only or best way to deal with such transgressions.

2.3 Inequalities in the impacts of environmental victimization

There is a further important dimension to environmental victimization that in many ways underscores all the above discussions. While Williams (1996) has criticized the characterization of the powerless as environmental victims and the powerful as environmental victimizers as promoting 'a stereotyped view that omits the victimization of those with power and wealth' (p. 201), the overriding evidence now points to endemic inequality in the distribution of the harms discussed in this chapter (Dobson, 1998). There are several elements to this inequality, one of which is geographical. Indeed the geographically unequal impact of environmental degradation is well recognized by the international legal order, with the preamble to the 1992 UN Framework Convention on Climate Change (FCCC) acknowledging the particular vulnerability of 'low-lying and other small island countries, countries with low-lying coastal, arid and semi-arid areas or areas liable to floods, drought and desertification, and developing countries with fragile mountainous ecosystems'.[23] More recently, the Outcome Document form the 2012 UN Rio+20 Conference on Sustainable Development acknowledges that

> small island developing States remain a special case for sustainable development in view of their unique and particular vulnerabilities, including their small size, remoteness, narrow resource and export base, and exposure to global environmental challenges and external economic shocks, including to a large range of impacts from climate change and potentially more frequent and intense natural disasters.
>
> (Para. 178)

Of course, as already discussed in this chapter and as hinted at in this extract, it is important that this focus on the inequalities of environmental harm fostered by physical geography do not distract us from the more complex – social, economic and cultural – aspects of environmental victimization. Examples like that of the Maldives reflect the important observation that victimization as a result of climate change is distributed very unevenly, with the poorest, most disadvantaged countries and groups within countries tending to suffer most. As acknowledged by the International Association for the Study of Insurance Economics (2009):

> unmitigated climate change may have significant adverse effects on the long-term development of the world economy, ranging from water shortages for food production to an increased severity of tropical windstorms. Developing countries are particularly vulnerable, facing the risk of social disorder and mass migration.
>
> (p. 108)

Beyond climate change, the unequal distribution of environmental degradation as a whole has been commented on by South (2010), who sees this as reflecting wider tendencies towards 'social exclusion' which have long been a topic of research and discussion in mainstream criminology (Byrne, 1999). In relation to environmental victimization, Lee (2009) has summarized the situation: 'Poor people are usually excluded from the environmental decision-making process, and once a policy is made, they are usually powerless to change it' (pp. 3–4). For South (2010), the depletion of resources caused by environmental derogation can only exacerbate existing social division between the well-off and the poor:

> In a world of increased scarcity, such inequalities will simply be embedded further and we will face the threat of new social constructions of hierarchies and needs emerging. The resulting competition for resources is likely to produce discrimination and violence based on ethnic, gender and other well established sources of 'difference' and discrimination.
>
> (p. 237)

Certainly, South's contention that environmental degradation leads to increased division on grounds of ethnicity is well documented in the literature, to the extent that it has been called 'environmental racism' (Spencer *et al.*, 2011). Economic theories as to why exposure to environmental harms apparently varies by race include 'pure discrimination by polluters or politicians in sitting decisions; differences in willingness to pay for environmental amenities linked to income or education levels; and variations in the propensity of communities to engage in collective action to oppose the location of potential polluters' (Hamilton, 1995: p. 1). Paulido (1996) provides a good overview of the development of evidence of a link between sites of environmental degradation (especially the dumping of toxic materials) and black communities within the US.[24] Similar results have been replicated at the international level (Alston and Brown, 1993). Boer *et al.* (1997) confirm that, statistically, the appearance of discrimination in the location of hazardous waste treatment, storage and disposal facilities (TSDF) proximate to areas where ethnic minorities live in Los Angeles is not explained by alternative, non-racial factors: '[E]ven controlling for income, industrial land use, and manufacturing employment, racial/ethnicity correlates with the location of TSDF' (p. 807).

Of course, the fact that ethnic minorities tend to fall victim to environmental harm reflects their increased susceptibility to general criminal victimization, another widely accepted finding of mainstream criminology (Clancy and Hough, 2001). This last observation adds weight to the contention that these matters are actually well suited to investigation by criminologists, as the underlying social causes of such inequality in victimization may well be similar, if not the same. Pulido (2000) has picked up on the notion that environmental racism is precipitated by wider social processes, in addition to more overt forms of racism such as 'discriminatory facility siting and malicious intent' (p. 12). As such, the author introduces the concept of 'white privilege', which suggests that there is a less conscious but hegemonic form of racism that over time has dramatic effects on the use of space:

> Although, in Los Angeles, nonwhites have always lived adjacent to industry, people of color have recently begun moving into the suburbs, and have taken over what were once white industrial suburbs. Over time, these industrial suburbs have become part of the inner city, and are increasingly populated by people of color. As a result, central Los Angeles with its concentration of industrial hazards, remains a nonwhite space. In contrast, whites continue to move to the periphery, which is relatively cleaner. These

patterns developed over a century and continue to inform the present, illustrating how various forms of racism shape our landscapes.

(p. 33)

The argument that environmental harm also disproportionately falls on women is of course the main contention of the feminist critique, as discussed in Chapter 1. As is the case with race, there are numerous studies that support this gendered interpretation of environmental victimization. Wachholz (2007) has summarized these effects as being linked to gendered division of labour in many developing countries, where women are disproportionately responsible for subsistence farm labour, child care, care of the sick and infirm and the gathering of household biofuels and water. Essentially, the effects of environmental degradation on traditional farming industries, water supply and health increase the workload of these women, 'reducing their opportunities for personal and social development' (p. 169), exacerbating the poverty that women the world over disproportionately find themselves subjected to. As the author summarizes, 'The IPCC[25] has warned that climate change is likely to actuate gaps between the world's rich and poor, and women are already among the poorest' (Wachholz, 2007: p. 171). This reality has also been acknowledged by the UN Development Programme (2010) in its advancement of UN Millennium Development Goal 3, to promote gender equality and empower women:

> Climate change, including increased severity and frequency of extreme events, puts women and girls especially at risk of loss of life and livelihoods, exploitation, and further marginalization. Inequitable access to food, shelter, and medicines also increases gender impacts post-disaster.
>
> (p. 2)

The Rio+20 Outcome Document published following the UN Rio Conference on Sustainable Development in June 2012 similarly has paragraphs on 'Gender equality and the empowerment of women', with particular focus on women 'in rural areas and local communities and among indigenous peoples and ethnic minorities' (Para. 238). Notably, however, this document makes no specific mention of the increased vulnerability of women to environmental harms per se.

One major concern about the impact of environmental degradation, and climate change in particular, on women is the possible link to violence. Essentially this is due to the fact that violence against women tends to increase in the aftermath of natural disasters of the kind precipitated by the effects of climate change. On this point, Wachholz (2007) compiles evidence of an increase in such violence following hurricanes, floods and droughts. In a comprehensive review of knowledge gaps in this area, Brody *et al.* (2008) conclude:

> There is also evidence that women and girls are more likely to become victims of domestic and sexual violence after a disaster, particularly when families

> have been displaced and are living in overcrowded emergency or transitional housing where they lack privacy. The increase in violence is often partly attributed to stress caused by men's loss of control in the period following a disaster, compounded by longer term unemployment or threatened livelihoods.
>
> (p. 3)

The mention here of family displacement links the question of inequality of impact on women to that of human trafficking discussed above, the vast majority of these victims being women and girls (Denton, 2000). Jasparro and Taylor (2008) have specifically commented on the vulnerabilities of women in this regard as climate change and other environmental degradation expands. Indeed, to give one example, it was reported in 2010 that Masaai parents in the Mar region of Kenya, where climate change was already having noticeable effects on crops, were 'selling off' their under-age daughters to a group of human traffickers posing as foreign tourists (Women's News Network, 2010).

Overall, what is clear is that the disproportionate impact of environment degradation on women comes about not as a result of 'new' harms per se, but rather as a result of the manner in which environmental harm exacerbates existing inequalities of vulnerability to existing crimes.

It is perhaps unsurprising given the above discussion that the inequality of impacts of environmental harm operates not just between different social and economic groups within jurisdictions, but also *between* jurisdictions as a whole. Thus, the impacts of environmental degradation tend to weigh most heavily on the poorest developing *countries* as well as the poorest people within those countries. An analysis by Mendelsohn *et al.* (2006) of statistical data and prediction on climate change puts the matter succinctly: 'Overall, the poor [countries] will suffer the bulk of the damages from climate change, whereas the richest countries will likely benefit' (p. 173). The authors' contention that rich countries may benefit from climate change is based on the observation that they are 'located in the mid to high latitudes and are currently cool' (p. 162); thus warmer temperatures may actually be closer to optimum for crop production. Indeed, Deschênes and Greenstone (2007) suggest an increase in annual profits from agricultural land of $1.3 billion in the US as a direct result of climate change over the next decade. Such observations and estimations are however contestable, especially if one expands the scope of the discussion beyond crop production. As noted by White (2011):

> One thing is certain, and that is that climate change generally is bound to affect everyone on the planet. While, to date, the impact of climate change has been felt disproportionately in the developing countries, recent estimates indicate that more affluent countries of the West are now beginning to experience climate-related disasters.
>
> (p. 25)

The true extent of the inequality endemic to environmental victimization lies not in the differential impacts on rich versus poor as dictated by geographical phenomena, but in the ability of the rich to postpone the onset of such harms or to shift their impacts to the poorer countries. In a process which Stebbins (1992) dubs 'garbage imperialism', industrialized nations are increasingly exporting unwanted waste materials to third-world and developing nations. Indeed, the United Nations General Assembly, in its Millennium Declaration of 2000, alludes to this point: 'For while globalization offers great opportunities, at present its benefits are very unevenly shared, while its costs are unevenly distributed' (Para. 5). A particular issue has been identified in this regard with the export of so-called e-waste,[26] one of the world's largest exporters being the US:

> Most U.S. E-waste simply is disposed of in landfills or is incinerated, but a considerable portion of it is gathered for recycling and is exported to developing nations for remanufacture or refurbishment (Environmental Protection Agency [EPA], 2007). Many recycling facilities in developing nations, however, are not equipped to handle e-waste properly, and much of it is not processed but is instead dumped in local villages near people and water sources (Pellow, 2007). Illegal dump sites have been documented in Nigeria, Ghana, China, the Philippines, Indonesia, Pakistan, and India (Greenpeace, 2008; Iles, 2004), and they pose severe threats to both human health and the natural environment.
>
> (p. 546)

The transfer of waste from rich nations to poor nations is not just a question of the former taking advantage of looser regulatory regimes in the latter, but rather the trade in such waste may actually become an industrial and economic necessity for developing countries. As Critharis (1990) notes, 'Third world nations are particularly good targets [for waste exporters] because of their need for capital' (p. 312).

Waste materials may not be the only exported environmental harms from the global rich to the global poor. Walters (2006), for example, has described 'the ways that powerful governments and corporations seek to dominate global food markets while exploiting, pressuring and threatening vulnerable countries' (p. 1). In particular, she discusses the political, economic and even spiritual pressure[27] exerted by the US on Zambia in the effort to convince the African nation to import its genetically modified crops. The long-term implications of such crops for human health and biodiversity are of course still the topic of heated debate (Malarkey, 2003).

This transnational element to the question of environmental victimization demands the consideration not only of national legal remedies, but also of remedies provided by the international legal order. It is clear from the above paragraphs that this is a highly complex, multifaceted problem which combines very practical consequences with economic and socially dependent variables. As always in such cases, developing a legal system which adequately encompasses all these elements, let alone provides effective redress or other solutions, is a significant task. It is to the beginnings of this task that the next section turns its attention.

2.4 Environmental victims as victims of abuse of power?

In an attempt to reconcile some of the above complexities in conceptualizing 'environmental victims', one possible solution that has been suggested by commentators (Williams, 1996; White, 2011) is to draw on the UN General Assembly's definition of 'victims of abuse of power' from its 1985 Declaration of Basic Principles of Justice and Abuse of Power, which might serve as a useful starting point for ascribing rights to environmental victims. The 1985 Declaration definition reads:

> [P]ersons who, individually or collectively, have suffered harm, including physical or mental injury, emotional suffering, economic loss or substantial impairment of their fundamental rights, through acts or omissions that do not yet constitute violations of national criminal laws but of internationally recognized norms relating to human rights.
>
> (Para. 18)

The inclusion of victims of abuse of power within the 1985 Declaration was intended to encompass victimization by the state[28], making this definition particularly relevant from the perspective of victims of environmental harms. As noted in Chapter 1, Kauzlarich *et al.* (2001) have drawn on this to develop a framework 'victimology of the state', which includes 'International-International Governmental Crime', or crime which occurs outside a state's geographic jurisdiction against international law or human rights. Such an understanding would theoretically encompass victimization not only by one's home state, but by other states as well, possibly covering situations like that of the Maldives. Another salient example can be drawn from the reaction of some states to environmental activists, a case in point being the sinking of the Greenpeace flagship *Rainbow Warrior* in Auckland harbour in 1985 by the French Secret Service. Carrabine *et al.* (2004) remark on this example of state victimization: 'States condemn "terrorism" but are perfectly capable of resorting to terrorist-type methods when in conflict with oppositional groups (p. 394). Furthermore, it is notable that, in keeping with the radical victimological critique discussed in Chapter 1, abuse of power is specifically conceived in the 1985 Declaration as actions and omissions that *do not* constitute crimes. In this light, states should:

> [P]eriodically review existing legislation and practices to ensure their responsiveness to changing circumstances, should enact and enforce, if necessary, legislation proscribing acts that constitute serious abuses of political or economic power, as well as promoting policies and mechanisms for the prevention of such acts, and should develop and make readily available appropriate rights and remedies for victims of such acts.
>
> (Para. 19)

On the face of it, 'abuses of political or economic power' has the potential to capture many of the activities discussed above, particularly in relation to the political pressures associated with the dumping of toxic materials and with the export of genetically modified crops. Importantly, the definition also employs the term 'harm' rather than 'injury', again giving it the breadth to encompass a wide range of environmental victimizations, and is in keeping with the social harms approach outlined in Chapter 1.

I will return to the legal implications of the 1985 Declaration in Chapter 3. At a theoretical level, however, the key drawback of the definition for these purposes is its reliance on 'recognized norms relating to human rights' as a means of distinguishing abusive from non-abusive exercise of power. Although this is a topic of increasing debate, Chapter 4 will demonstrate the difficulty of establishing the existence of any human right to a clean environment recognized by the international legal order. Furthermore, the definition does little to address the political reality that, whatever understandings are employed by commentators, legal reform tends to be enacted for the benefit of 'ideal' and 'innocent' victims, as opposed to the many environmental victims discussed above who may turn to, or find themselves forced into (or even defined into), criminal activities. This is significant because, while general evaluations of victim reform across jurisdictions suggest that it is now common to define victims of all kinds by reference to 'harm suffered' rather than 'crime' in theory, in reality reform agendas across these same jurisdictions tend to emphasize certain kinds of (ideal, cooperative) victims and certain kinds of suffering (often experienced as a result of cooperating with criminal justice agencies; Hall, 2010). Indeed, although the 1985 Declaration has existed for over 20 years, only a very small percentage of reforms derived from it have related to victims of abuse of power, as opposed to victims of crime. In effect, therefore, the definitions of victimhood in use in most jurisdictions are much narrower than they first appear (Hall, 2010). It can be predicated that similar political pressures will be in place as national and international legal systems are adapted to (ostensibly) cater for victims of environmental harm.

2.5 Ways forward

What the preceding discussions clearly confirm is that, as suggested by White (2011), environmental victimization is indeed an active, social process. Indeed, as a report published by the Royal Institute of International Affairs (Hayman and Brack, 2002) noted, '[S]ociety as a whole is often unaware of its [environmental] victimization, so regulators may not set levels of enforcement effort and restitution properly' (p. 6). While victims may in theory be bound together by overarching concepts such as 'abuse of power', it is important, as with addressing any victimization, to appreciate that different people experience 'harm' in unique, subjective ways. We cannot assume for example that *all* aboriginal Canadians experience a deep cultural loss as a result of their ancestral lands being poisoned by toxic dumping, just as not all (or, indeed, most) victims of burglary suffer long-term psychological damage and loss of security in their homes (Shapland and Hall, 2007). Of course, this leads us back to the problem with which this chapter commenced: whether such a wide understanding of environmental victimization could ever be incorporated within a working legal system (nationally or internationally). In fact the problem may be even greater if we acknowledge that, the experience of harm being so subjective, in many cases victims of environmental harm can only be *self*-defined.

Bell and McGillivray (2008) makes the point that, in a great deal of environmental regulation at present, enforcement depends very much on the working practices and cultures of enforcement agencies. While using 'harm' as a common denominator in the identification of environmental victims should result in a wide definition, or self-definition, of victimhood based on an individual's subjective experience of suffering, in fact the availability of legal redress mechanisms (or access to other support beyond the justice system) for such victims may largely depend on the *recognition* of such victim status by these agencies. Again, this suggests that the real problem faced is not so much legal or definitional as cultural.[29] The alternative is to offer mechanisms for self-defined environmental victims to pursue their own cases against parties identified as causing them environmental harm, which of course many are free to do now in domestic civil-law systems. The question to be addressed in the following chapters, however, is what scope exists for these individuals to gain redress under national and international criminal law, particularly when the accused party is their own state, or indeed another state. The next chapter examines these legal issues in greater depth.

3 Environmental victims across jurisdictions: criminal law and state responsibility

The previous chapters have set out the theoretical basis for the consideration of victims of environmental harm by criminologists and victimologists, followed by arguments concerning the nature of such victims and such victimization. The next step, from a green criminological perspective, is an examination of how such victims are acknowledged by and fit into legal systems at the national and international levels, with particular attention being paid to *criminal* justice.

Once again, such a discussion is largely absent from the existing literatures in both international and national environmental law as well as in victimological critiques. This discussion in nonetheless vital in in the endeavour to provide meaningful and useful answers (for policy-makers and legal practitioners) to the research questions set out in Chapter 1. This chapter will be split into two main sections: the first dealing with the application of *criminal law* at the national and international level in relation to the victims of environmental harm, and the second dealing with the possibilities of holding *states* to account for such harm under international law. As is often the case when debating green issues, this choice of direction for the present volume is not above contention. As discussed in both Chapters 1 and 2, the assumption that the law, let alone the *criminal law*, is best placed to 'resolve' cases of environmental harm or offer redress to its victims is far from settled. Nevertheless, we have already seen that there has been in recent years an appreciable trend towards addressing such matters in a criminal context both nationally and internationally, and this will be highlighted further in the present chapter and in Chapter 4. One example, discussed in greater detail below, is that of EU Council Directive 2008/99/EC on the protection of the environment through criminal law.[1] The Directive essentially requires member states to criminalize certain defined breaches of existing EU environmental law. What is significant about this development and others like it is that, previously, member states had the discretion to individually determine the appropriate sanction for breaches of such laws (criminal, civil or administrative[2]) and the severity of any penalties or sanctions imposed. This led to a high degree of variability between countries. The advent of the Directive thus signals a Europe-wide acceptance that *criminal law* is the preferred mechanism for dealing with environmental transgressions. That said, it should not be thought that the *criminalization* of environmentally destructive activities is an entirely new phenomenon. As noted by McMurry and Ramsey: 'In fourteenth century England the Crown prescribed capital punishment for Englishmen who defied a royal proclamation on smoke abatement' (1986: p. 113). As mentioned previously, Roughton (2007) similarly notes that religious scholars have begun to rediscover and reapply environmental precepts from centuries-old Islamic law (shariah law).

In the second part of this chapter, the discussion will turn to state responsibility for environmental harm under international law. Such a discussion is important in this context because, despite developments in the application of domestic criminal law to these issues, a persuasive argument has been made by a number of commentators from the fields of criminology (Walters, 2006) and international law (Berat, 1993) that it is *states*, not just corporations or individuals, that are ultimately responsible (or at least partly responsible) for a large proportion of environmentally destructive activities and the subsequent harms they cause to individuals and ecosystems. Kramer *et al.* (2002), for example, have argued that the state is often complicit in the crimes of large, economically powerful corporations based within its territory:

> State-corporate crimes are illegal or socially injurious actions that result from a mutually reinforcing interaction between (1) policies and/or practices in pursuit of the goals of one or more institutions of political governance and (2) policies and/or practices in pursuit of the goals of one or more institutions of economic production and distribution.
>
> (p. 271)

Furthermore, in reference to the Bhopal Gas leak in India in 1984, Groombridge (1991, citing the previous work of Pearce and Tombs, 1990) makes the following point concerning the liability of the Indian state for the disaster:

> They (Pearce and Tombs, 1990) open their arguments with a quote which suggests that the Indian State may have negligently licensed Union Carbide to operate a plant at Bhopal by relying on an inadequate[ly] staffed and inexpert inspectorate. They make no further reference to the quote which, out of context, may be open to a number of interpretations. It might be presumed that they intend us to understand that Bhopal may not have happened if the Indian State could afford to employ more and better inspectors and followed the policies they advocate.
>
> (p. 8)

In this light of such examples, it is vital to establish to what extent international law facilitates *states* being held accountable for such environmentally destructive actions.

3.1 The challenges of incorporating environmental harms into criminal law

Despite the developments in criminal law in many national and international jurisdictions alluded to in the last section, conceptually ascribing *criminal* blame for environmental destructive activities is a difficult proposition, even before one begins considering the role of the individual or collective victims in such a process. Often it is difficult in such cases to ascribe direct (or even indirect) causation between the actions or inactions of a specific party (or state) accused of bringing about the harm and the undesirable outcomes themselves. Indeed, Du Rées (2001) has commented on this issue in relation to methods of neutralization employed by supervisory agencies with regard to environmental crime, whereby any victim(s) and/or the harm caused is effectively denied:

> It is often claimed that environmental crimes have no directly or clearly defined groups of victims. It is difficult, for example, to connect a specific discharge of a prohibited substance to a specific form of damage to the environment or to people's health.
>
> (p. 649)

Furthermore, as noted by Bell and McGillivray (2008), the extended range of perpetrators of environmental crime can be hopelessly wide: 'A diverse range of individuals and corporate bodies carry out the activities that lead to breaches of environmental law, from solo fly-tippers, to huge multinational corporations' (p. 264). In the absence of a generally recognized 'right' to a clean and unpolluted environment,[3] the basis of any criminal liability for such activities and their resulting harms at a jurisprudential level is often unclear. Indeed, Passas (2005) has highlighted the particular difficulty in relation to cross-border practices which are legal in one country but not in another:

> Cross-border malpractices make the best candidates for crimes without any lawbreaking whatsoever. Whether the offenses and offenders cross domestic state lines or international borders is immaterial. Asymmetries in legal definitions and law enforcement enable corporations to do what is prohibited at home in other jurisdictions without breaking any laws. Processes of globalization have multiplied the opportunities for that.
>
> (pp. 773–774)

Although Passas is not primarily concerned with *environmental* crime or harm, it is clear that the asymmetries he speaks of are precisely what render specific parts of the world and specific groups within a society especially vulnerable to environmental victimization, as highlighted in the last chapter.

In light of such jurisprudential difficulties, Mares (2010) has developed a conceptual framework for understanding the criminalization of environmentally destructive acts. For him, the harm caused by such activities is ultimately reflected by a reduction in the 'carrying capacity' of the planet (that is, its ability to sustain a given amount of human, plant and animal life). In this sense, for Mares, any person, corporation or state which allows, facilitates or engages in behaviour or actions that undermine our (future) means of existence carries a degree of responsibility for reducing the earth's carrying capacity and therefore engages in a crime against both the planet and humanity at large. As the author continues, the notion of carrying capacity is a fundamental omission from the majority of modern legal systems:

> Most legal systems have highly specific laws that regulate only the most severe forms of ecological damage (toxic dumping, illegal logging practices, selling unsafe foodstuff, depriving people of food), but none recognize the harm done by individuals or human societies to the future sustainability of the earth. This is glaringly obvious when examining actions that are considered critical to the economic and social wellbeing of current residents.
>
> (p. 287)

Although somewhat broad-brush, from the perspective of critical criminology the necessary inclusion of corporate and state offenders within this conceptual framework is appealing. The limitation of Mares's framework from a victimological perspective, however, is that he advocates an almost entirely anti-anthropocentric philosophy, where the primary victim is always 'nature'.[4] Indeed, central to Mares's conception is the notion that the use of *legal* systems to address environmentally destructive activities (even one based on notions of carrying capacity) is likely to fail; he advocates instead a more fundamental cultural shift towards a shaming[5] approach:

> It remains to be seen whether criminalization of ecological harm is a fruitful avenue in anything but the clearest and most outrageous cases. Part of the problem is that the connection between offender (human) and victim (nature) is not clear cut; the human damages to carrying capacity are simply too complex.... Rather than relying on strict criminalization of behaviors harming our carrying capacity, I would suggest that we emphasize both collective and individual responsibility for our actions and that we underline their negative impact by employing a shaming approach.
>
> (p. 289)

While there is much to commend this approach in the long term, the difficulty recognized by victimologists is that the kind of wholesale cultural change Mares envisions is unlikely to be achieved in the short term. In the meantime, a great number of individuals, groups and communities will fall victim to environmental harm. There is a clear parallel to be drawn here between Mares's (and others': see South, 1998) arguments in favour of a shaming approach in cases of environmental harm (or, in his language, threats to carrying capacity) and the arguments advocating restorative justice as a solution to the problems faced by 'mainstream' victims in criminal justice (see Dignan, 2004). Of course, restorative justice is often conceived as the very antithesis of 'shaming' (in an exclusionary sense), but for present purposes the point is that both arguments advocate a move away from traditional, formal criminal justice. Contributing to more traditional victimological debates, I have previously argued that this recent focus on restorative justice has to some extent fostered a dearth of up-to-date (empirical) research on the notion of achieving victim-centeredness in the existing criminal justice system (Hall, 2009). Given that the vast majority of victims must still deal with the traditional criminal justice model even in the light of restorative options, it is argued that we ignore this model at our peril, or certainly the peril of victims. Nevertheless, in taking this stance I by no means dismiss the significance of the restorative movement, as this will clearly continue to gather pace and become increasingly important to crime victims in the future, and most probably to victims of environmental harm. Many advocates of restorative justice retain in their theorizing a place for more traditional forms of case disposal (see Dignan, 2002; Braithwaite, 2002). The following discussions adopt the view of Bottoms (2003), who argues in terms of a separation between the criminal justice and restorative justice systems.

3.2 Victims of environmental harm in domestic criminal justice systems

As noted previously, victims of crime in general have recently been the focus of considerable criminal justice reform in many jurisdictions in the developed world. Significantly for the present discussion, this reform agenda has included a general move towards defining victims by the *harm* they endure rather than falling back on exclusive, legalistic categories linked directly to specifically defined offences (Hall, 2011). Nevertheless, any assumption that victims of environmental harm will necessarily be 'caught' by the domestic rules and policies in place in many national criminal justice systems aimed at victims of crime in general is problematic, especially given the 'invisible' nature of such persons (Du Rées, 2001), many of whom may not even identify themselves as victims. The difficulty of applying such broad-brush victim reforms to environmental harm is further reflected by Skinnider (2011), who argues:

> The characteristic of the collective nature of this kind of victimization needs to be understood, particularly with its implications for victims to seek assistance, support and redress which have predominately developed for traditional crimes involving individual victims.
>
> (p. 26)

Notwithstanding such arguments, there are isolated exceptions to the general proposition that something 'more', or at least 'different', is needed for environmental victims over and above that which is already being provided for victims of crime in general, the most significant being the application of the US Crime Victims' Rights Act of 2004 (CVRA)[6] to victims of environmental crime.

Heralded as a major breakthrough by proponents of a more judiciable form of victims' rights (Doyle, 2008), the 2004 CVRA introduced the concept of victims' rights into the US penal code for the first time. The Act contains provision for 'service rights' for victims (Ashworth, 2000) including the provision of information to them by the justice system, protection, and compensation, as well as a procedural right for victims of crime[7] 'to be reasonably heard at any public proceeding in a district court involving release, plea, sentencing, or any parole proceeding'.[8] The most significant feature of the legislation, however, is the enforcement mechanisms it creates. Here, individuals or the federal government may assert victims' rights at the district court level. If the victim or the government are still not satisfied with the enforcement of these rights they may file a petition with the Court of Appeals for a writ of mandamus. A court's decision to deny any of these rights may also be asserted as an error by the prosecution in the case. Even more significantly, in limited circumstances a victim may move for a new trial on the basis of the denial of their rights.[9] The Crime Victims' Rights Act does not apply to the states, as it is not an amendment to the Bill of Rights or the US constitution. Nevertheless, the Act was incorporated into the Federal Rules of Criminal Procedures, which is followed by all judges in federal criminal cases, in April 2008. The Act does not give victims the right to sue the federal government for breach of their rights, but remains one of the most robust systems of rights enforcement for victims seen in any jurisdiction.

The first application of the CVRA to victims of *environmental* crime followed an explosion of a British Petroleum (BP) oil refinery in Texas in 2005. In this case, the US Fifth Circuit Court ruled that the government had violated victims' rights under the CVRA by failing to consult with those locals affected by the explosion (mostly in the form of personal injury and property damage) in the agreement of a plea bargain with BP (Starr *et al.*, 2008). This was despite the fact that the number of victims stretched into the hundreds and the CVRA neither includes nor, on a standard reading, conceives harm caused by environmental damage. More recently, in the case of *W.R. Grace & Co.*, the named company was prosecuted under environmental legislation for 'knowingly endangering' the residents of Libby, Montana, by exposing them to asbestos through mining activities. The federal judge in the case had ruled that 34 prospective victims of these activities (local residents) did not fall under the definition of victim within the Crime Victims' Rights Act[10] and therefore excluded them from the trial proceedings. At appeal, in *Re Parker; U.S.* v *U.S. District Court* and *W.R. Grace & Co.*[11] the United States Ninth Circuit Court of Appeals reversed this decision, thus confirming that prospective victims of environmental harm are indeed included within the ambit of rights provided under the 2004 Act. The case is interesting not only for the specific result, but as a demonstration of the breadth of the term 'victim', and gives weight to the contention that the term includes (or should include) environmental crimes even where there is no specific mention of this category of harms within the rights-enabling legal instrument.

Another potential route for individual victims of environmental harms to be involved in any criminal justice proceeding at the national level surrounding activities resulting in such harm is to mount a private prosecution against the polluter. Private prosecutions are still possible in most jurisdictions (Burns, 1985; Lidstone *et al.*, 1990) although, generally speaking, they are rare and often unsuccessful, principally because they require access to investigatory and legal resources beyond the reach of most individuals or non-governmental organizations (NGOs).[12] This arguably becomes an even greater challenge in the area of environmental crime, where in many cases a great deal of highly complex, scientific and medical evidence may be needed to establish guilt. As noted by Skinnider (2011):

> Cost remains a major obstacle for private prosecution since gathering evidence, hiring experts, hiring a lawyer, etc., fall on the shoulder of the individual or the NGO. In some cases, to mitigate the impact of cost for public interest litigants, the courts have order[ed] advance cost award[s] be paid before the trial to facilitate access to justice.
>
> (p. 63)

Private prosecutions for environmental offences are therefore relatively rare, although accurate figures are difficult to come by. In the UK, Crowhurst and Murphy (2006) report that in 2005 there had been 15 private prosecutions by individuals and NGOs against water companies for pollution offences and 17 private prosecutions of British Coal for pollution from abandoned mines. The most prolific private prosecutor of environmental crime in the UK is the Royal Society for the Prevention of Cruelty to Animals (RSPCA), which regularly brings actions against offences under the Wildlife and Countryside Act 1981 (RSPCA Prosecutions Department, 2010). The RSPCA achieved 2,441 convictions in the Magistrates' Courts in 2010, which the Society puts at a 97.5 per cent success rate for prosecutions (RSPCA, 2012). Ironically, one of the most influential cases of private prosecution on environmental matters in the UK to date involved the principal regulator and prosecutor of such crimes, the Environment Agency, itself as the defendant. This followed the Agency having contracted a firm to build a gauging station on the River Barle, during which the company released a large quantity of cement gout into the water, killing hundreds of fish. As Crowhurst and Murhy (2006) argue:

> Mr Cook's [the prosecutor's] case sets a precedent for future private prosecutions of the Environment Agency. It may even open the floodgates to a whole range of private prosecutions under environmental law. It is conceivable that there could be an increase in private prosecutions of the Environment Agency, central government departments, and local authorities in relation to breach of their duties under environmental legislation.
>
> (p. 236)

Further examples of private prosecutions for environmental crimes can be drawn from the US. In this jurisdiction the public's right to bring prosecutions for criminal acts is somewhat more restrictive than in the UK, as it is limited to those who can show 'standing' in a case: meaning they have suffered actual, or serious potential of, injury directly caused by the defendant. I have already mentioned the difficulties of establishing such lines of causation in cases of environmental harm, which might make such prosecutions difficult to achieve. However, federal environmental law is generally one of the few exceptions to this need for 'standing'. Thus, The Clean Air Act, Clean Water Act, Endangered Species Act, Toxic Substances Control Act and several other federal statutes permit 'any person' (including organizations, municipalities and states) to take action against parties who violate the substantive provisions of those laws, even when there is no direct effect on the prosecutor (Friedman, 1997). Skinnider (2011) also notes the example of a Canadian case, *R* v *Kingston,*[13] in which a biologist found evidence that the city of Kingston was depositing a deleterious substance in water frequented by fish contrary to s.36 of the Fisheries Act, and launched an ultimately successful private prosecution of the city (albeit later backed by provincial prosecutors).

The lack of further examples of the application of 'standard' victim assistance or participation mechanisms in domestic criminal justice systems illustrates the absence of consideration of environmental victims in the formation of these measures. In all probability, this is at least partly due to the difficulty in identifying such victims, as alluded to above. In additionm, though, like criminology itself, domestic criminal justice systems have traditionally had difficulties dealing with cases that involve large numbers of victims (or offenders). As noted by Skinnider (2011):

> The victim of crime is usually defined in legislation as a person who is directly and proximately harmed as a result of the commission of a crime. One of the main challenges in accessing the criminal justice system for victims who suffer from environmental harm is the individualist nature of criminal law – it is formulated with individual victims and individual perpetrators in mind.
>
> (p. 169)

Furthermore, as discussed in the previous chapters, environmental harm is often *transnational* in nature, making purely domestic approaches largely irrelevant. For such reasons, and further to the third research question set out in Chapter 1, incorporating an international focus is especially important for this volume as a whole. Indeed, White (2011) has distinguished the conceptualization and structuring of an *international* system of criminal justice equipped to deal with environmental crime as a 'key challenge' (p. 122) for what he terms eco-global criminology. With this in mind, this chapter will now broaden its focus beyond national criminal justice systems, first to examine developments at the European level.

3.3 Victims of environmental harm in European criminal justice

Beginning with the 1987 Single European Act, the European Union has been expanding its competence in relation to the legal protection of the environment over the last three decades (see Cardwell *et al.*, 2011). In a parallel and overlapping development, a new category of jurisprudence has emerged (both in legal practice and academic rhetoric), commonly referred to as 'European criminal law'.[14] It is now widely accepted that cooperation on areas traditionally beyond the scope of EU competence (including migration law and policy as well as criminal justice) is now one of the fastest-developing areas of EU policy-making. At the same time, the EU has increasingly concerned itself with the place of the victim in the criminal justice systems of member states. It is at this intersection of legislative competences (environmental protection and criminal justice), regulatory measures (regulations/directives and framework decisions) and the concurrent emergence and recognition of the victim in EU policy-making that I wish to position this section of the discussion. This notwithstanding, the key argument put forward by this section is that in fact there has been a distinct *lack* of interaction between the EU's consideration of victims of traditional crimes on the one hand and of environmental harm on the other.

Starting with victims of crime more generally, to date the most significant expression of this relatively new area of EU interest[15] has been the introduction of the 2001 EU Council Framework Decision on the Standing of Victims in Criminal Proceedings. More recently, a proposed EU Directive establishing minimum standards on the rights, support and protection of victims of crime has also been drafted, and is expected to go into force in the near future.[16] The European Court of Justice has also recently had the opportunity to interpret the meaning of 'victim' in a way that may, over time, have a bearing on emerging and contradictory national interpretations.[17]

While the 2001 EU Council Framework Decision is undoubtedly the most progressive source of recognition to date for victims of more traditional crimes at the European level, it is clear that victims of environmental harm (or environmental crime) are, as with the domestic measures to assist victims discussed above, largely excluded from its ambit. Indeed, even mainstream victimologists (Groenhuijsen and Pemberton, 2009) and victim assistance organizations (notably Victim Support Europe, 2009) have criticized the Framework Decision for its narrow conception of crime victims, defined here as 'a natural person who has suffered harm, including physical or mental injury, emotional suffering or economic loss, directly caused by acts or omissions that are in violation of the criminal law of a Member State' (Article 1). Although the range of possible impacts listed here is wide, and indeed to some extent reflects the range of possible impacts of environmental victimization discussed in the last chapter, the strict limitation to those affected *by proscribed breaches* of the *criminal law* is problematic, given the fact that many relevant activities are not strictly speaking breaches of the criminal law, especially in relation to activities and decisions carried out by *states*. In addition, by requiring that harm or loss is 'directly' caused by the relevant crime, the Framework Decision effectively excludes any notion of *indirect* victimization. This is especially problematic given the difficulty discussed above of establishing direct causation in environmental cases, at least to the criminal standard.[18]

It will be recalled from Chapter 2 that Williams's (1996) solution to this problem of defining victims of 'environmental harm (or 'injury' as he would prefer[19]) is to draw on the UN's 1985 Declaration of Basic Principles of Justice for Victims of Crime and Abuse of Power, conceiving relevant environmentally destructive activities as 'abuse of [state] power'. This route will be discussed in detail in the next section. In terms of *EU* instruments, however, although the 2001 Framework Decision looks likely to be replaced by the newly proposed Directive, the definition of 'victims' in the drafts of that document extends the 2001 definition only in the sense that it now includes 'the family members of a person whose death has been caused by a criminal act' (Article 2), which does little to incorporate environmental victims.

Just as EU policies on victims of crime have apparently failed to factor in environmental issues, likewise the developments made in the environmental arena have failed to account for the *victims* of environmental harms. In relation to environmental degradation, the most significant measure taken by the EU, at least in relation to the criminalization of such harms, has been the 2008 adoption of EU Directive 2008/99/EC on the protection of the environment through the criminal law mentioned above.[20] Nevertheless, no provisions are found within the Directive relating to victims of either environmental harm, or indeed environmental crime.

That the Directive should exclude victims in this way is somewhat puzzling, given the pedigree of this instrument. Like most such measures, the Directive is in fact not an isolated development, but rather should be understood in the broader context of a series of attempts by the EU to use the criminal law to ensure more effective enforcement of environmental law (see Cardwell *et al.*, 2011).[21] Of course, using the criminal law to enforce environmental provisions has not been the traditional method adopted by many member states, which have been keen (in many cases) to redress environmental harm through regulation and administrative sanctions (Holder and Lee, 2007).[22] Key among the previous European (although not EU) initiatives in this regard is the 1998 Council of Europe Convention on the Protection of Environment through Criminal Law. Though this treaty has not yet entered into force (and indeed has secured little support from member states) it is significant as the precursor to the adoption of the 2008 Directive within the European Union. Most significantly for present purposes, the 1998 Convention seems to confer rights of *participation* for victims of environmental harm in criminal justice procedures. The full implications of this will be discussed in greater detail in Chapter 4, but for present purposes the key point is that, in the light of wider reforms in the EU concerning victims of crime, the fact the 2008 Directive does not contain similar language is both unfortunate and somewhat surprising.

Indeed, while clearly following the lead of the Council of Europe,[23] on the face of it the 2008 EU Directive is a more modest document than the 1998 Convention, although its impact is likely to be more keenly felt. Moreover, as the European Court of Justice noted in 2005 in judicial proceedings brought over the correct legislative base for the Directive, criminal law has a clear role to play in environmental matters:

> As a general rule, neither criminal law nor the rules of criminal procedure fall within the Community's competence ... the last-mentioned finding does not prevent the Community legislature, when the application of effective, proportionate and dissuasive criminal penalties by the competent national authorities is an essential measure for combating serious environmental offences, from taking measures which relate to the criminal law of the Member States which it considers necessary in order to ensure that the rules which it lays down on environmental protection are fully effective.[24]

The Directive therefore requires member states to 'criminalize' certain defined breaches of EU environmental law. Previously, member states had complete discretion to determine the appropriate sanction. As studies for the European Commission on this issue make clear, there was high variability in both the nature (criminal, civil and administrative) and severity of penalties and sanctions imposed (Lepage *et al.*, 2007). The range of acts which now require the imposition of criminal law include:

- instances of pollution, the generation, disposal and other activities related to hazardous waste, nuclear materials and radioactive waste, and the operation of a plant in which a dangerous activity is carried out, but in all cases only where they 'cause ... or [are] likely to cause death or serious injury to any person or substantial damage to the quality of air, the quality of soil or the quality of water, or to animals or plants';
- the illegal shipment of hazardous waste;
- the destruction of wild fauna and flora and habitat;
- trading in protected specimens of wild fauna and flora or parts or derivates thereof;
- the various production, transit and marketing stages involving the sale of ozone-depleting substances.[25]

Clearly the inclusion of 'death or serious injury to any person' is especially significant for the present (admittedly anthropocentric) discussion, as it implies that such new crimes must take into account the impact of environmental offences on individuals and groups of human victims.

On the one hand, the development of EU Directive 2008/99/EC is a strong indicator of the growing importance of criminal law in tacking environmental harms in Europe, and implies affirmative answers to the first research question in Chapter 1. On the other hand, however, the notable absence of the victim from these developments betrays a failure by EU policy-makers to engage with the victimological literature, or indeed with other aspects of what is now quite well-established EU policy in its developing competence in criminal law matters. Once again this highlights the need for an interdisciplinary, unified discussion of these issues, which is what the present volume is seeking to contribute. Previous work by the Council of Europe in the form of the 1998 Convention further suggests that such measures are possible, but they remain absent in the European context. At present, therefore, it appears that if we are to identify potential avenues for the inclusion of environmental victims within criminal justice processes we will need to look beyond the purely European context. To this end, the next section examines the potential role of international law in this regard.

3.4 Beyond Europe: the 1985 UN declaration and international law

The difficulty of incorporating appreciation for harmful effects on individuals in public international law and international criminal law is well recognized in the literature (Redgwell, 2010; Thirlway, 2010). Nevertheless, Skinnider (2011) has discussed how the UN Commission on Crime Prevention and Criminal Justice in fact adopted a resolution on environmental crime as early as 1994, in which member states were called upon to:

> consider in the framework of the constitution and the basic principles of the legal system, the rights of identifiable victims, victim assistance, facilitation of redress and monetary compensation, by removing legal barriers such as standing to sue, participation in proceedings and actions by citizens, including class action suits and citizen suits.[26]

In Chapter 2 I highlighted Williams's (1996) assertion that the definition of victims of abuse of power in the 1985 UN Declaration of Basic Principles of Justice for Victims of Crime and Abuse of Power might serve as a starting point for the incorporation of environmental victims both within national criminal justice system and internationally, and it is here that this assertion will be tested more thoroughly. The other instrument of some interest to the present discussion is the International Law Commission's (2006) response to the issue of compensating victims of environmental harm in its draft principles on the allocation of loss in the case of transboundary harm arising out of hazardous activities. The issue of compensation will be returned to in Chapter 5 but, for present purposes, Principle 6(2) of this document is especially interesting, requiring that:

> Victims of transboundary damage should have access to remedies in the State of origin that are no less prompt, adequate and effective than those available to victims that suffer damage, from the same incident, within the territory of that State.

Further illustrations from the sphere of international environmental law largely relate to the question of whether or not there is a *right* to an unpolluted environment or whether other, more established rights could be read as including this. This section deals largely with the 1985 Declaration, leaving these wider arguments to Chapter 4, which is dedicated to the questions surrounding the establishment of such 'green' rights.

Certainly the 1985 UN Declaration is the most wide-ranging and influential document on the issue of victims' rights at the international level. The Declaration speaks of victims being afforded access to justice and fair treatment, and of compassion and respect for their dignity. While an essentially non-binding, soft-law instrument, the Declaration has influenced most of the domestic provisions relating to the place of victims in criminal justice (which usually take the form of non-binding Codes of Practice) in the world today (Hall, 2010). Nevertheless, in line with the observations set out in Chapter 1 concerning the general focus of the victim movement on human agency as opposed to legal structure, the Declaration is very much lacking in mechanisms for the enforcement of the principles it champions (at the national and international levels), and is in fact a self-confessed aspirational document.

It is significant for present purposes that the definition given for victims of abuse of power in Article 18 of the 1985 Declaration[27] includes actions and *omissions* which do not constitute crimes, but simply lead to a person or persons suffering harm. As noted above, the activities leading to climate change are often not illegal in nature. More significantly, however, one might consider this provision alongside the 'no-harm' principle under customary international law (to be discussed in greater detail below) that essentially requires states to actively prevent causing environmental harm to other states. Thus, the case could be made that a state is responsible under the 1985 Declaration for failure to regulate activities (that is, failure to show 'due diligence'; see Barnidge, 2006) within its borders which lead to transboundary environmental victimization, this constituting an abuse of power.

While it may seem fanciful to read environmental victims into a document conceived long before the term was in popular use, or indeed before the problem was widely accepted and understood, in domestic law at least I have already discussed a precedent for such an adaptation in the form of the US Crime Victims' Rights Act (Ferguson, 2011). This domestic application of (traditional) victims' rights to environmental harm is admittedly several steps away from the acceptance of individual victims of environmental harm into international law, but it does demonstrate how instruments usually presumed to extend only to victims of traditional domestic offences (and in this case one heavily based on the 1985 Declaration) can be applied to environmental harm. The critique here is not that international law has considered and rejected this argument in relation to environmental victims specifically, but rather that, through its championing of legal rules and process over substantive *outcome*, such arguments are rarely even considered.

As noted in Chapter 2, the other crucial point concerning the 1985 Declaration's definition of victims of abuse of power is its centring on the concept of 'harm'. It is clear from the definition as a whole that 'harm' in this context is defined widely and applies to the individual, 'including physical or mental injury, emotional suffering, economic loss or substantial impairment of their fundamental rights'.[28] This seems eminently compatible with the concept of social harm (as opposed to *crime*) discussed in Chapter 1. In other words, the

Article is concerned with the infliction of harm on individuals and groups, broadly defined, rather than violations of national criminal laws per se. Again this reflects the championing by the victims' movement of individual agency over legal structure. From the perspective of environmental degradation, the significant implication of this is that abuse of power can include the grey legal areas alluded to earlier into which environmentally destructive activities often fall. Furthermore, it is notable that the draft principles produced by the International Law Commission (2006) on the allocation of loss in the case of transboundary harm arising out of hazardous activities similarly draw on the concept of harm (or 'damage'), defining victims as 'any natural or legal person or State that suffers damage',[29] 'damage' here including loss of life, personal injury and financial costs attributed to environmental harm.[30]

While the 1985 Declaration (and certainly the ILC draft principles) remains non-binding, it can be argued that the principles espoused within it could form the basis of future international obligations relating to those affected by environmental harms conceived as victims of abuse of power. While there is at present insufficient evidence to argue that this aspect of the 1985 Declaration has attained the status of customary international law,[31] it is significant that the instrument has already prompted substantial reform and policy development at the national and international levels (Hall, 2010).

Indeed, it should not be thought that the creation of *formally binding* principles of international law is a prerequisite to attaining justice or redress for victims of environmental harm. For example, some international lawyers have championed the concept of 'soft law' that has the capacity to form the material basis of customary law[32] and can be converted into 'hard law' though its enshrinement in treaties.[33] The concept of soft law is greatly contested in the relevant literature (Boyle, 2006). In practice, whether or not one chooses to call the 1985 UN Declaration, or indeed the ILC (2006) draft principles, soft law has little bearing on arguments concerning their potential either to become hard law or to constitute an important step in the process towards the establishment of internationally binding legal principles relating to victims of environmental harm. Indeed, d'Aspremont (2008) has reflected on the argument that, given the operation of policy networks, legally binding instruments are not always needed to achieve significant ends:

> Many recent developments, like networks among governmental officials or transnational law, have shown that non-legal instruments may prove more adapted to the speed and complexity of modern international relations and are more and more resorted to in practice. Non-legal instruments can be at least as integrative for a community as legal ones.
>
> (p. 1062)

Given the generally non-binding nature of most national and international provisions and principles relating to *both* environmental harm *and* victims of crime as a whole, such insight is important for both fields of study. What victimology also contributes to these debates is a wealth of experience in dealing largely (indeed, almost totally) with such non-binding instruments in attempting to attribute rights or 'legitimate expectations' (JUSTICE, 1998) to victims. Such 'rights' are almost exclusively found in non-binding declarations and codes of practice issued by national governments and international organizations.[34] The important observation is that such instruments have brought about significant changes in many jurisdictions concerning the place of victims in criminal justice, notwithstanding their non-binding or persuasive character (Groenhuijsen and Pemberton, 2009; Hall, 2010). This again implies that 'hard law' is not the only mechanism for enhancing the position of victims of environmental harm, both politically and legally.

3.5 International criminal law: prospects for the International Criminal Court

I have chosen to focus attention principally on the International Criminal Court (ICC) in this section largely because, as will be discussed below, as a relatively new institution it has had the greatest opportunity to establish itself from the outset with a mind for the victims of the crimes that come before it. The court also represents something of the state of the art in terms of institutional handling and prosecution of cases under international criminal law, although it is certainly not the only such institution in existence or historically.[35] At present, the only mention of the environment included within the Rome Statute of 1998, which established the ICC, is at Article 8 (2)(b)(iv), where 'War Crimes' are defined as including:

> Intentionally launching an attack in the knowledge that such attack will cause incidental loss of life or injury to civilians or damage to civilian objects or widespread, long-term and severe damage to the natural environment which would be clearly excessive in relation to the concrete and direct overall military advantage anticipated.[36]

Sills *et al.* (2001) have commented that the stringent requirements that must be met in order for the ICC to hear a war crimes case makes it extremely unlikely that such environmental crimes would reach it 'in respect to multilateral UN peace-keeping and/or peace-making operations, though more likely following unilateral actions, since there would be fewer parties to decisions' (p. 1).

Along with war crimes, the jurisdiction of the ICC at present covers genocide, crimes against humanity, and crimes of aggression. These offences are described in Article 5 of the Rome Statute as being 'the most serious crimes of concern to the international community as a whole'.[37] Given such a description, both criminologists (see Akella and Cannon, 2004) and international lawyers (see Schwartz, 1998) have argued that a crime of wanton destruction to the environment fits within this remit and thus should be added to the Statute. The International Law Commission has proposed that such a crime, for serious wilful acts causing environmental harm, have an international element.[38] Activists have made arguments to the effect that the Rome Statute should incorporate a crime of 'Ecocide', which has been defined as 'The extensive destruction, damage to or loss of ecosystem(s) of a given territory, whether by human agency or by other causes, to such an extent that peaceful enjoyment by the inhabitants of that territory has been severely diminished' (Eradicating Ecocide, 2012). Notably, this definition extends beyond human victims of such activities to include aspects of what White calls ecological justice. Gray (1996) has argued that all the components of an international crime of ecocide, namely (1) serious, and extensive or lasting, ecological damage, (2) international consequences, and (3) waste, can already be identified as established principles of international law, and he contends therefore that ecocide is itself not such a radical proposition. He further postulates that ecocide can be identified on the basis of the deliberate or negligent violation of key state and human rights. The argument that existing human rights might form the basis of greater victim involvement in international criminal procedures concerning environmental harm will be taken up in Chapter 4.

Although it is largely theoretical at present, the workability of an international crime of ecocide was tested in September 2011 at a mock trial conducted in the Supreme Court of the United Kingdom. The experiment has been called a success both in signifying the feasibility of such a crime while also demonstrating that *restorative justice* options may be particularly appealing when it comes to the sentencing phase (Rivers, 2012). Certainly, the incorporation of an international crime of environmental destruction or ecocide within the Rome Statute would, in the context of the present discussion, have significant implications for the victims of such environmental harm. This is because the International Criminal Court is an almost unique example of a discrete judicial system developed from the outset with a firm appreciation for the arguments of the victims' movement. As Holder notes:

> Of course, the International Criminal Court is young and untested. It is nonetheless significant that this and the other initiatives I have mentioned show that court leadership and indeed court delivery of assistance to crime victims is not intrinsically incompatible with court independence and impartiality.
>
> (Holder and Lee, 2007: p. 11)

In March 2005 the ICC adopted a Code of Judicial Ethics, which included the following requirement:

> Judges shall exercise vigilance in controlling the manner of questioning of witnesses or victims in accordance with the Rules and give special attention to the right of participants to the proceedings to equal protection and benefit of the law.
>
> (ICC, 2005: Art.8(2))

The rules mentioned here are the ICC's Rules of Procedure and Evidence (ICC, 2002). These contain many safeguards to what are called the rights of victims, including the right to participate in proceedings as a party with legal representation.[39] For example, under these rules the prosecution and defence can agree that an item of evidence will be treated as 'proven' without needing to present it formally in court 'unless the Chamber is of the opinion that a more complete presentation of the alleged facts is required in the interests of justice, in particular the interests of the victims' (ICC, 2002: Rule 69).

Indeed, the ICC rules often bring together an 'interests of justice' test with an 'interests of victims' test. This means that victims' views must be canvassed under many of the rules, and their privacy protected. Perhaps most significantly, the rules provide the following general principle for the ICC to work under:

> A Chamber in making any direction or order, and other organs of the Court in performing their functions under the Statute or the Rules, shall take into account the needs of all victims and witnesses in accordance with Article 68, in particular, children, elderly persons, persons with disabilities and victims of sexual or gender violence.
>
> (ICC, 2002: Rule 86)

While there is clearly a special focus here on ideal victims, the general principle applies to all victims. It is also to be noted that, should victims of environmental harms be brought within the Rome Statute, they would then qualify for the compensation mechanisms so provided, an issue to which Chapter 5 will return.

Bottigliero (2004) argues that the victims' movement has tended to focus on what she calls 'ordinary' crimes such as assault and theft, which can be dealt with in the domestic context, while ignoring the victims of atrocities such as war, genocide and crimes against humanity. She argues that the infrastructure set up by the International Criminal Court begins the process of addressing the needs of such victims, particularly their need for restitution. Her argument may be applied equally to the field of environmental crime and environmental victims. Regrettably, however, such arguments are at this stage entirely theoretical.

3.6 State responsibility for environmental degradation under international law

So far, the potential for bringing environmental victims within the ambit of domestic, European and international criminal law has been demonstrated to be somewhat limited. The work of the UN on the area of victims in general offers some hope for a future widening of interpretations to include such victims, but such applications of the 1985 Declaration are at this point speculative. In addition to the problems and limitations outlined above, critical criminologists would point out that, even if the instruments discussed above fully incorporated environmental victims, this leaves the inherent problem of holding governments and *states* as a whole responsible for activities which they bring about (or perhaps fail to prevent) leading to such environmental harm. Given the importance of state actions in contributing towards environmental victimizations, as discussed throughout this volume so far, it is impossible to separate a discussion concerning the place of victims of environmental degradation within the international *criminal* legal order from the wider debate concerning the obligations and responsibilities of states in this regard. Clearly, if states cannot be held accountable for environmental degradation more generally, the prospect of them also being held responsible for the environmental victimization vested upon individuals seems remote. This section will therefore discuss the difficulties inherent in attributing (legal) responsibility to states for environmentally degrading activities, arguing that this proposition becomes even more problematic when thought is given to the position of individual victims.

A number of arguments have been put forward in favour of states taking legal responsibility for the impacts of environmental degradation, although few have won universal acceptance as principles of international law. This latter point is significant because, in the general absence of legally binding multilateral rules determining state responsibility for environmental degradation,[40] such responsibility can only be established as a binding principle of *customary* international law if it can be shown to constitute a common practice by states, with particular regard to those states most affected by that practice.[41] This section will demonstrate how the already complex problem of establishing responsibility on the part of states for environmental degradation itself becomes even more challenging when an attempt is made to attribute that responsibility to harm suffered by *individuals*, affording such victims some form of redress. Picking up the argument made in Chapter 1, the contention here is that this represents a significant and ultimately restrictive disregard for the role of agency in the formation of international legal systems.

Attempts to identify responsibilities of states concerning environmentally polluting activities as a whole have generally been based around broad principles argued by some to have become implicit in customary international law. For example, Principle 21 of the 1972 UN Declaration on the Human Environment (known as the Stockholm Declaration) imposes upon states the obligation to ensure that activities within their jurisdiction or control do not cause transboundary harm. This standard was also contained in Principle 2 of the 1992 Rio Declaration on Environment and Development. These are non-binding instruments, although there is a body of supporting evidence to suggest that the no-harm principle at least has entered into the corpus of customary international law, tracing back to the seminal judgment made against Canada by the Mixed Arbitral Tribunal[42] in the *Trail Smelter Arbitration* concerning cross-border air and water pollution.[43] In this case the arbitrator of the tribunal posited that 'A State owes at all times the duty to protect other states against injurious acts by individuals within its jurisdiction'.[44] In addition, the International Court of Justice in the *Corfu Channel Case* has pronounced that a state is under an obligation not to 'knowingly allow its territory to be used for acts contrary to the rights of other states'.[45] As noted by Redgwell (2010), however, the no-harm principle is limited in that it constitutes only a negative obligation on states not to allow their territories to be used for activities that cause harm to the environments of other states, or the global commons.[46] This falls far short of a positive obligation to protect the environment.[47] There is also no real or substantial attempt in any of these pronouncements to recognize the harm caused to *individuals* within states. 'Harm' in this context seems to mean harm against another state in general.

Redgwell has labelled other general principles which have been applied to environmental degradation attributable to the actions or inactions of states as 'even more controversial' in terms of their status as customary law (Redgewell, 2010: p. 695). One prominent example is the 'precautionary principle': the belief that society should seek to avoid environmental damage through forward planning and blocking the flow of potentially damaging activities despite an absence of full scientific certainty on the matter. The principle is found under the Rio Declaration[48] and has the advantage that it is able to operate despite scientific uncertainties as to the causes of some environmental degradation, in particular climate change. The principle has been adopted more in Europe than the US; again there seems to be a lack of universal application that would cause it to be recognized as customary international law (Wybe, 1997). In addition, from an evidential perspective, if there is no scientifically proven relationship between specific acts or omissions by states and the harms caused to victims, this would make it very difficult to establish specific responsibility or to ground compensation claims on this basis.

Other general principles which have been applied to environmental degradation include that of *sic utere tuo, ut alienum non laedas* or 'use your own property in such a way that you do not injure others', which was incorporated into Principle 21 of the Stockholm Declaration in 1972, and the principle of sustainable development, which is stated in Principle 3 of the Rio Declaration: 'The right to development must be fulfilled so as to equitably meet developmental and environmental needs of present and future generations'. While this pronouncement does incorporate the human element, it does so only in the forward-reaching, collective sense of humankind and intergenerational justice, rather than acknowledging human agency in the here and now. In this respect, the 'polluter pays' economic principle seems to have greater potential for attributing to the state some degree of responsibility for the harms caused to individuals by pollution. The thrust of this principle is that the wrongdoer (polluter) is under the obligation to make good the damage caused. The principle has already become widely accepted as a means of paying for the cost of pollution and domestic control (Tobey and Smets, 1996), and is of particular interest in the context of the present discussion because it tends to encompass the public interest, as in Principle 16 of the Rio Declaration:

> National Authorities should endeavour to promote the internalization of environmental costs and the use of economic instruments, taking into account the approach that the polluter should in principle bear the cost of pollution with due regard to the public interest and without distorting international trade and development.

The difficulty, though, is that the 'polluter pays' principle has so far not been applied to *nation states* as responsible parties for pollution (Tobey and Smets, 1996). This is in contrast to the no-harm principle that, while aimed at member states, does not concern itself with the harm caused *to individuals*, but rather to other states. In both cases, then, the established principles fail to connect the nation state, as a responsible party, with the individual victims who are harmed. Again, there is a lack of unified consideration of structure and agency. In terms of substantive legal instruments concerning environmental degradation, Redgewell (2010) offers a comprehensive overview of the areas in which international law has made significant strides. These areas include: protection of the marine environment; protection of the atmosphere; nuclear risks; other hazardous substances and activities;[49] the conservation of nature; and the conservation of marine living resources.

3.6.1 Climate change: an illuminating example?

Inevitably, the entire body of international environmental law is too wide to conduct an exhaustive review of state responsibilities and the (potential and actual) roles of individual victims in every aspect of the field. The specific topic of climate change will be discussed here in some detail as an exemplar of how international law in general deals (or fails to deal) with individual victims of environmental harm. This restriction seems justifiable for two main reasons. First, as has already become apparent during the course of this chapter, *individual* victims of environmental degradation as a whole in fact figure very little in international law, to the extent that narrowing the focus to climate change for these purposes is not to exclude vast quantities of relevant international instruments. Second, the issue of state responsibility for the effects and harms of climate change is an especially contentious area of international environmental law, and thus will serve as a good indicator of how the international legal order is able (or unable) to adapt itself to the needs of individual victims of such 'novel' harms. More general discussion of wider international obligations to protect the environment as a whole and their implications for victims of environmental harm will be discussed in Chapter 4 in the context of human rights.

The key response of the international community to the problem of climate change is the 1992 Framework Convention on Climate Change (FCCC), which embodies obligations for states to take action to mitigate its adverse effects. The 1997 Kyoto Protocol to the Framework Convention sets legally enforceable emissions targets for countries. Some commentators have also suggested that the Kyoto Protocol might embody obligations *erga omnes*, or obligations that are owed to the international community as a whole by all states (Higgins, 1978). In theory, any state (but not individuals) can seek redress in the event that such obligations are breached, although there is little evidence that such an obligation relating to climate change has been accepted, as a principle or as a custom, into the corpus of international law.

The above paragraph notwithstanding, the Kyoto Protocol is not universally applicable given that, significantly, the United States has stated that it will never ratify the Protocol. Therefore the US, as the world's biggest polluter per capita, is not bound by any emissions reduction targets. Arguably the US still has an obligation to limit its emissions of carbon and greenhouse gases because it remains a *party* to the FCCC and, under Article 18 of the Vienna Convention on the Law of Treaties,[50] a party to a treaty is under an obligation not to do anything that would defeat the object and purpose of a treaty. Perhaps the more significant impact of the US failure to ratify Kyoto is the implications this has for customary international law. That is to say, it becomes somewhat unconvincing to argue that the obligations contained in the FCCC and in Kyoto constitute the required generality of practice when the world's biggest per capita polluter has rejected them. Moreover, the climate change omission targets within the Kyoto protocol are based on a principle of shared but different responsibilities between countries. While no party to the Protocol is entirely excused responsibility for climate change, developing countries – more than half of the world's nations – do not face the same level of omissions targets, including major emitters like China and India. As such, although the harm and victimizations caused by climate change and environmentally destructive activities in general is morally recognized by most states, obligations in this regard are not in themselves customary international law.

Significantly for the present discussion, neither of the above instruments includes provisions expressly aimed at the *individuals* harmed by climate change. The FCCC acknowledges in its preamble that climate change is 'a common concern of humankind' and in Article 1(1) adopts a definition of the 'adverse effects of climate change', which includes 'significant deleterious effects on human health and welfare'. Article 4(1)(f) of the Convention requires parties to minimize the adverse impacts of climate change 'on public health'. Article 3(1) also speaks of protecting the climate system 'for the benefit of present and future generations of humankind', reflecting the notion of intergenerational justice discussed in Chapter 1. Notably all of these references are collective, rather than specific to particular groups of citizens, or individuals, affected by climate change. This of course very much reflects the state-centred paradigm in international environmental law, as in international law in general.[51]

To summarize, some 70 years after the *Trail Smelter Arbitration* provided high hopes for those individuals seeking to assert the responsibility of states for environmental harm, the difficulties of establishing such responsibility are still great. While progress has been made both in terms of substantive treaty-based international law and in terms of general principles in the international legal community, it is generally still difficult to argue that most such rules have been accepted as universal principles of international law. The no-harm principle may be an exception, although the 'harm' conceived here clearly suggest harm caused to states rather than to individuals within states. Again, then, we are confronted with this lack of consideration of individual human agency within international legal instruments. However, some of the more recent international pronouncements on the future of the environment appear to make far greater mention of the individual. Indeed, the Outcome Document from the Rio+20 UN Conference on Sustainable Development goes as far as to state:

> We recognize that people are at the centre of sustainable development and in this regard we strive for a world that is just, equitable and inclusive, and we commit to work together to promote sustained and inclusive economic growth, social development and environmental protection and thereby to benefit all.
>
> (Para. 6)

The Outcome Document also goes on to stress 'the need to provide social protection to all members of society, fostering growth, resilience, social justice[52] and cohesion'. The reference to 'social justice' here in particular is a notable, if vague, hint that states need to concern themselves more with how environmental degradation impacts upon individuals and communities. A similar message may be gleaned from other recent documents, including the Johannesburg Plan of Implementation[53] and the United Nations Millennium Declaration of 2000.[54] As with other such statements, these documents remain at best soft law and, indeed, the Rio+20 conference in particular has already received criticism from journalistic commentators as producing a 'largely meaningless document' (Pearce, 2012: unpaginated).

Of course, in legal terms, establishing state *responsibility* for environmental harms is only a start. Once an obligation has been established in principle, there is the need to demonstrate conclusively that a state has breached that obligation, and causation would need to be established between the actions of that state and the harm caused to the individual (in the home state or another state). There is insufficient scope here to examine these significant legal hurdles in more detail, but it can be confidently predicted that, while states have taken to compensating domestic victims of violent crimes without necessarily accepting fault,[55] it is extremely unlikely that they will do the same for those affected by environmental degradation in their own or other countries,[56] not least because this would have very different cost implications.

3.7 Conclusions and ways forward

Victims of more mainstream crimes have in the last three decades made enormous strides towards full recognition by legal systems both nationally and internationally. Those affected by environmental harm, however, seem to fall into a lacuna in which they are largely ignored. The options available to such victims are in fact remarkably narrow. In Europe, for example, while the 2008 Directive is a great step forward, by failing to incorporate the rights of victims within this progressive development the Directive has missed an important opportunity. At the international level, victims of environmental harm are excluded, as they are from much of the international legal order, with references to individuals scarce and, in many cases, aspirational or symbolic. This is especially noticeable not only because victims of crime are gradually being supported by the criminal justice process more generally but also, as recent developments in environmental law itself have shown, citizen participation is now considered an essential element for effective regulation (Bynoe, 2006). This has been recently affirmed in the Outcome Document from the UN's 2012 Rio+20 Conference on Sustainable Development, where Para. 99 reads, 'We encourage action at the regional, national, subnational and local levels to promote access to information, public participation and access to justice in environmental matters, as appropriate'. Yet this chapter has also demonstrated that the incorporation of individual victims within such national and international legal systems is far from unthinkable. As both the 1998 Council of Europe Convention and the US Crime Victims' Rights Act demonstrate, it is wholly appropriate to combine the addressing of environmental crime with allowing victims to participate in the criminal justice process. While the victim has traditionally been excluded from much of intentional law, the mechanisms put in place by the International Criminal Court demonstrate that this can be rectified, the difficulty here being a failure to acknowledge some environmental destruction as an international crime. Furthermore, it has been argued that the same document that prompted so much of the victim reform agenda in national jurisdictions, the UN Declaration of Basic Principles of Justice for Victims of Crime and Abuse of Power, has real potential to be applied to victims of environmental harm. One way to achieve this, of course, is to look at the question from the perspective of the rights of environmental victims, to which this book next turns attention.

4 Human rights, victim rights, environmental rights?

So far this volume has employed the term ‘victim rights’ in a number of guises. Principally this reflects the pervasiveness of a ‘rights discourse’ in policy-making and criminal justice reform internationally, especially in Europe following the introduction of the European Convention on Human Rights and, in the UK, the Human Rights Act 2000 (see Risse *et al*., 1999). More recently, the 2001 EU Council Framework Decision on the Standing of Victims in Criminal Proceedings, requiring all EU states to afford victims basic levels of services and support, has again spurred a revival of ‘rights’ language (and non-governmental pressure) associated with victims across Europe.[1] In this context, it is perhaps inevitable that greater and greater interest is now being paid by victimologists to the notion of victims of crime having ‘rights’ as a means of alleviating the long-term difficulties which victims face when dealing with criminal justice systems, as highlighted by the victims’ movement.

In the previous chapter I discussed a number of instruments that were intended to incorporate victims of traditional crimes within criminal justice processes or at least to afford them some recognition and support from those processes. The actual or potential application of these instruments to victims of *environmental* crime (and broader harms) was then discussed. By way of review, particularly important examples included: the 1985 Declaration of Basic Principles of Justice for Victims of Crime and Abuse of Power; the 2001 EU Council Framework Decision; the US Crime Victims’ Rights Act of 2004; the 1998 Council of Europe Convention on the Protection of Environment through Criminal Law; and provisions relating to the International Criminal Court.

In many cases, the above instruments draw on the language of ‘rights’, and it is to this concept of ‘victim rights’ that the present chapter turns attention. In so doing, a number of the instruments mentioned above will be revisited with a particular focus on their conception and application of such ‘rights’. Central to the chapter is the argument that there are distinct parallels to be drawn between the relatively recent moves to ascribe ‘rights’ to victims of crime more generally and recent developments within international legal scholarship concerning environmental harms. In particular, in the light of the difficulties in applying domestic, European or international law to individuals or to environmental harms,[2] international legal scholars have increasingly turned to the question of human rights – including so-called environmental rights – as a means of attributing responsibility to states and other parties for harms to individuals. Birnie and colleagues have recently described this developing focus on rights as 'perhaps the most significant shift in the focus of international law' (Birnie *et al.*, 2009: p. 269). In this chapter it is argued that such a move also provides considerable impetus to the cause of critical victimology and the acknowledgment of victimization by the state in particular, especially in relation to environmental harms.

Among international environmental lawyers, the application of human rights to instances of environmental degradation remains distinctly underdeveloped. This reflects the continued state-orientated nature of the debate conveyed in previous chapters. A further level of complexity lies in debating the degree to which any such environmental rights should be purely anthropocentric, and the extent to which the rights of the individual should be weighed against any damage to the wider environment, the ecosystem, animal rights and so on (White, 2008a). As noted previously, the focus in this chapter (and this volume as a whole) on individual human victims should in no way detract from the importance of these wider questions. Indeed, by way of illustration, at the time this chapter is being written it is being reported in the media that experts in philosophy, conservation and animal behaviour are calling for the recognition of a 'non-human persons' status for dolphins and whales via a Declaration of Rights for Cetaceans (BBC, 2012a).

Of course, 'rights for victims of crime' more generally is itself a complex and contentious proposition, victims of crime generally lacking the usual taken-for-granted rights enjoyed by defendants under most conceptions of natural (criminal) justice. The next section of this chapter will introduce the main conceptual debates and issues raised by victimologists concerning the rights of victims of *crime* more broadly, before the chapter moves on to examine the 'green' question more closely.

In sum, this chapter aims to combine debates concerning 'environmental rights' found within international legal scholarship with the established victimological literature on rights for victims of crime. Pursuant to the third research question set out in Chapter 1, this combined approach aims to expose notable parallels between the progress of victims' rights more generally and the development of international environmental law as it relates (or fails to relate) to environmental victims. Given such parallels, and further to the third research question, there is marked potential for these two areas of academic debate and policy development to learn from each other; taking a holistic view should progress our understating of all the relevant issues and further the development of workable legal structures which take account of environmental victims at both the national and international levels. Given the growing importance of environmental issues within the criminal justice sphere, and beyond it, coupled with the new prominence of 'rights' in modern (international) legal discourse, it is submitted that such a combined analysis is an important addition to the literature, and indeed one that is long overdue.

4.1 Conceptualizing victims' rights[3]

The provision of rights to victims of crime is a controversial issue, provoking significant conceptual debates in the literature. The most divisive discussions have primarily concerned the degree to which such victims should be permitted to influence decision-making within a criminal justice system while still safeguarding defendants' right to due process. This debate itself betrays a more fundamental underlying assumption informing much of the literature in this area: that there exists a 'zero sum game' between victims' and defendants' rights, such that giving rights to one group means taking them from the other.[4] This assumption has been disputed by numerous authors (Jackson, 2004; Hall, 2009). For Ashworth (1998), the key distinction to be drawn in such discussions is one between 'service rights' for victims and 'procedural rights'. The service rights Ashworth has in mind include respectful and sympathetic treatment; support; information; the provision of facilities at court; and compensation from the offender or state. Also according to Ashworth (2000), victim participation should never be allowed to stray beyond this and into the domain of 'public interest'. Falling within this latter category, Ashworth is particularly concerned with the possibility of victims exerting influence over sentencing decisions through victim impact statements (see Hall and Shapland, forthcoming). In support of his position, Ashworth cites the inability of courts to test robustly the accuracy of such statements. In addition, he argues that it is unjust to allow unforeseen, unpredictable, or unusual impacts of crime on victims to affect sentencing. For Ashworth (1993, 2000) the international spread of victim impact statements constitutes a means of legitimizing a punitive stance against offenders.

Of course, given that the majority of offenders are not caught, the majority of 'traditional' crime victims who approach the criminal justice system deal only with the police (and perhaps with victim support agencies) as opposed to prosecutors and/or the court process. It can therefore be argued that the prioritization of 'services' over 'rights' is rational and a good way of supplying *most* of these victims with *most* of what they require. This is backed by the majority of the literature in which (traditional) victims have been questioned directly concerning their needs (Bradford, 2011). Hall and Shapland (forthcoming), however, have argued that participatory rights for such victims become more essential further into the criminal justice system. Criminal procedure in all legal systems is shaped and operated through legislated rules. If victims are to receive consideration during prosecution and at court (and in relation to compensation or restitution measures), then the rules need to provide them with those means, and key decision-makers within criminal justice must be appointed to ensure they are operationalized. Jackson (2003) makes a similar point in relation to the development of victims' rights: 'One of the problems with putting obligations on criminal justice agencies, however, is that they are unlikely to be taken seriously unless consequences attach to non-compliance' (p. 139). While it seems likely that, broadly speaking, a similar line of reasoning would apply to victims of *environmental* crime, one cannot simply *presume* that for most environmental victims, as for most traditional victims, service rights will suffice. Of course, establishing the truth of this one way or the other would involve consultation with the victims themselves, and it has already been observed that even traditional victims in general have often found themselves the subjects of policies put in place with little reference to what *they* feel they need (Rock, 1990). It is therefore perhaps unsurprising that there is an absence of research in which victims of environmental crime, or environmental harm more generally, have been so questioned,[5] and a direct comparison between the needs of traditional victims verses the special needs of environmental victims has not been carried out.

Of course, even if service rights in some form *would* in fact suffice for most environmental victims, the next question concerns the extent to which 'generic' service rights, aimed at victims in general, would meet the needs of environmental victims specifically, and whether in any case victims of environmental crime find themselves in a position to take advantage of such service rights to the same extent as other victims. For example, in the UK, most traditional victims of crime are put in contact with Victim Support as a result of being referred there by the police (Victim Support, 2009). If the police do not appreciative that victims of environmental crime may also need such support, they may not so refer them. Indeed, on this point, it was demonstrated in the last chapter that environmental victims were often not envisioned in the drafting of most existing victim instruments and procedures, so the concern that more generic victim assistance measures may fall short of the mark (whether in theory or in practice) is a significant one.

A new dimension to these debates is introduced by Sanders and Young (2000), who argue that both service and procedural rights fail to cater for the interests of (traditional) victims, as does the recurring 'due process verses crime control' dichotomy (p. 51). The authors disagree with Ashworth's view of service rights as a solution to victims' grievances because they feel that such rights can also marginalize victims when they are poorly implemented. As an alternative, Sanders and Young (2000) seek to replace the service/procedural rights distinction (along with notions of a zero-sum-game between victim and offender rights) with a more sophisticated tool. Unlike Ashworth, Sanders and Young propose a mechanism whereby the rights of victims and defendants are balanced, by maximizing the net *freedom* within the system. Sanders (2002) illustrates this perspective by arguing that the provision of *information* to victims within a criminal justice system increases the freedom of victims without reducing the freedom of defendants. Conversely, Sanders and Young (2000) contend that if victims' opinions are permitted to sway decision-making then this will reduce the freedom of offenders more than it increases the freedom of victims, and hence constitutes an unacceptable 'right'. Consulting victims on the discontinuance of their cases is, however, justified provided the final decision is made by the relevant prosecuting agency based on an objective evaluation of the balance of freedoms.

The notion of balancing the rights of victims, and in particular their views and expectations, alongside other factors relevant to decision-making has been influential in the courts' handling of victims in a number of jurisdictions. Indeed, Jackson (1990) has remarked on the dominance of 'balance' rhetoric within the transnational and international criminal justice discourse generally, and in relation to victim and offender rights specifically (Jackson, 2004). The same logic might also apply to decisions made by corporations and states in relation to the siting of potentially environmentally hazardous operations or materials in the locality of potential victims of environmental harm. Indeed, factoring the perspective of such potential victims into such decision-making is a key component of the 1998 UNECE[6] Convention on Access to Information, Public Participation in Decision-Making and Access to Justice in Environmental Matters, to be discussed below, and (as we have already seen) appears in the recent Outcome Document.[7] Furthermore, decisions concerning cases of environmental harm might frequently require a court to balance the needs of individuals or groups of victims with the economic needs of a state to promote industry, construction or even the profitable receipt and disposal of environmentally harmful waste products from other states (see Widmer *et al.*, 2005). This balance of interests will be returned to later in this chapter and again in Chapter 5, as part of a discussion on systems of compensation and restitution for environmental victims.

Not all commentators have argued so fervently against a more active form of procedural involvement for victims within criminal justice. In the US, Edna Erez has advocated victim impact statements as a means of affording victims participation rights (see Roberts and Manikis, 2011; Erez, 1994, 1999, 2000).[8] In challenging Ashworth's warnings, Erez (1999, 2004) begins by conceding that these statements have little impact on sentencing (see also Morgan and Sanders, 1999). Nevertheless, for her this is a product of the resistant cultures of practitioners and their widely held view that only 'normal' levels of impact should affect sentences (Erez, 1999). Conversely, Sanders *et al.* (2001) see the use of victim impact statements as fundamentally flawed because they rarely contain unexpected information.[9] Nevertheless, the debates surrounding victim impact statements have particular relevance to the question of 'rights' for victims of environmental harm: these kinds of victims may prove especially difficult to identify, while the full range of impacts upon them (their families, their livelihoods, their cultures) may be especially obscure, at least from an objective standpoint, and certainly while courts remain inexperienced in dealing with such cases (see Chapter 2). An example is provided by Skinnider (2011) in the form of the New Zealand Criminal case of *R* v *Koebel*,[10] where water treatment operators were convicted under the Criminal Code following an E. coli epidemic that 'damaged the health of several citizens and killed others' (p. 54). Victim impact statements were used at the sentencing stage by the judge in the case and, as Skinnider goes on to say:

> [The court] specifically held that the property owners affected by the commission of the offence of illegal clearing of native vegetation on private property were victims of a crime and victim impact statements ought to have been before the sentencing court. Potential implications in providing all

> victims the right to speak during sentencing might mean that the sentencing phase of environmental crime cases could be extended significantly, at added cost, when there are multiple victims wanting to exercise this right.
>
> (p. 54)

This of course returns us to the debate introduced above concerning whether the same assumptions and findings regarding the significance of procedural rights for traditional victims can apply to environmental victims. If the impacts of such victimizations are indeed especially difficult for courts to identify and understand, then victims of environmental crimes may ultimately require *stronger* guarantees of some form of procedural participation in the criminal justice system, certainly at the sentencing stage.

A central component to Erez's argument is the understanding that victims derive *therapeutic* benefit and vindication from expressing information about the impact of crime during the sentencing process, which in turn boosts satisfaction with the criminal justice system and may also achieve restorative ends (Erez *et al.*, 1997; Erez, 2004). Indeed, studies carried out in Australia, Canada and the UK show that victims seem to make a victim personal statement primarily for expressive reasons (desiring a voice at court), though instrumental reasons, such as affecting sentence, are also important (Erez *et al.*, 1997; Miller, 2008; Roberts and Manikis, 2011). Erez's argument is therefore that normative issues matter to victims, which is also the conclusion of Tyler (1990; Tyler and Huo, 2002). On a similar point, Shapland (2003) notes that one of the key benefits afforded to victims from having a judge order an offender to pay restitution to them is that such action constitutes official acknowledgement of their pain and suffering or, as Miers (1980) puts it, a recognition of their 'victim status'. Once again the lack of empirical evidence makes it impossible to conclude whether or not *environmental victims* value symbolic outcomes more, less or equally compared with traditional victims of crime.

Broadly speaking, the above debates concerning victim rights share the general limitations of victimology (and criminology) as a whole in being concerned primarily with individual victims (of crime) and individual (non-corporate, non-state) offenders. How such discussions should translate into the context of environmental crime or indeed wider environmental harm – which is dominated by corporate and state actors – is an important question for this volume. It may for example be argued that while it is unjust for sentencers to allow unforeseen, unpredictable, or unusual impacts of crime on victims to affect sentence in relation to the actions of individuals (as per Ashworth's criticisms), states and corporations can be held to a higher standard, particularly when considering principles borrowed from international law such as the no-harm rule or 'polluter pays', as discussed in the last chapter.[11] In addition, mass victimizations of the kind frequently generated by environmental crime, and environmental harm more widely, raise questions of balancing one victim's set of rights against other victims' rights, the distribution of a limited pot of compensation being an obvious example (see Chapter 5).

In terms of substantive instruments, rights for victims of crime in general have clearly received more explicit attention at national and international levels than rights for victims of environmental harms specifically. So, for example, the 1985 UN Declaration speaks of victims (of crime and abuses of power) being afforded access to justice and fair treatment, and of compassion and respect for the dignity of victims.[12] The instrument also makes reference to victims being informed about their role and about the scope, timing and progress of proceedings, as well as the disposal of their case.[13] The Declaration further maintains that victims should be guaranteed assistance from the criminal justice system (including information that such assistance is available),[14] as well as formal and/or informal procedures providing them with redress, restitution and compensation for wrongs suffered.[15] The document also has provisions protecting victims from unnecessary delay or inconvenience within the criminal justice system[16] and ensuring their concerns are considered.

Domestically, the 1985 Declaration has closely influenced the development of (usually non-binding) codes of practice in most developed jurisdictions regarding the treatment of victims by criminal justice systems (Brienen and Hoegen, 2000; Hall, 2010). The 2001 EU Council Framework Decision makes similar guarantees to victims, including respect and recognition by criminal justice actors, the right to protection from intimidation, and the provision of mediation schemes. Unlike the 1985 Declaration, however, the 2001 Framework Decision defines victims narrowly as those suffering harm 'directly caused by acts or omissions that are in violation of the criminal law of a Member State', which would exclude many victims of environmental harm. The replacement Directive for the 2001 instrument was criticized in Chapter 3 for similarly restricting the scope of victimhood quite narrowly and probably therefore excluding environmental victims. This is unfortunate, as the proposed Directive does contain a number of newly named 'rights' which might have particular relevance to victims of environmental crimes, including a right to understand and to be understood (Article 5), a right for victims to have their complaint acknowledged (Article 8) and a right to be heard (Article 9).

The above paragraphs notwithstanding, the question of whether such developments afford even 'mainstream' victims of crime genuine 'rights' is a complex one. In particular, because the mechanisms for the realization of such rights within individual jurisdictions are usually limited to the internal complaints mechanisms of justice agencies, the *enforceability* of such rights is left open to question (see Hall, 2010). As will be seen below, such concerns might equally be applied to any conceivable right to an unpolluted and clean environment, and again begs the question of how those who are affected by environmental damage brought about through criminal acts, or indeed 'abuses of power' by states, can seek to assert such a right in the domestic or international legal order. Having set out the key issues and debates concerning rights for victims of crime more generally, this chapter will now turn to applying such concepts to environmental victims specifically.

4.2 The human rights of environmental victims

It is clear that the development of specifically tailored rights for victims relating to any *criminal* proceedings which result from environmental degradation are much less developed than the concept of 'environmental rights' more generally. The exceptions to this are the cases in which environmental victims have been (or could be) included within the ambit of procedures and guarantees that were in the first instance put in place for victims of more traditional crimes in different jurisdictions (and at the international level), as was discussed in the last chapter.[17]

What we are left with essentially is a gradual progression of rights for those affected by environmental harm, mainly relating to the *civil* and/or *administrative* procedures put in place to allow them to challenge relevant decisions made by local or national governments which led to them being harmed. This reality should not however detract from the value of synthesizing debates about *these* rights with the largely criminal-justice-orientated perspective of mainstream victimology discussed above. This is partly so because, as discussed in Chapter 2, the propagation of references to 'harm', even in criminal justice policy-making circles, has increasingly blurred the distinctions between 'civil' 'administrative' and 'criminal' justice, particularly in an area where relevant (polluting) activities by corporations or states frequently fall into a legal grey zone. Indeed, Skinnider (2011) points out that while the term 'environmental crime' has raised much debate in many jurisdictions, the Canadian courts have established that the nomenclature of environmental 'crimes' or 'offences' or 'regulatory offences' is irrelevant for the purposes of guaranteeing the Canadian Charter of Rights and Freedoms. This means that regulatory provisions that amount to actual prohibition of blameworthy conduct are found to be constitutional under the criminal law power.

To continue my argument advocating closer synthesis between literatures (and in line with the first and third research questions set out in Chapter 1), it will be argued below that one of the key questions relating to victims in either criminal or civil procedures is often that of their *standing* to participate in those procedures. As such, a combined examination of how 'ordinary' victims have been given participatory rights in criminal justice and the participation of environmental victims in civil and/or administrative procedures and, perhaps more importantly, the handling of their complaints concerning such procedures by human rights courts, should benefit both areas of study. In any event, *all* legal proceedings (whether civil, administrative or criminal) will ultimately be compelled to reflect established human rights principles, and thus the development of environmental rights is equally relevant to victims of crime and to victims of wider environmental harm in their dealings with the authorities. Finally, but of considerable significance, both nationally and internationally the *criminal law* is increasingly being utilized to address cases of environmental degradation brought about by the actions of individuals, corporations and states. The parallels between mainstream victim rights and the rights of victims of environmental harm look set to converge in the near future, and indeed this may already be occurring. In short, the fact that, as noted in Chapter 3, much 'environmental harm' is dealt with other than through *criminal* law does not itself negate the utility of synthesizing the literature on so-called environmental rights with that of mainstream victimology.

Of course, it is important to appreciate from the outset that support for the advance of environmental rights in some form is not unanimous across the literature. Boyle (1996) in particular has argued that the development of such rights is redundant, given the speedy expansion of international environmental law as a whole. In this context, Boyle essentially questions what more a right to a clean and unpolluted environment could achieve. This perspective, however, fails to consider the full range of implications and potential benefits that the recognition of such human rights would entail for victims of environmental harms. Indeed, it is submitted that such a dismissal of the human element to these questions once again exemplifies the prioritization of structure and the under-consideration of agency[18] in international legal scholarship, which this volume sets out to address. A similar point is made by DeMerieux (2001):

> Boyle's argument is cogent except in one regard. Environmental rights and in particular procedural rights would enable persons, and no doubt groups, to challenge actions detrimental to the environment. One problem of environmental law, international or domestic, relates to standing to challenge infringements of that law, so that enforcement of treaties, directives of regional authorities and domestic law is largely left in the hands of states and other bodies.
>
> (p. 524)

The implied suggestion here that further incorporation of victims into the justice process in relation to environmental harms might actually assist with the overall enforceability of relevant laws seems worthy of closer examination. Certainly one might draw parallels with how the victims' movement has facilitated serious attention being paid by police and prosecutors to certain kinds of crime which previously were often dismissed as 'minor' or beyond the 'proper' scope of criminal justice work, the most obvious of which is domestic violence (Association of Chief Police Officers, 2008).

Turning now to specific debates concerning rights and the environment, two broad approaches have been taken to ascribing the victims of environmental harm (including climate change) with relevant rights: theorizing a new right to a clean and unpolluted environment (the less anthropocentric path),[19] and arguing that such an environment, while not a distinct right in itself, is necessary in order to guarantee a more recognized human right such as, for example, the right to life or the right to privacy.[20] A similar distinction can be drawn in the victimological literature, and associated policy movements, between the development of specific victim-focused schemes (such as the rollout of victim impact statements in many jurisdictions; Erez, 1999), the introduction of information services for victims of crime (Williams, 1999) and the general courteous treatment of such victims mandated by relevant (often non-binding) guidelines on the one hand, and broader legal arguments concerning the application of existing human rights to victims *as well as* to defendants on the other (Sanders and Young, 2000). Each of these approaches to 'environmental rights' will now be considered in turn.

4.2.1 A 'right' to a clean, unpolluted environment?

While considerable progress has been made in both victimology and international legal scholarship in recent years towards the assimilation of human rights, there have also been significant challenges to what in both cases is undoubtedly a novel application of the rights concept. Indeed, human rights have generally not been conceived as extraterritorial in nature (D'Amato, 1982). As such, no right to a healthy or clean environment has yet been widely recognized by the international legal order,[21] although there are examples of such a right at a more regional level. For example, Article 11 of the American Convention on Human Rights Protocol of San Salvador reads:

1 Everyone shall have the right to live in a healthy environment and to have access to basic public services.
2 The States Parties shall promote the protection, preservation, and improvement of the environment.

Notably, this places a positive obligation on states in relation to environmental protection and improvement, as opposed to merely requiring them to refrain from destructive activities. Such positive obligations are significant when one considers that states generally do not accept responsibility for other kinds of victimization (thefts, violence and so on) on the basis that they have a positive duty to 'protect' citizens from crime. This is commonly reflected in the rationales given for state-funded compensation systems for crime victims, most of which make it very clear that the money is paid from the public purse not out of recognition that the state has failed in some protective duty, but rather on welfare, communitarian or other grounds (see Miers, 1991 and Chapter 5 of this book). By contrast, such a right as described in Article 11 of the American Convention might imply that a state is directly responsible if through a failure to promote and improve the environment, and certainly if its actions lead to hazardous pollution, individuals are caused environmental harms.

In a different localized context, the 1981 African Charter on Human and People's Rights states in Article 24: 'All peoples shall have the right to a general satisfactory environment favourable to their development'. This Article has achieved special prominence within the international legal scholarship on human and environmental rights following its interpretation by the African Commission on Human Rights and Peoples Rights in the *Ogoniland*[22] decision as follows:

> The right to a general satisfactory environment, as guaranteed under Article 24 of the African Charter or the right to a healthy environment, as it is widely known therefore imposes clear obligations upon a government. It requires the State to take reasonable and other measures to prevent pollution and ecological degradation, to promote conservation, and to secure an ecologically sustainable development and use of natural resources.
>
> (Para. 52)

The *Ogoniland* case concerned complaints made against the Nigerian government by two non-governmental organizations (NGOs)[23] that it had 'condoned and facilitated' gross environmental damage caused by State Oil companies and Royal Dutch Shell, leading to 'environmental degradation and health problems resulting from the contamination of the environment among the Ogoni People' (Para. 2). The decision goes on to lay out the full harms and health impacts in particular on local communities on which, significantly for present purposes, it had received evidence via the NGOs: 'The resulting contamination of water, soil and air has had serious short and long-term health impacts, including skin infections, gastrointestinal and respiratory ailments, and increased risk of cancers, and neurological and reproductive problems' (Para. 2). The Commission further reiterated the Charter's direction that African states were obliged to 'prevent pollution and ecological degradation, to promote conservation, and to secure ecologically sustainable development and use of natural resources'.[24]

Coomans (2003) makes the point that the Commission in this case was adopting an 'obligations' approach, whereby states are required to *respect*, *protect*, *promote* and *fulfil* relevant (in this case, environmental) rights. Significantly, Coomans argues that this effectively puts civil and political ('first generation') rights on an equal footing with cultural, economic and social ('second generation') rights of the kind which, as was demonstrated in Chapter 2, may well be compromized by environmental victimization:[25]

> The use of the typology [of obligations] implies that realization of each separate right in the African Charter may involve duties to respect, to protect, to promote and to fulfil. In other words, a State Party may not limit itself to observance of one specific obligation only. In most cases, implementation of civil and political rights as well as economic, social and cultural rights will require observance of all levels of duties: all types of obligations are interrelated and interdependent.
>
> (p. 753)

While this is only a local judgment, conferring what can be viewed as a collective right on a community of people rather than an individual right,[26] Birnie *et al.* (2009) have called it 'a remarkable decision which goes further than any previous human-rights case in the substantive environmental obligations it places on states' (p. 273). Indeed from the (critical) victimological perspective, if the juxtaposition within this judgment of official state (economic) interests and those of victims of environmental harm is significant, the fact that the impact on victims essentially won through is extraordinary.[27] Furthermore, the ruling emphasized potential victims' rights to *information* concerning environmental hazards – this being a staple of the victims' (service) rights literature as a whole – appealing to the Nigerian government to begin 'Providing information on health and environmental risks and meaningful access to regulatory and decision-making bodies to communities likely to be affected by oil operation' (pp. 15–16).

The African and South American examples cited above are interesting and significant cases of *local* applications of what might be called rights to a clean and unpolluted environment. More generally, however, while such a right was suggested by the 1972 UN Conference on the Human Environment, and is reflected in Principle 1 of the Stockholm Declaration,[28] the Rio Declaration of 1992 neglected to develop this suggestion any further. Possibly the most progressive source of legally binding environmental obligations in the corpus of international law is found in the 1998 UNECE Convention on Access to Information, Public Participation in Decision-Making and Access to Justice in Environmental Matters (the 'Aarhus' convention), although this provides victims of environmental harm with participation and procedural rights (to be discussed below), along with rights to information, as opposed to a blanket right to a clean environment per se. A right to a healthy and decent environment has also been suggested by the UN Sub-Commission on the Prevention of Discrimination and Protection, on the grounds that it would enhance the standing of environmental concerns when balancing conflicting rights and objectives (see Sierra Club Legal Defence Fund, 1993), although this recommendation was not taken forward.

4.2.2 The 'greening' of existing rights

The second main option for establishing rights both for victims as a whole and for victims of environmental harm in particular is to ground such expectations in *existing* rights that have already met with wider acceptance. Here the European Court of Human Rights (ECtHR) has taken the lead in both areas (victims generally and environmental rights specifically) in adapting its Convention to meet such needs. Several rulings from the Court now appear to offer traditional victims of crime giving evidence in court a degree of protection from undue intimidation. For example, the cases of *Baegen* v *Netherlands*[29] and *Doorson* v *Netherlands*[30] confirm that keeping witnesses (including victim witnesses) anonymous in order to reduce intimidation and enhance protection does not breach a defendant's Article 6 rights under the Convention[31] to a fair trial, provided the witnesses' evidence can still be effectively challenged. In addition, the case of *Sn* v *Sweden*[32] confirms that Article 6 does not grant the defence an unlimited right to secure the appearance of witnesses in court. The *Sn* case also maintains that witnesses can give evidence through recorded interviews without breaching Article 6. In England and Wales, domestic cases have similarly reaffirmed the basic principle that special facilities may be provided to assist witnesses to give evidence in court, especially those witnesses deemed 'vulnerable' by reason of physical or mental handicap, so long as similar mechanisms are available to the defence: *R* v *Camberwell Green Youth Court*[33] and *R (TP)* v *West London Youth Court*[34] being important cases in point.

Doak (2003) has gone further to argue that victims might be in a position to argue for a breach of Article 3 (freedom from torture or degrading treatment) and Article 8 (right to a private life) of the European Convention on Human Rights if they are treated in a degrading manner by the criminal justice system or if the state fails to protect their rights to privacy when giving evidence in court.

In matters of environmental harm, the ECtHR has also adopted the Convention in particular to compel states to regulate and actively prevent activities that infringe upon a person's right to (healthy) life[35] and to the use of their private property. This approach has the advantage that it does not require consensus on what a good or healthy environment is (as does the less anthropocentric option), merely that the activities in question infringe upon other rights. Indeed, Doak's (2003) argument that Article 8 might be utilized by victims of crime in general has a direct parallel with developments at the ECtHR, where Article 8 has been the most commonly cited provision in relation to environmental cases, principally because of the inclusion of 'home life' within the Article (DeMerieux, 2001). Thus, in *Powell and Rayner* v *UK* the European Commission of Human Rights argued that a State has the obligation to *protect* (as well as *respect*) the rights under Article 8 and that excessive noise pollution would indeed constitute interference with a person's right to enjoy their home and, therefore, to a private life. The case concerned an alleged breach of Convention rights owing to noise emanating from low-flying planes near Heathrow Airport. The ECtHR's ruling that no such breach of Article 8 had occurred raises questions of the relative weight given to individual victims' rights (residents living in the vicinity of Heathrow) when compared with wider economic advantages for a region or the state as a whole, especially when compared to the outcome of the African *Ogoniland* case discussed above, where state economic interests apparently ranked second to the victims' interests.

A landmark ECtHR case in this jurisprudence is that of *Lopez Ostra*:[36] in relation to an alleged breach of Article 8 caused by the siting of a waste disposal plant near the complainant's home, the court ruled that 'Naturally, severe environmental pollution may affect individuals' well-being and prevent them from enjoying their homes in such a way as to affect their private and family life adversely, without, however, seriously endangering their health' (Para. 51). Furthermore, the Spanish State did

> not succeed in striking a fair balance between the interest of the town's economic well-being – that of having a waste-treatment plant – and the applicant's effective enjoyment of her right to respect for her home and her private and family life.
>
> (Para. 58)

Notably the ruling once again draws on 'balance' rhetoric, whereby a state's economic benefit is weighed against the likely impact on individuals. The

ECtHR has continued to rule in favour of breaches of Article 8 in cases of what it ruled to be excessive pollution in *Tatar* v *Romania*[37] and *Olui* v *Croatia*.[38] In the case of *Borysiewicz* v *Poland*[39] the court set out the test to be applied in assessing the level of interference with family or home rights required to raise an issue under Article 8:

> the interference must directly affect the applicant's home, family or private life and the adverse effects of the environmental hazard must attain a certain minimum level of severity. The assessment of that minimum is relative and depends on all the circumstances of the case, such as the intensity and duration of the nuisance, and its physical or mental effects.
>
> (Para. 100)

The court was silent here on how such a minimum impact threshold would need to be established, and whether this would include direct consultations with victims themselves. Much of the victimological literature argues that in such cases this kind of direct engagement with victims is essential, while at the same time pointing out that in practice it often does not occur (Shapland *et al.*, 1985). In making this ruling the Court also emphasized 'that there is no explicit right in the Convention to a clean and quiet environment, but where an individual is directly and seriously affected by noise or other pollution, an issue may arise under Article 8 of the Convention' (Para. 98). This understanding was repeated in *Leon and Agnieszka Kania* v *Poland*.[40]

The ECtHR has also considered claims for breaches of the rights to life in Article 2 in relation to environmental degradation.[41] In particular, in *Budayeva and others* v *Russia*[42] the court held that the public authorities had failed to provide adequate warnings to the public of dangerous mudslides, of which they had received advance warnings of possible danger to residents in the local area from scientific experts, and had failed to put in place containment mechanisms against the mudslides. As summarized by Wilson (2011):

> When the government has knowledge of an imminent risk to lives or severe failures in current protections from natural disasters, the government must take all diligent measures to protect the right to life. In this case, the government took essentially no steps to remedy the known risk to life from mudslides, so there seems to be a very clear violation of Article 2. This decision is notable because natural disasters are almost inherently unforeseeable, but there was enough information available about the risks such that, in this instance, the risk was still considered imminent.
>
> (p. 6)

Beyond the ECtHR, the 'greening' of existing recognized human rights for both the victims of environmental harm and the adaptation of such rights for victims as a whole is notably less developed. Judge Shigeru Oda of the International Court of Justice has referred to the notion of victims having rights in his dissenting opinion in the case of *LaGrand* (*Germany* v *United States of America*),[43] in a form which once again emphasizes a 'balance' between victims and offender rights:

> I am and have always been fully aware of the humanitarian concerns raised by the fate of the LaGrand brothers. However, I also drew attention to the rights of the victims of the LaGrand brothers ... if Walter LaGrand's rights as they relate to humanitarian issues are to be respected then, in parallel, the matter of the rights of victims of violent crime (a point which has often been overlooked) should be taken into consideration.
>
> (p. 18, per Oda J.)

Likewise, in the case of *Port Hope Environmental Group* v *Canada*[44] the UN Human Rights Committee accepted that dumping nuclear waste raises serious right-to-life issues in relation to both present and future generations. Nevertheless, the general lack of development beyond the ECtHR of rights for either group (victims as a whole or those of environmental harm more specifically[45]) makes it difficult to establish a foothold for such concepts in international customary law.[46]

4.3 Victim participation?

So far this chapter has focused on the recognition of victims of environmental harm as wronged parties in the sense that their human rights have been breached. Perhaps more significant, however, is the question of their *participation* in any process (civil, criminal or administrative) in which corporations, states or any other parties are held to account for the harms caused by polluting activities: in legal terms, their *locus standi*. The International Law Commission, in its draft principles on the allocation of loss in the case of transboundary harm arising out of hazardous activities (discussed in Chapter 3), remarked in its commentary that '[t]he definition of victim is thus linked to the question of standing' (ILC, 2006: p. 137) and then went on to outline various instances in domestic and regional law (including some of the examples mentioned above) where affected individuals and NGOs have been given the right to seek legal redress for environmental harm.

Indeed, legal standing is at the heart of most of the debates concerning victims' rights in general because, in recent history, victims have lacked party status in most domestic criminal justice systems (Hall, 2010).[47] As a consequence of this legal reality, it is the state that acquires the rights of individual victims, effectively forcing those affected by crimes and other social misfortunes to take a subsidiary role in proceedings. This was famously captured by Nils Christie (1977), who argued that the state effectively 'steals' conflicts from their rightful owners, namely the victim and the accused. The same could aptly be said of the victims of environmental harms being excluded from the international legal order; indeed, in this instance the victims' plight is almost entirely taken over by the state because, as already discussed, under international law it is the state and not the individual which can draw on the international legal order against another state. As noted already, one of the arguments in favour of environmental rights for victims, particularly in relation to procedural rights of participation, is that they will allow for better and more effective enforcement of environmental laws. As noted by DeMerieux (2001), 'procedural rights go beyond redundancy and can allow for better enforcement of the law itself' (p. 524).

It is important to appreciate that a 'right to participate' covers a breadth of possibilities, ranging from the nominal to the much more substantive. In the victimological literature, Edwards (2004) has labelled participation 'a comfortably pleasing platitude', which is rhetorically powerful but conceptually abstract. In his discussion, Edwards describes four possible forms of victim participation in criminal justice. The most significant casts victims in the role of *decision-makers*, such that their preferences are sought and applied by the criminal justice system. Less far-reaching would be *consultative* participation, where the system seeks out victims' preferences and takes them into account when making decisions. Edwards sees the traditional role of victims in terms of *information provision*, where victims are obliged to provide information required by the system. Finally, under *expressive* participation, victims express whatever information they wish, but with no instrumental impact; here Edwards highlights the danger of victims wrongly believing their participation will actually affect decision-making.

For victims affected by environmental degradation, the 1992 Rio Declaration, in one of its most forward-reaching provisions, reflects this move towards individual participation. In Principle 10, states are encouraged to ensure 'public awareness and participation by making information widely available'. It goes on to say that '(e)ffective access to judicial and administrative proceedings, including redress and remedy, shall be provided'. Under ECtHR jurisprudence, such a right of participation in environmental cases has most frequently been upheld in relation to Article 6 (the right to a fair and public hearing to determine civil rights). Thus, in *Zander* v *Sweden*[48] the court held that a couple's inability under Swedish law to contest the granting of a licence by the government permitting a company to dump waste adjacent to their property, leading to the pollution of their drinking water (which was drawn from a nearby well), violated Article 6.[49] Article 6 requires a 'civil' right to be admissible, and on this question the Court ruled that the relevant right that had been affected was the right to peaceful enjoyment of one's possessions (Article 1).

Principle 10 of the Rio Declaration has been adopted and adapted by the 1998 UNECE 'Aarhus' Convention on Access to Information, Public Participation in Decision-Making and Access to Justice in Environmental Matters, which requires governments to bring individuals who may be affected into the process when environmental issues are at stake, what Edwards would call *consultative participation*.

Analogous views are found in the 2012 Rio+20 Outcome Document, which acknowledges that 'broad public participation and access to information and judicial and administrative proceedings are essential to the promotion of sustainable development' (Para. 46), although here it is to be noted that access to justice is separated from the notion of 'participation'. Indeed, in terms of holding states to account for the harm caused by environmental degradation, what is significant about the Aarhus convention is that, almost uniquely within international law, under Article 15 it is envisioned that members of the public are able to refer possible breaches of their rights under the Convention to its Compliance Committee:

> The Meeting of the Parties shall establish, on a consensus basis, optional arrangements of a non-confrontational, non-judicial and consultative nature for reviewing compliance with the provisions of this Convention. These arrangements shall allow for appropriate public involvement and may include the option of considering communications *from members of the public* on matters related to this Convention.
>
> (emphasis added)

The key question from a victimological perspective is whether these provisions under Aarhus are the equivalent of giving victims a level of discretion over what in the criminal context would be prosecution decisions (a 'procedural right'), something that has thus far been vigorously avoided in all jurisdictions, or whether it is merely akin to the complaints mechanisms offered to many other types of victims the world over (a 'service' right). So far there have been few (63) applications made to the Compliance Committee.[50] The body cannot issue binding decisions, but rather makes recommendations to the full Meeting of the Parties (Birnie *et al*., 2009). This is remarkably similar to the most common mechanism of affording 'rights' to victims of traditional crime in most domestic jurisdictions, whereby such victims can complain in the event of poor treatment or breach of the relevant codes of practice by a criminal justice agency to an independent arbiter or ombudsman, who can then investigate the claims, although usually not enforce any penalty (see Hall, 2009; 2010). Hence, in this instance the apparent absence of genuinely enforceable rights for individuals concerning the impacts of environmental decisions that affect them mirrors the absence of judiciable rights afforded to victims of crime in domestic jurisdictions (and by international bodies). In both cases, such rights as are purported to exist for victims lack specific enforcement mechanisms or consequences for those breaching the alleged rights. Thus, while the Aarhus convention offers something of a 'way in' to the international legal order for the individual, in practice its compliance mechanisms can be subject to many of the same criticisms more generally leveled at victim empowerment provisions: there is a lack of real compulsive power on behalf of the Compliance Committee to address victims' complaints and ensure that restitution and/or apologies from perpetrator states are forthcoming.

Key among the previous international initiatives relating to the criminalization of environmental harm in this regard is the 1998 Council of Europe

Convention on the Protection of Environment through Criminal Law, discussed in Chapter 3. Although this treaty has not yet entered into force, it is significant as the precursor to the adoption of EU Council Directive 2008/99/EC within the European Union. While the latter instrument almost entirely excluded victims, the 1998 Convention contains a significant provision relating to the participation of environmental victims in criminal justice mechanisms. Article 11 reads:

> Each Party may, at any time, in a declaration addressed to the Secretary General of the Council of Europe, declare that it will, in accordance with domestic law, grant any group, foundation or association which, according to its statutes, aims at the protection of the environment, the right to participate in criminal proceedings concerning offences established in accordance with this Convention.

This article has the potential to be ground-breaking, raising the very real possibility of opening up environmental criminal proceedings to wider participation by the victims of environmental harms themselves. In the context of EU environmental (and criminal) law, the adoption of the language of 'participation' in relation to such organizations is a significant step forward, although it remains a moot question whether the groups envisioned in this Article represent the majority of 'real' environmental victims.[51]

It should be noted that Article 11 of the 1998 Convention is carefully worded to omit any sense of the individual victim. Nevertheless, its inclusion is an important indication of changing attitudes. No longer is the state viewed as the sole trustee of the public good, as is often still the case in international environmental law. As the explanatory report to the Convention notes:

> The main reason for allowing NGOs access to environmental proceedings is that criminal law in the environmental field protects interests of a highly collective nature, in view of the fact that the various forms of pollution potentially affect the interest not only of single individuals, but also of groups of persons.
>
> (Council of Europe, 1998)

While some member states have already implemented such a right, many others have not. As the explanatory report continues, because of this variability, 'as mandatory provisions were found inappropriate, the Committee drafted the Article in a facultative form'. Nevertheless, as a model of progressive development, it ties into many contemporary trends. As the International Law Commission's (2006) Commentary noted in its draft principles on the allocation of loss in the case of transboundary harm arising out of hazardous activities, 'In France, some environmental associations have been given the right to claim compensation in criminal cases involving violation of certain environmental statutes' (p. 137).

Another notable example of participatory rights for victims of environmental harms, albeit again concerning only the *administrative* (rather than criminal) liability of polluting operators, is that of the 2004 EU Environmental Liability Directive.[52] That instrument includes a key role for those affected by environmental harm. Article 12 (entitled 'request for action') and Article 13 ('review procedures') of that Directive state:

> Article 12
>
> 1 Natural or legal persons:
> a affected or likely to be affected by environmental damage or
> b having a sufficient interest in environmental decision making relating to the damage or, alternatively,
> c alleging the impairment of a right, where administrative procedural law of a Member State requires this as a precondition,
>
> *shall be entitled to submit to the competent authority any observations relating to instances of environmental damage or an imminent threat of such damage of which they are aware and shall be entitled to request the competent authority to take action under this Directive.*
>
> What constitutes a 'sufficient interest' and 'impairment of a right' shall be determined by the Member States.
>
> To this end, the interest of any non-governmental organisation promoting environmental protection and meeting any requirements under national law shall be deemed sufficient for the purpose of subparagraph (b). Such organisations shall also be deemed to have rights capable of being impaired for the purpose of subparagraph (c).
>
> Article 13
>
> 1 The persons referred to in Article 12(1) shall have access to a court or other independent and impartial public body competent to review the procedural and substantive legality of the decisions, acts or failure to act of the competent authority under this Directive (emphasis added).

Notably, these provisions include *individual* victims as well as groups and NGOs purporting to represent them. It should also be mentioned in this sections that EU citizens (as individuals or represented by groups) have the right to 'petition to the European Parliament on a matter which comes within the Union's fields of activity and which affects him, her or it directly' under Article 227 of the Treaty on the Functioning of the European Union. Lenaerts and Gutiérrez-Fons (2010) have argued that this provision could be utilized by (directly harmed) citizens who feel that national legislation is conflicting with EU environmental law.

One final example of an instrument in which victims of environmental harms are granted participatory rights on an administrative level is that of the North

American Agreement on Environmental Cooperation (NAAEC).[53] Under this instrument, submissions can be made to the secretariat of the Commission for Environmental Cooperation asserting that a 'party to the agreement is failing to effectively enforce its environmental law'.[54] If the submissions satisfy criteria specified in the NAAEC, the secretariat may request a response from the party named in the submission. While such representations will usually be made by another of the parties to the agreement (these being the US, Mexico and Canada), the agreement also stipulates at Article 22(3) that 'a third Party that considers it has a substantial interest in the matter shall be entitled to participate in the consultations on delivery of written notice to the other Parties and to the Secretariat'. In addition, Article 29 – entitled 'Third Party Participation' – reads:

> A party that is not a disputing Party, on delivery of a written notice to the disputing Parties and to the Secretariat, shall be entitled to attend all hearings, to make written and oral submissions to the panel and to receive written submissions of the disputing Parties.

Although the NAAEC procedure is strictly administrative, it is particularly significant for present purposes in that it relates to a state's lack of enforcement of (environmental) *criminal* law. A similar provision can also be found under the Canadian Environmental Protection Act 1988, which gives citizens the right to sue authorities if environmental laws are not enforced. Girard *et al.* (2010) have remarked on the increasing use of this provision by environmental activists in Canada in the face of what they term 'the Conservative government's continued intransigence' (p. 233) on environmental matters.

4.4 Discussion and ways forward

This chapter has examined the application of human rights principles to both victims as a whole in the victimological literature and specifically to victims of environmental harms. In so doing it has shown that both groups face common difficulties in terms of the recognition of any such rights in the first instance – bringing into question their categorization as 'rights' at all (Jackson, 2004) – and the enforcement potential for those rights. Despite the parallels in both fields, it is important to acknowledge that international environmental lawyers and mainstream victimologists are in fact approaching human rights from a slightly different perspective. This is because the key difficulty faced by victimologists is the lack of enforcement and redress mechanisms in traditional law for victims of crime. Victimology has made considerable progress towards the *recognition* of such individuals, but often lacks the structural basis in law to take the needs of those individuals forward in a substantive way. Conversely, while international environmental lawyers do face similar difficulties in terms of the *enforcement* of rights for victims of environmental harm, this is not because a structure of dedicated international environmental law and redress is not *present* (international environmental law now being a well-established field with over 1,000 international instruments in force on all aspects of environmental degradation; Weiss, 1995) but rather because the structure which does exist has not recognized the needs or harm of those *individuals*. In light of the above discussion, it is argued that the convergence on human rights by international environmental lawyers and by victimologists in fact reflects the structure/agency biases in both disciplines, which have been considered in earlier chapters.

Following on from Chapter 3, the above discussion has noted that 'rights' for victims of traditional crimes are now fairly well established, at least on a rhetorical level, in a number of national and international instruments. Such rights include important service rights – which have been largely uncontroversial (JUSTICE, 1998) and, as discussed above, might well be equally applicable to environmental victims – and also a slowly developing field of procedural rights of participation. It was suggested that such participation may be particularly important in some cases of environmental harm, where the full impact of crime on victims may be obscure. It was also suggested that some of these rights are susceptible to questionable enforcement mechanisms which lack compulsive powers, although in relation to environmental victims it is submitted that this is at present a secondary concern. The main difficulty, rather, lies in the fact that narrow conceptions of 'victimization' in almost all of the relevant criminal justice instruments mean that such rights (if rights they are to be called) as have been afforded to victims of traditional crime are not easily applied to environmental victims, especially when the relevant polluting activities are not 'crimes' per se (because, for example, they are ultimately state-sanctioned or state licensed). As noted in Chapter 3, while the 1985 UN Declaration's definition of 'victims of abuse of power' has the potential to offer victims of environmental harms which do not amount to officially prescribed crimes a way to access the pantheon of victims' rights contained in that document, the problem lies in the fact that that the Declaration relies on 'recognized norms relating to human rights' as a means of distinguishing abusive from non-abusive exercise of power. As such, victims are left facing the position of having to prove 'general' environmental rights before gaining access to victim-specific ones.[55]

The development of such rights has, we have seen, been somewhat restrictive. Certainly there is little evidence on which to base the acceptance of a separate right to a green and unpolluted environment at the international level, and in Europe the ECtHR has specifically excluded this concept in a number of rulings. This must be considered unfortunate because, as more local decisions have shown in Africa and South America, courts in these jurisdictions have not only apparently recognized such rights but, in so doing, they have directly addressed the 'balancing' of individual/state/corporate interests which seems to lie at the heart of environmental victimization issues, and indeed of critical victimology more generally.

Generally speaking, the adapting of existing rights to fit green issues seems to have proceeded more quickly, although its direction can be criticized for its anthropocentric bias. Clearly the ECtHR is increasingly prepared to interpret

Convention rights in this way although, as noted above, beyond Europe even this solution is less tried and tested. The other difficulty with the ECtHR jurisprudence on this matter is that while it recognizes that grounds of action (in the form of breaches of rights) have occurred, it goes into less detail about how, for example, 'a certain minimum level of severity' is to be established in relation to the harm suffered, or whether victims are to be consulted directly. In other words, the ECtHR cases recognize that rights are breached, but has done little to shed light on the participation rights of green victims in the same way it has examined participation rights of victims of traditional crimes. Furthermore, DeMerieux (2001) notes that because victims must show some form of present injury to bring a case to the ECtHR, this in fact precludes consideration of longer-term damage to culture for the next generation. In other words, relying on the ECtHR to enforce environmental rights for victims would be to exclude all notions of intergenerational justice.

It has been argued above that the question of 'standing' to participate in proceedings is often at the centre of rights discussion, in relation to both victims of traditional crimes and victims of environmental crime or environmental harm. In the latter case, there are now a number of progressive instruments at the intentional level, which seem to facilitate such participation by environmental victims, although only in *administrative* proceedings.[56] The main exception in this regard would be the draft Council of Europe Convention on the Protection of Environmental through Criminal Law, although this document has yet to meet with widespread acceptance by states.

The overall impression one gets from the above discussion is that there has been a lack of holistic or joined-up thinking in relation to the rights of victims of environmental harm. Many of the relevant arguments concerning the creation of such rights have in fact already been made. Mainstream victimology provides a solid basis for the development of such rights, having considered such issues as the right to be heard, the right to have a victimization acknowledged, and so on, for many years. This literature also points the way towards consulting victims themselves as to what rights and services they require. Many instruments designed for traditional victims of crime similarly contain a number of relevant provisions for victims of environmental harm, including the right to information, support and courteous treatment. The difficulty, though, is that there has been a lack of consideration of the victim of environmental harm in relation to these instruments, and the result is that such victims are effectively excluded from them. From the perspective of international law, while we have seen that the development and incorporation of rights for victims of environmental harm or crime are strikingly underdeveloped in a number of ways, the overall picture actually very much supports the proposition that rights are possible (indeed in *local* contexts they *do* exist) and that international courts and administrative bodies are equipped (although inexperienced) to address issues such as the 'balancing' of state and individual perspectives and even the 'standing' of such victims to participate in the process. Much of this development has been along administrative lines, but this has significant implications for the developments of criminal procedures as well. For example, the development of environmental victims' rights in *administrative* law has also had the positive effect of promoting rights to information about environmental matters. In the light of the growing use of criminal law to deal with environmental harms at the national and international levels, such literatures must be considered together and policy-makers must be prepared to transpose the ideas that are demonstrably workable in both areas.

5 Responding to environmental victimization: compensation, restitution and redress

Following the overall theme of this volume, and in particular the first research question set out in Chapter 1, this chapter represents the first attempt in a somewhat disparate literature to examine and compare the different avenues of compensation and restitution available to victims of environmental harm (in theory and in practice), taking a holistic approach and drawing on victimological as well as legal insights. It is hoped that the results of this combined critical analysis of the relative merits of each process will contribute significantly to the literature as a whole as well as offering important insights into both the first and third research questions posed by this volume.

The preceding chapters have concerned themselves largely with the place and recognition of victims of environmental harm in criminal (plus administrative and civil) proceedings at the national and international level. In the victimological literature, one line of argument – emphasizing 'procedural justice' (Tyler, 1990; Tyler and Huo, 2002) – suggests that this *recognition* by a justice system is in fact a key (some argue paramount[1]) variable affecting victims' satisfaction with the process. In other words, victims of (traditional) crime care more about how a justice system treats them, including its sensitivity to their concerns and needs and how it recognizes the harm they have suffered, than about the instrumental outcomes of such procedures (whether they result in convictions, restitution and so on).

In relation to environmental victims the situation is markedly less clear, due to the almost total absence of empirical research directly asking *these* victims what they would hope to take away from a justice systems (of any kind) when that system endeavours to respond to environmentally destructive activities perpetrated by individuals, corporations or states. If we were to assume (and in the case of many victims of crime we know this would be a false assumption; Shapland, 2003; Wright, 1998) that environmental victims require some kind of monetary recompense for the harms they have endured (or will endure in the future), the next question is where these payments should come from. Should they come from the perpetrator of the environmental degradation, or from the state, or, alternatively, from domestic or international funds constituted for this purpose? Furthermore, even in cases of officially recognized environmental crimes, should such payments be imposed as part of a *sentence* (as part of the criminal justice process), or would civil or administrative mechanisms be more appropriate? A further issue is whether such monies should cover only the identifiable physical and economic costs of currently affected individuals and groups, whether provision should be made to restore the damaged ecosystem to its previous state, and whether further provisions should be made for future generations affected by present environmental degradation.

This chapter will address the questions posed above by examining what provisions exist for restitution and/or compensation[2] for victims of environmental harm, with a particular focus on environmental *crime*, at national and international levels. Of course, constraints of space coupled with an absence of empirical evidence means it will be impossible to offer truly conclusive answers to these questions. Furthermore, the picture here is in fact very complex because environmental harm, as we have seen, may be addressed through national or international systems, which are criminal, administrative or civil. Indeed, in principle at least there is scope for victims to approach *all* these sources for restitution and compensation.

For the purpose of this chapter the term 'compensation' will generally be used (unless otherwise stated) to refer to monies paid to victims of environmental harm by *states*: in other words from public funds. This will be contrasted to 'restitution', which will normally come from perpetrators of environmental harm (whether individuals or corporations). I will refer to both terms collectively as 'redress'. It should be noted that in the wider literature these terms are sometimes used loosely and interchangeably, and in markedly different ways to their use here. Furthermore, given that states may themselves be the perpetrators of (or at least contribute to) environmental harm, it cannot be assumed that all monies coming from public funds would constitute 'compensation' as it is understood here. Arguably it is precisely these kinds of conceptual uncertainties that have contributed to a situation where the questions noted above (and others) have not been the subjects of detailed analysis in relation to environmental victims for either victimologists or international lawyers. This further underlies the necessity of engaging in such an analysis here.

5.1 What do victims of environmental crime want? What do they need?

As noted above, there is at present a dearth of empirical research on what victims of environmental crime might actually want from a criminal justice (or other) process (Williams, 1997). There is a real sense of history repeating itself in this state of affairs. In the UK, for example, the 1964 introduction of the Criminal Injuries Compensation Scheme (discussed below) was largely based on a presumption that victims wanted it, and indeed might turn to vigilantism without it (Rock, 1990). Such examples are far from unique to victim policies. Ellis (2005), for example, recounts how 'youth' became a policy concern for the Conservatives in the 1960s based on a mistaken belief that this group threatened Conservative values. In the modern context, with the focus being on so-called evidence-based policy-making (see Lawrence, 2006), the lack of direct consultation with environmental victims is worrying. Indeed, in a more general sense it is truly fascinating how in environmental crime fields, the definition of victims by victims themselves is largely being ignored. Hall and Shapland (forthcoming) have suggested that this is because more direct consultation would mean confronting what victims themselves say and think, rather than 'using' them as exemplars of damaged people in line with Garland's view of 'the culture of control' (2001). Of course, in this sense environmental victims are threats not only to lawyers and the state, but also to environmental activist groups wishing to attack states, if (for example) it turns out that victims desire only respectful treatment, information, understanding and an apology as opposed to more retributive outcomes. Certainly in relation to victims of crime more generally, this latter impression is supported by Bradford's (2011) analysis of the national victimization survey for England and Wales, the British Crime Survey, which found that victims who did have contact with Victim Support had more favourable views of the fairness of the criminal justice system and higher levels of confidence in its effectiveness. The link between contact with Victim Support and confidence in the criminal justice system was mediated by trust in the fairness of the system: it appears that if victims have someone who listens to their concerns (and may take action in relation to them), they trust the system more and have greater confidence in it. This continues to support Tyler's (2006) theory of procedural justice noted above: that those members of the public who have contact with the system view the system through the lens of their perceptions of how fairly it takes decisions and how it treats them (with respect, sensitivity and dignity scoring highly). Of course, definitive answers as to the question of whether this same effect applies to *environmental* victims can only follow detailed empirical work.

Given the above situation, green victimologists are at present forced to retreat to theoretical discussion to anticipate what victims of environmental crime might need. On this point, Lee (2009) has emphasized the importance of a holistic, welfare-centred approach to environmental harms, rather than concentrating purely on financial compensation or restitution:

> The social welfare needs of residents in environmentally polluted communities are a multi-dimensional, long-term issue. The distribution of cash reparations alone will do little to bring about sustainable development, but will simply alleviate poverty temporarily.
>
> (p. 26)

As an alternative to simple, blanket, monetary compensation, Lee puts significant weight on the provision of long-term, tailored support and restoration packages in individual communities. Given that 'different localities inherit different cultural norms and characteristics' (p. 29), Lee also emphasizes the vital role of *local* government in developing and facilitating the delivery of such packages. Further indications that at least some victims of environmental degradation need much more than simple monetary recompense can be found in a telling case study by Wheatley (1997), concerning the significant cultural impacts on Canadian aboriginal peoples following mercury poisoning of their traditional lands and supplies of food and water: ‘Even after compensation was paid social problems persisted, especially in Whitedog, where solvents are smuggled into the community and 4 suicides were reported in the spring of 1995’ (p. 78). Although only one (perhaps atypical) example, this does raise questions as to whether compensation or restitution schemes should focus on the short-term needs of individuals affected by environmental harm, or the longer-term needs of the community as a whole, along with the needs of *future* generations of potential (cultural, economic and physical) victims of such harm. The importance of non-monetary restitution is further supported by the more established victimological literature, which consistently holds that payments from offenders themselves carry greater symbolic value to victims of crime than monies allocated from taxation (Shapland, 2003). Malsch (1999) too has emphasized the importance of ‘immaterial damages’ to victims of crime and the complexities inherent in addressing these in the criminal justice context:

> Material damages are, in general, relatively easy to assess, in contrast to immaterial damages. The latter includes invasions of privacy and feelings of security, and increased fear of crime. It is difficult to translate these aspects into a monetary claim. The presence of immaterial damages may, moreover, impact more widely than only on the direct victim. People surrounding the victim (family, friends, colleagues) are affected in one way or another, and will be confronted with the complicated task of offering support to the injured person.
>
> (p. 244)

Shapland (2003), having interviewed victims directly on the question of compensation, concluded that victims feel that their pain and suffering has been duly recognized by the judge when offenders are ordered to pay compensation: as Miers (1980) put it, a recognition of their ‘victim status’ (see also Wright, 1998). The recognition of such a status by a criminal court (and by offenders) may be especially significant to environmental victims, given the often hidden or indirect nature of their suffering. Of course, in the absence of empirical evidence, we have at present no idea whether victims of environmental harm value symbolic gestures more than, less than or equally to other types of victims.

In sum, although we lack direct evidence, if we apply what we do know based on both theory and empirical evidence from the more established victimological literature, it can be seen that the simple payment of money to individuals harmed by environmentally destructive activities (whether they constitute crimes or not) is likely to constitute at best a broad-brush means of addressing the impacts of such activities, and at worst it may fall far short of full redress (see Malsch, 1999).[3] The remainder of this chapter will examine various mechanisms for providing such redress, in an effort to evaluate how they measure up to these rather difficult criteria.

5.2 Mechanisms of redress

5.2.1 Criminal justice

In the context of the present volume, and in particular seeking answers to the first research question set out in Chapter 1, the most directly relevant means of providing victims of environmental harm with some form of redress is to seek this though *criminal justice* mechanisms. The most likely method of achieving this seems to be the granting of court-based restitution orders imposed as part of a criminal sentence against environmental offenders. Not only might such a route provide some financial redress, it would arguably also have important symbolic impact. The latter point has been acknowledged by the European Commission (2001), which has argued that imposing criminal sanctions in environmental cases 'demonstrates a social disapproval of a qualitatively different nature compared to administrative sanctions or a compensation mechanism under civil law' (p. 238). The intended overall effect, it is suggested, is to increase condemnation of such acts and raise awareness as to their dangerousness and the social harms they engender.

Criminal penalties, and in particular criminal-based restitution, have also on occasion proved a strategically beneficial option for the recovery of monies from environmental offenders. Richardson (2010) describes how, following the 1989 Exxon oil spill off the coast of Alaska, the US federal government sought recovery of natural resource damages to Prince William Sound 'not by pursuing a civil claim against Exxon ... but by filing criminal charges' (p. 4). The Exxon Shipping Company was charged with criminal violations of the Migratory Bird Treaty Act (having caused the death of protected birds) and the Refuse Act. Significantly, both these crimes carried penalties that would require restitution to injured parties. In this case the injured party was deemed to be the United States, for damage to its natural environmental. The criminal route was chosen because, at the time, the relevant legislation in the US imposed significant limitations on the amount that could be claimed from polluters under civil law.[4] The outcome was that Exxon pleaded guilty, and a settlement was reached through negotiation with the government that involved significant financial payments to the US.

In the light of previous discussion, and the subject of this volume as a whole, it is somewhat ironic that one of the successful examples of utilizing the criminal law to achieve restitution for environmental crimes involved the *state* as the victim. Of course, the ensuing clean-up operation paid for from the settlement naturally benefited individuals affected by the disasters (and indeed their descendants), but this was achieved only via the state effectively acquiring their conflict with the company: the very act of states 'stealing' conflicts from victims criticized by Christie (1977).[5] Notably, Richardson doubts the utility of criminal law to settle the restitution claims of *individual victims directly*, and the remainder of this section will serve to test this hypothesis.

5.2.1.1 Restitution as part of sentencing for environmental crimes

As a general trend in recent years, many countries have, as part of their criminal justice processes, turned increasingly to offenders to provide monetary restitution to victims of crime: either directly though the imposition of court-based orders, or through the establishment of victims' funds maintained by offender surcharges and fine payments (Whitehead and Block, 2003; Canadian Department of Justice, 2012). Such a move is well supported by the established literature, which, as noted above, consistently holds that payments from offenders themselves carry greater symbolic value to victims of crime than monies allocated from taxation. As such, restitution has become an integral and indeed mandatory component of many of the world's criminal justice systems (see Hall, 2010). The importance of the *symbolic* benefit to victims of receiving money directly from offenders is often used to counteract the observation that individual offenders themselves are often unable to afford to pay much, if any, restitution (at least if such restitution is reckoned in monetary terms), and therefore the sums involved cannot be said to compensate the victim for the harm suffered in a strictly financial sense (Newburn, 1988; Nagin and Waldfogel, 1998). That said, it is notable that in the US the national Mandatory Restitution Act 1996 makes it explicit that the purpose of imposing restitution orders is *not* merely symbolic, but in the words of the Californian scheme is intended 'to help victims recover from any financial hardship caused due to [a] criminal activity' (California Department of Corrections and Rehabilitation, 2009). Of course, herein lies one of the primary distinctions between 'ordinary' offenders who commit traditional crimes and environmental offenders, who might well be large corporations. Such corporations will often be in a position to afford much more in the way of financial restitution. We might speculate that such concrete (not merely symbolic) restitution could be of greater importance to victims and communities affected by serious economic impacts or impacts on their livelihoods as a result of environmental crime, although again to do so risks the same criticisms that have been levied at the development of existing victim support schemes: presuming what victims want.

What we do know, at least in England and Wales, is that court-based restitution for environmental crimes has not been widely utilized. On this point, the House of Commons Environmental Audit Committee (2004) received evidence from the Environmental Industries Commission suggesting:

> Whilst there is statutory provision for the criminal courts to order an offender to remedy the environmental harm caused, it is not apparent that this is often used. Earlier guidance to magistrates recommended a greater use of compensation orders but this does not appear to have occurred (this may be because of uncertainty in applying the concept to environmental offences).
>
> (p. 63)

The guidance notes mentioned here are based on those issued by the Sentencing Council, which says that if a specific victim in environmental cases is identifiable, a court should consider imposing a compensation order[6] against offenders. Indeed, s.130(3) of the 2000 Act requires courts to give reasons why they have *not* imposed compensation orders in all cases, and s.130(12) mandates that compensation orders must take precedence over fines if offenders are only able to afford one of the two.[7] Bell and McGillivray (2008) argue that the explanation for the under-utilization of compensation orders in cases of environmental crime in England and Wales lies mainly with the existence of many statutory powers of clean-up and cost recovery available to regulatory agencies in defined situations (for example, s.59 of the Environmental Protection Act 1990 and s.161A of the Water Resources Act 1991). In addition, the authors point out that under s.131 of the 2000 Act, compensation orders are restricted to a maximum of £5,000, a sum that in fact may often be insufficient to fully restore victims or their environment to their previous state (see Chapter 2), if indeed *any* sum of money can achieve this. A further problem in some jurisdictions, notably Canada, is that restitution orders are sometimes restricted to certain proscribed offences, which do not include environmental crime (see Canadian Department of Justice, 2012).

Of course, the fact that the sums involved may be insufficient to restore victims to the state they were in prior to the effect of an environmental crime is in keeping with the notion that the purpose of restitution, at least in England and Wales, is largely symbolic. Elsewhere, as in the Californian example noted above, the situation is less clear-cut. For example, in the South African criminal justice system, 'restitution' is defined as the return or repair of property by the offender 'in order to restore you [the victim] to the position you were in prior to the commission of the offence'[8] (South African Department of Justice and Constitutional Development, 2008: pp. 13–15). This was also the rationale given for the introduction of restitution orders in the Netherlands in the Terwee Act 1995 (Wemmers, 1996). Such an unfettered version of restitution orders, if applied against large, rich corporations responsible for environmental harm, has the potential to be a very powerful mechanism for environmental victims – including large groups of victims – both in terms of the amount of money available and the symbolic benefit of being recognized as criminally harmed. Skinnider (2011: p. 55) has commented on the difficulty of applying restitution orders in cases of 'mass' or 'community' environmental victimization, although he suggests a number of solutions, including:

- an order for restoration of any harm to the environment caused by the commission of the offence;
- payment of the costs and expenses incurred by a public authority in restoring any harm to the environment;
- payment of the costs for carrying out a specified project for the restoration or enhancement of the environment in a public place or for the public benefit;

- payment of a specified amount to an environmental trust or a specified environmental organization for the purpose of a specified project for the restoration.

An argument that could be raised against all these solutions, however, is that they lack direct recognition of individual victims or their suffering, and of course in the more practical sense do nothing at all to assist such victims with incurred costs (health costs, insurance costs, repair costs and so on).

A more fundamental difficulty with relying on such restitution orders is that achieving criminal convictions in such cases is very difficult, for reasons already alluded to in previous chapters. The question of causation is often extremely difficult to resolve, and there may be underlying issues concerning the cultural willingness of prosecutors to pursue such cases. Even assuming a conviction is achieved for the original crime, ascribing that crime to the full ambit of possible impacts discussed in Chapter 2 would be close to impossible (as well as costly for the criminal justice system itself). O'Hear (2004) has rightly highlighted how one of the key difficulties in applying the social harms perspective within *criminal justice* more broadly is that of establishing *culpability* for wide-ranging and diverse impacts:

> From a culpability standpoint, the underlying problem is that punishing actual harm effectively punishes a defendant for circumstances beyond his or her control.... While this approach may make sense for a compensation scheme ... the approach is far more problematic in a culpability-based punishment scheme.
>
> (pp. 229–230)

Such difficulties reflect broader problems that criminal justice systems face when confronted with environmental offenders and environmental victims. In particular, the concept of mass victimization is still difficult for many justice systems to assimilate, recalling of course that most such systems around the world are still struggling to incorporate individual victims of traditional crimes where matters such as causation are fairly clear-cut (as in, for example, a non-contentious assault case).

It has been suggested that initial low take-up rates of restitution orders for *any crime* in a number of jurisdictions were largely based on cultural reticence within the judiciary to use them, and by implication to put the needs of victims above a perceived need to, say, punish an offender through a fine (see Newburn, 1988; Moxon *et al.*, 1992). On this point, matters are improving (Ashworth, 2010), but it seems clear that criminal justice systems still have a way to go before restitution orders are routinely used in *environmental* cases, even though, ironically, corporate environmental offenders may be in a much stronger position to pay financially meaningful sums to large groups of victims.

5.2.1.2 State-based criminal compensation systems

In the majority of western jurisdictions it is possible for victims of some crimes to receive monetary compensation from the state, paid out of public funds. In most cases, however, the particulars of these schemes restrict the availability of compensation to those who have suffered physical injury as a result of violent crime (see Hall, 2010 for a full review). Consequently, environmental victimization will almost always fall beyond the remit of such existing mechanisms. Strictly speaking, these schemes are administrative in nature,[9] rather than falling within the criminal justice system per se (at least in most jurisdictions). They are introduced here largely because to include environmental victims within such officially labelled *criminal* compensation schemes would imply an official and social recognition of environmental harms as *criminally* perpetrated, which might prove significant from the perspective of both the individual victims and that of wider society (as alluded to above). Indeed, as with restitution orders, it is acknowledged in a number of jurisdictions that the payments made by such schemes are symbolic, even though the sums involved are often greater than that which can be paid by most offenders. This perspective is demonstrated by the system in operation in Queensland since 1995, which was revised in December 2009:[10]

> The purpose of the COVA [Criminal Offence Victims Act 1995] scheme is to recognise the impact of crime on victims and help with the financial cost of injuries. However, as in all other jurisdictions, it is not intended to reflect the amount of compensation a victim may receive at common law.
>
> (Queensland Department of Justice and Attorney General, 2009: p. 13)

Similarly, the Dutch scheme makes the following stipulation: 'The Fund does not pay full compensation, but rather an allowance for personal injury. The amount of this one-off payment may therefore differ from the actual amount of damage you suffer' (Schadefonds Geweldsmisdrijven, 2008: p. 6). That this should be the case is in one sense quite surprising, given that originally (in England and Wales and elsewhere) such schemes were modelled after pre-existing systems of common law damages (Fry, 1951).[11] Of course, a key reason such schemes present themselves as offering symbolic rather than full economic compensation is to control escalating costs, which have been witnessed in almost all jurisdictions that have introduced them (see Miers, 1997; Zhang, 2008). Notwithstanding this, the overriding impression given by the available reviews of state-based criminal compensation mechanisms in operation in most developed nations is that they are aimed at ideal (individual) victims and at stereotypical notions of suffering, both of which, as we have seen, tend to exclude environmental victims (see New Zealand Law Commission, 2008; Irish Criminal Injuries Compensation Tribunal, 2009; Hall, 2010). This is especially unfortunate in the environmental context given that a key advantage of seeking compensation though these systems is that, in most cases, a conviction does not have to be achieved and indeed an offender need not even be identified. This in effect avoids the problem of establishing culpability. Indeed, this seems particularly attractive in the case of environmental crimes, given the difficulties alluded to above in achieving convictions against offenders. Of course, the same advantage would in fact apply to any administrative environmental compensation scheme, whether or not the damage being compensated is recognized by the scheme as a 'crime' and whether or not the funding for this compensation came from public funds. This chapter will turn to these wider administrative compensation systems in the next section.

While the schemes set up to compensate victims of traditional *crimes* through administrative mechanisms do not at present accommodate environmental victims, their development over the last 50 years has spawned a great deal of academic debate concerning their rationale and justifications, which may provide important insights for the application of such a scheme to cases of (criminal or non-criminal) environmental harm.

Of course, not least among the debates surrounding such schemes is whether *states* should in fact be paying anything at all to those who have suffered harm (criminal or otherwise). England and Wales, for example, introduced the world's second criminal injuries compensation scheme in 1964[12] and, although this was based on common law damages, originally the campaigners for its introduction conceived such a system as based around the existing industrial injuries scheme in operation in England and Wales (now known as Industrial Injuries Disablement Benefit), and grounded on the same *welfare* principles (Fry, 1951).

In relation to victims of environmental harm, the notion of grounding an administrative compensation scheme on welfare principles seems appealing, especially in the light of Lee's (2009) strong advocacy of a welfare-based system discussed earlier in this chapter. Nevertheless Miers (1997) in particular has argued that in reality states do not pay compensation to victims (of crime) based on welfare needs. Indeed, his argument is that these schemes are rather based on perceived political necessity:

> [O]ne of the most notable features of the introduction of criminal injury compensation schemes in common law jurisdictions has been that they have often been immediately preceded by the commission of a particularly serious crime of violence against a vulnerable or altruistic victim, which in turn occasioned a public campaign in favour of 'doing something' for victims of crime.
>
> (p. 10)

Both Miers and Elias (1983) emphasize the heavily political character of state compensation as a concept. This echoes the earlier statements of Harland (1978), writing from a US perspective, to the effect that state compensation programmes are often grounded in the contemporary emotional and political climate, created in the wake of tragic and dramatic events or victim rallies:

> The reality of state-funded victim compensation seems to be that it is an extremely limited service available to only a minute proportion of those who suffer loss or injury as a result of crime. Too often, however, this reality is cloaked in a political show of concern for victims, while the underlying fears of costs continue to emerge in the form of programme restrictions.
>
> (p. 213)

It seems that these views can be applied beyond the sphere of 'significant' *criminal* events or victimizations, to encompass a wide range of ad hoc administrative state compensation schemes. Indeed, if we examine the range of examples of such schemes we can see they are often in fact pre-empted by such eye-catching, mediatized events as the September 11th Victims Fund and the Claims Fund set up following the Deepwater Horizon oil spill in the Gulf of Mexico in 2010, discussed in more detail below.

The New Zealand Law Commission (2008) has recently called for a major rethink of the groundings of their own criminal injuries compensation system and, in so doing, raised questions concerning the special consideration being afforded to victims *of crime*, as opposed to wider social harms:

> [V]ictims' compensation schemes cannot be justified on the basis of abstract notions about the social contract between state and citizen. Furthermore, while some initiatives may be able to be justified on a cost-benefit analysis, it is generally difficult to justify special treatment of crime victims on grounds of social utility.
>
> (Para. 4.3)

Why victims of *crime* should be singled out for special attention, assistance, and (public) funding compared to victims of other social misfortunes is a moot point.[13] The history of most state compensation systems betrays confusion on this issue: as demonstrated by the further reasoning of the 1968 Alberta report:

> [W]hy should victims of crime be singled out for assistance from the public purse? We base our recommendation on the plight of the victims and the fact that his injuries have arisen from the wrongful acts of an element in society. There is a connection between the social breakdown manifested in crime and injury to innocent citizens.
>
> (Institute of Law Research and Reform, 1968: p. 3).

What makes this justification unclear (and contradictory) is that the same report goes on to present a disclaimer that its recommendation for the introduction of a state compensation scheme 'does not rest on the argument that the machinery of law enforcement has broken down, or on the proposition that the state is under a duty to compensate' (p. 3). Indeed, all state compensation systems for victims of crime are careful to emphasize that, while their justification might be obscure, this is certainly *not* based on any notion that the state has 'failed' in a duty to protect its people from criminal victimization, and is therefore culpable for any injury. Given the discussion earlier in this volume concerning the *state's* own role (or co-role) in some instances of environmental degradation and victimization, however, this is an argument which may not apply so readily to environmental victims. Of course the question of why victims of *crime* are so important also recalls some of the earliest debates of the victims' movement prior to the widespread focusing of victimology on victims of crime specifically.[14] It also returns us to the question of *criminal* verses *social harms* discussed in Chapter 1.[15]

5.2.2 Administrative compensation schemes

O'Hear (2004) has argued that administrative compensation systems for environmental damage (in this case brought about through climate change) carry numerous advantages over both civil and criminal court procedures. His main argument is that such schemes can operate under a more comprehensive set of pre-defined rules.[16] Lin (2005) adds to this argument by noting the benefits of such schemes' use of standardized schedules of damages. This is certainly the case under most *criminal* compensation schemes, although a criticism of this is that while it offers greater certainty it also allows for very little adaptation of the rules to specific situations. Given the broad range of environmental harms discussed in Chapter 2, and the general gaps in our knowledge concerning the full range of these effects, a rigid system may not serve some victims of environmental harm particularly well.

Following on from the last point, O'Hear argues that more diverse forms of environmental harms (in this case impairment of 'characteristics of the landscape' and disruption or impairment of lifestyles of indigenous communities) have 'traditionally not received nearly as sophisticated consideration in the legal system as have others' (p. 162). O'Hear supports his argument with a further comment from Bowman (2002), in which the latter argues that such compensation schemes that have been implemented around the world in response to environmental degradation 'have not really involved recognition of harm to the environment at all, but have been concerned with the infringement of established human interests relating to the person or property caused through the medium of the environment' (pp. 12–13). This recalls questions from Chapter 1 concerning the anthropocentric focus of much of green criminology, but also raises the more specific point that administrative compensation schemes are indeed often concerned with individual claimants rather than restoration of the environment as a whole, although monies from such funds can be channelled into more generalized efforts to repair the environment.[17] On a more affirmative note, however, such schemes are usually designed to cater for large groups of victims/claimants, one of the rationales being that approaching such mass victimization in this manner is more efficient (in terms of time and costs) than multiple civil tortious cases going through the courts for a protracted period, as occurred (and is still occurring) after the Bhopal disaster in India in 1984.[18] Indeed, Lin (2005) has argued that a key advantage of administrative compensation schemes in cases of environmental harm is that they have the potential to compensate those who are *not yet* affected by environmental damage but are at a significant risk of becoming so:

> The goal of corrective justice generally receives less attention in an administrative system than in a tort system where individualized adjudications focus on the causal link between the defendant and the plaintiff. But if an

> administrative system provided ex ante compensation to persons who would otherwise receive nothing in tort (such as future victims who do not yet display symptoms of an illness), that system would provide some marginal benefit of corrective justice.
>
> (pp. 1468–1469)

Lin's argument is grounded on his notion of a 'risk-based' compensation system for victims (or potential victims) of environmental harm, whereby claimants are made awards based on their scientifically verifiable increased *risk* of environmental harm as a result of polluting activities.

Farber (2007) has argued along similar lines that the problem of establishing full (or even partial) causation in cases of environmental crime can be avoided by offering victims what he calls 'proportional recovery':

> There is considerable scholarly support for a different approach to probabilistic harm. Rather than providing full compensation for victims who have proven at least a fifty percent probability of causation and none for those who have not met that burden of proof, the new approach would provide proportional recovery to all victims. Thus, if there is, for example, a sixty percent chance that a victim's injury was caused by exposure to the toxic chemical, the victim would receive compensation for sixty percent of her loss. Similarly, if the probability is only twenty percent, twenty percent of the loss would be compensable.
>
> (pp. 1637–1638)

In cases where different groups of victims have different chances of becoming subject to environmental harm, O'Hear too advocates the risk-based approach. This again avoids the difficulty of proving causation in the criminal (or indeed civil) courts. For Lin (2005) the advantages of administrative compensation systems over civil courts are very clear. He argues that administrative systems typically employ specialized or expert decision-makers who can conduct their own studies and consider a broad range of information. He also suggest that administrative systems can provide more continuous oversight and distribute compensation more fairly among a class of victims, while being more politically accountable than the judicial system. Lin's notion of a risk-based, administrative compensation system for victims of environmental harm is encouraging, although he does place considerable faith in the ability of modern science to assess risk accurately.[19] This may be over-generous given the continuing development in knowledge of environmentally induced harms along with the still considerable gaps in that knowledge. To give one pertinent example, Cross (1989) has highlighted the difficulties in drawing verifiable conclusions in relation to environmentally induced cancers. In addition, of course, it might be argued that administrative systems such as this lack the symbolic recognition afforded to victims by a ruling in a criminal, or even a civil, court.

One of the most recent high-profile administrative compensation systems related specifically to environmental victimization is the $20 billion fund constituted through talks between BP and the US government following the 2010 Deepwater Horizon oil spill in the Gulf of Mexico. Unlike the state-funded criminal schemes discussed previously, this fund is financed by BP. The fund is administered by an 'Independent Claims Facility' that, controversially, is managed by an employee of BP (2010). Consequently, this is perhaps better thought of as an administrative *restitution* scheme which can pay monies to businesses, state departments and, significantly for present purposes, *individuals* demonstrating 'legitimate claims including natural resource damages and state and local response costs' (BP, 2010). Given the worldwide interest in the case it might be speculated that the speed and efficiency with which the US and BP brokered the deal may reflect the kind of political underpinnings to the scheme predicted by Elias (1983) and Harland (1978). The continued high degree of controversy and interest in the workings of the scheme on the part of the US media in particular[20] has maintained the disaster as a political issue.[21] While overall the scheme is a positive step in the direction of addressing the needs of environmental victims more broadly, some commentators have used it to exemplify the disparity between the treatment of environmental victims in such particularly newsworthy cases[22] compared to provisions for such victims more broadly at the national and international level. Indeed, even within the United States it is notable that when the Comprehensive Environmental Response, Compensation, and Liability Act (CERCLA)[23] was passed by Congress in 1980, proposed provisions relating to the compensation of individual victims of environmental damage were removed at the last minute to ensure its passage (Bronston, 1983). As explained by Farber (2007), compensation for injury to natural resources is payable under the Act only to: the US government; to any state for resources 'within the State or belonging to, managed by, controlled by, or appertaining to such State';[24] and to any Indian tribe in specified situations. CERCLA does not extend any procedural rights to individual victims, with the authority to sue under the Act being vested in the President on behalf of the United States or 'authorized representatives of any state'.[25]

Returning to the Deepwater Horizon example, Van Tassell argues (2011):

> The Gulf of Mexico oil spill and British Petroleum's quick efforts to pay for clean-up and compensation for victims may lead many people to falsely conclude that national and international laws operate effectively to make the polluter pay for harm. In truth, clean-up and compensation is rarely accomplished so efficiently, and laws operate to insulate polluters when [such a] disaster occurs in poorer countries.
>
> (unpaginated)

In this instance the author draws particular comparison with the large number of environmental victims going uncompensated in Nigeria, following the widespread pollution caused by the oil industry. This example will be returned to below. The criticism is that while highly visible, relatively lucrative compensation schemes are available for major one-off polluting events in developed jurisdictions that have the ability to put pressure on large multinational corporations, this does little to address the more general absence of such compensation or restitution mechanisms internationally for more endemic, but perhaps less media-friendly, examples of environmental victimization. This disparity also reflects the inequality of impact of environmental harm between rich and poor nations discussed in Chapter 2.

Another example of an administrative compensation system set up to compensate victims of environmental harms (among other classifications of injury) is the United Nations Compensation Commission established in the wake of the 1990–1991 Iraq war (Wyatt, 2010). Of particular relevance to this discussion is the fact that a *state* (Iraq) was being held accountable for wartime environmental atrocities (mainly the setting alight of oil wells during Iraq's withdrawal from Kuwait) and their aftermath. According to UN Security Council resolution 687 of 3 May 1991, Iraq was 'liable under international law for any direct loss, damage, including environmental damage and the depletion of natural resources, or injury to foreign Governments, nationals and corporations, as a result of Iraq's unlawful invasion and occupation of Kuwait' (Para. 16). Notably this statement refers to the injuries done to *individuals* as well as other states, although in terms of procedural involvement (see Chapter 4) the Commission will only receive claims from and communicate with governments, rather than corporate, group or individual victims. Wyatt (2010) describes how the Panel of Commission for environmental claims

> drew on tests for causation elaborated in the context of peacetime environmental damage to determine what constituted a direct cause, taking a very liberal approach to 'direct causation' in one particular case where the Commissioners held that, even where there were intervening events, a direct causal link could be established so long as those events did not break the chain of causation.
>
> (p. 621)

This again illustrates how administrative systems are able to avoid the difficulties faced by courts in demonstrating causation in such cases.

A number of other proposed administrative environmental compensation systems from the US are discussed by Lin (2005), although as noted above he ultimately dismisses these in favour of a risk-based model. These include an Environmental Law Institute Proposal from 1983 to raise a fund from 'a tax on petroleum and chemical production, an annual hazard fee that roughly reflected the risk-generating characteristics of the substances produced, and public revenues' (p. 1482). The idea was that potential tort claimants could instead apply to the fund for compensation, which would pay monies to compensate 'only for pecuniary losses, not for pain and suffering' (p. 1483). The scheme would be run on a no-fault basis, with claimants only having to show they had been affected by the pollution, not establishing the direct culpability of any particular organization or business. Of course, a difficulty with imposing new taxes or levies on polluting industries is that they will simply pass on such costs to the consumers, thus removing any *deterrent* effect of the measures. Indeed, it was for this reason that recently the British Shippers Council – a democratic arm of the UK's Freight Transport Association (FTA) – resolutely rebuffed proposals to impose a bunker levy on shippers to fund environmental compensation schemes (see FTA, 2011). Perhaps more significantly, however, is the fact that corporations may resist levies placed upon them arbitrarily when no direct fault has been attributed to them. This issue will be discussed in more detail below.

Another proposal reviewed by Lin is that of Fisher (2001), who suggested that polluting companies be compelled to buy pollution compensation insurance, and victims of environmental harm would thus apply directly to insurance agents for compensation rather than the court. Fisher argued that this system would be both efficient and cost-effective, although one of Lin's key criticisms is that 'the cost and efficiency benefits of the proposal would be relatively modest – the proposal would simply replace individualized judicial determinations with individualized administrative ones' (p. 1486). In addition, at its heart the scheme is once again compelling polluters to pay for harm they are not proved to have caused.

A rudimentary administrative pollution compensation scheme has also been running in some form in Japan since 1973 (see Bronston, 1983). Implemented in the wake of growing industrialization after the Second World War, originally the scheme essentially paid monetary compensation to victims resident in predefined areas of the country who contracted specifically defined diseases. The geographical areas were split into 'Class I' and 'Class II' locales. Class I locations were areas where air pollution was especially prevalent. Victims falling ill with one of a number of specifically defined respiratory illnesses could claim from a fund raised from levies and taxes placed on polluting corporations, specifically emitters of sulphur oxides. In Class II areas, a causal relationship had been established between a polluting agent and certain health effects. In these areas monies could be reclaimed directly from the polluter. Politically Class I payments proved to be the most contentious, and in the long term the government bowed to pressures to cancel all the Class I area designations in 1988. Lin (2005) describes the fundamental difficulties with the Class I levy system as follows:

> Japan's experience is instructive in several ways. First, thoughtful and equitable design is critical. Using levies on sources of present pollution to fund the compensation payments to victims of past pollution ultimately undermined the Class I system. For this reason, emitters reasonably contended that it was unfair to hold them financially responsible for illnesses caused by other polluters. From the perspective of industry, causation standards were so relaxed that the system became a no-fault compensation scheme.
>
> (p. 1498)

This perspective illustrates that while a lower threshold of showing causation is one of the befits of applying administrative compensation schemes to environmental harm, as opposed to criminal or civil standards of proof, if the system becomes too open it will not be perceived as fair by those who must fund it. This is important, because such (largely industrial) actors are also likely to have the economic and political sway to lobby against such a system, as was the case in Japan. Lin's argument is thus that the corporations were unwilling to accept levies to pay compensation for harms they themselves had not been shown to have caused. Indeed, for both Class I and II claims victims did not have to show any but-for causation between the pollutant and their disease specifically. The other chief criticism of the Japanese model is that, much like the criminal injuries compensation schemes discussed previously, the system was narrowly focused on specific types of harm (pre-defined diseases) and even to specific areas of the country. Furthermore, the compensation was available only to cover medical costs. This is many steps removed from a system covering the full range of environmental harms discussed in Chapter 2, and does nothing towards repairing the environment itself. Indeed, the classification of areas in this manner seems to betray official acceptance that some areas are to be surrendered to pollution for the benefit of the greater economic good, and with this an acceptance of the environmental victimization of their residents.

Aside from schemes directly related to environmental harm, it is possible to draw pertinent examples from the systems put in place to compensate victims of the London bombings of July 2005 (Home Office, 2005: p. 17) and the operation of the US compensation systems after 11 September 2001 (BBC, 2006; Walklate, 2007b). In the latter case, compensation was available for distribution to the spouses, children, or other relatives of people killed in the attack (Maginnis, 2002), which is broadly the same as the UK Criminal Injuries Compensation Scheme (Criminal Injuries Compensation Authority, 2008). However, the English scheme limits compensation in fatal cases to a £12,000 payment, whereas the US scheme paid out considerably more in individual cases and at a considerably faster rate, and included economic and psychological costs far more readily than the UK scheme. Indeed, the US compensation figures were high enough to provoke some criticism of the federal government for using the taxpayers' money 'to make millionaires out of the 9/11 victims' (Maginnis, 2002: p. 2). In addition, there appeared to be inconsistencies of approach between different claimants and claim levels. Farber (2007) argues that, in terms of a potential administrative mechanism for distributing compensation for the adverse effects of climate change, the operation of the September 11th Fund teaches us both the importance of utilizing *standardized* payment schedules and that such schemes may become necessary in some cases if large numbers of claims on tort are to be avoided: 'Clearly, the threat of tort liability pervaded the construction of 9/11 compensation, and the potential for tort liability also will likely prompt climate change compensation in other forms' (p. 1618). Of course, it might be argued that schemes set up in the aftermath of the terrorist attacks in New York and London are clear examples of the mediatized effect Miers (1980) and

Harland (1978) argue is at the heart of most victim compensation schemes (see above). The attacks were also of course discrete events (in terms of causation) with very obvious victims, which distinguishes them from environmental harm more generally or at the international level. Nevertheless, the operation of these schemes once against illustrates that such administrative mechanisms can be constituted when the political will is present, can run more cheaply than the courts, and can deal with large groups of victims.

5.2.2.1 Administrative compensation systems: an appraisal

Overall, administrative compensation systems have much to recommend them, both from the perspective of victims of environmental harm and indeed from the perspective of those running and financing these systems. The evidence does point to such systems being more efficient and less time-consuming that their court-based equivalents (Farber, 2007). Furthermore, the removal of the need to prove causation (to either the criminal or civil standard) should in theory facilitate more pay-outs. Questions do however remain as to how these systems could be adapted to address environmental victims. The funding of the schemes, for example, brings a number of complex issues. Direct payments from the polluter to the victims seem the most beneficial option, both financially and symbolically. In addition, such payments might have specific and general deterrent effects on polluters. However, in a scheme like this either the standard of proof and the certainty of causation to be established would need to be high, *or* such schemes must be restricted to very specific events and groups of people (such as those living in the vicinity of oil spills, or those present in the area at the time of a particular man-made environmental disaster). The latter option obviously excludes a great number of victims, while in the former option the systems loses some of the benefits of the administrative model; as noted by Bronston (1983),

> A system stressing compensation, however, is almost a necessity in this field because an alternative system stressing both compensation and deterrence would be limited to injuries where a hazardous substance and a firm responsible for that substance could be identified. In such a mixed system, victims of injuries where substances and firms were not identified would be denied compensation. Consequently, the moral arguments for compensating innocent victims of hazardous substances quickly and inexpensively are stronger than for deterring identifiable firms from polluting by making them absorb the costs.
>
> (p. 516)

Thus, Bronston argues strongly against prioritizing deterrence as the basis of such schemes. The difficulty, however, is that this clearly restricts the degree of compensation victims can expect, as is the case with traditional criminal injuries compensation schemes.

As an alternative to compelling the polluters responsible for environmental harms to pay victims directly, we have seen that some systems have employed a blanket levy on polluting companies to fund compensation schemes. This, however, raises real questions of fairness and, as in Japan, the possibility that powerful corporate parties will render the scheme politically unworkable. In addition, the costs of such levies might simply be passed on to consumers, meaning they would have no deterrent effect.[26] Another option is for states themselves to fund compensation payments from administrative schemes, on a welfare basis. In theory such schemes could be directed at a wider range of environmental harms and are in line with the development of critical arguments that question why at present only victims of *crime* should receive such support from the state. On the other hand, the more mainstream victimological literature suggests that victims of environmental harm would find payments from the state less symbolically beneficial than payments from those responsible for this victimization. As noted previously, without direct research on the needs of such victims this can only be a hypothesis.

Another question raised by the above review of administrative schemes is *what* precisely they should be compensating for.[27] Many such schemes have been limited to compensating for specific health impacts and medical expenses. From our discussion in Chapter 1, however, we know that this is a very anthropocentric approach, and it may be argued that such schemes should provide something towards remedying the actual environment. We have seen that such payments were made available through a *criminal* procedure in the Alaskan Exxon case. This does however raise the further question as to whether such schemes should apply compensation *ex post* or *ex ante*. If the schemes are limited to the former, then this rules out any appreciation of intergenerational justice or very long-term impacts which do not present themselves for many years. This is a core reason for Lin's focus on *risk* in his model of an administrative compensation scheme. The counter-argument, however, is that such schemes rely on us being relatively certain that our scientific knowledge can predict accurately how people, places and communities might be affected in the future by environmental degradation going on today. The rapidly developing nature of scientific evidence on environmental matters suggests that such assurance may be misplaced. Nevertheless, Farber (2007) notes that the longer such systems wait to award compensation, the less likely it will be that victims will actually see it:

> One of the lessons of the reparations debate is that the passage of time makes compensation increasingly difficult. Moral responsibility becomes diffused, and damages become progressively more difficult to trace. Similarly, [greenhouse gas] emissions today may have harmful effects over many decades, but delaying compensation in the meantime would be a mistake: compensation denied at any time is very likely to be compensation denied forever. Thus, the compensation scheme should prefer ex ante measures of damages rather than waiting for harm to occur.
>
> (p. 1643)

Several commentators noted above have argued the merits of applying set schedules of payments to these schemes, although this brings with it a lack of flexibility to tailor compensation to meet the diverse range of needs victims may have in these cases. Of course, the wider the net of compensation is cast by these schemes the more expensive they will become, whoever is providing the funding. Indeed, the core reason for the restrictiveness of most state criminal compensation schemes is that to open them up to wider victimization would increase costs, when the costs of almost all such schemes have already risen exponentially since their inception (see Duff, 1998).

The key difficulty with administrative compensation systems is that it is difficult to see how they could be rolled out to meet the full range of environmental victimizations discussed in Chapter 2. In reality such schemes appear to be largely ad hoc, or focused on very specific forms of environmental harm. There also seems to be a connection between the formation of these schemes and the mediatization and politicization of high-profile pollution catastrophes. Moreover, such schemes are far more prevalent in developed, rich jurisdictions than in less developed poor ones. Consequently, while they seem particularly suited to one-off or perhaps especially serious events, it is more difficult to advocate their use as the primary means of compensating victims of environmental crime when so many of these victims would be missed by them. Thus there appears to be a need to retain court-based compensation for more 'everyday' events, or where victimization is less clear-cut. The possibility of applying criminal courts to this task has already been discussed, and we will now turn to examine the role of civil courts.

5.2.3 Civil resolutions and 'toxic torts'

Although, in keeping with the overall theme of this volume, I have elected to discuss criminal and administrative remedies before coming to civil measures, in fact by default civil-law suits represent the more 'traditional' mechanism of victims acquiring restitution payments (damages) from polluters whose actions have caused them to suffer environmental harm. Indeed, McEldowney and McEldowney (2011) have described how, in nineteenth-century England, 'The law of nuisance came to encompass the amenity value of land, which included things affixed to the land such as trees and crops' (p. 8), and how 'in rare cases this was extended by the courts to include the physiological and psychological needs of the population' (p. 8). In supporting their argument the authors cite a number of relevant cases, including *Bamford* v *Turnley*,[28] in which 'it was decided that burning bricks on the defendant's land was unreasonable because of the resulting smoke and smell' (p. 12) and *St Helen's Smelting Co* v *Tipping* where the court drew upon the demonstrable scientific link between fumes from a smelting company and harm to adjacent land. Indeed, we can trace back to this period in English tort law one of the first applications of what international lawyers would now call the precautionary principle:[29] the understanding that a person can use their own land in any way so long as it causes no harm to anyone else or their property, which was established in the famous case of *Rylands* v *Fletcher*.[30] In short, McEdldowney and McEldowney observe:

> Nineteenth century case law fitted environmental damage into the compensation culture prevalent at the time and was based on a crude cost-benefit analysis. Reflections of current dilemmas on how far the public benefit could excuse dangerous or injurious activity can be traced back to this time.
> (p. 181)

Despite this pedigree, however, generally speaking the tone of the recent literature in this area is disparaging of 'toxic torts' (Gold, 1986) as a means of adequately compensating environmental victims, although Lin (2005) recognizes (if perhaps grudgingly) that tortious remedies do bring at least two advantages over (in this case) administrative systems. In the first instance, this is because the public agencies that administer such schemes may be more vulnerable to regulatory capture than the judiciary or the executive. Second, it is argued, remedies in tort are based on fuller information about the precise impacts of the alleged environmental harm, whereas administrative mechanisms may not have access to such detailed information. The same advantage may naturally also accrue to criminal proceedings. Of course, claims in tort are not the only civil remedies available. In some jurisdictions the state has legislated for specific causes of civil action in cases of environmental pollution. One example from Canada is the Alberta Environmental Protection and Enhancement Act 2000, which creates a civil cause of action for any victims suffering loss or damage as a result of conduct constituting an offence for which the defendant was convicted under the Act. Victims can thus recover 'an amount equal to the loss or damage proved to have been suffered' (s.219).

The above notwithstanding, civil actions also present considerable difficulties for environmental victims, Skinnider (2011) summarizes these: 'Limitations for such remedies include where the perpetrator is not in the same jurisdiction as the victim; where the perpetrator is not readily identifiable; evidentiary burden of proof; and costs of litigation' (p. 74). Although naturally requiring a lower standard of proof than the criminal penalties discussed above, tort action must still establish culpability on the part of specified respondents, which given the nature of polluting activity is likely to be problematic in many cases. Furthermore, and significantly, civil cases cost considerable amounts of money for which, in most jurisdictions, there is little or no public funding. This means the cost of such actions must be borne by victims or victims' groups (Castle, 1996).

One potentially very important advantage of civil litigation as a means of securing compensation and restitution for environmental victims is the class action process available in many jurisdictions, allowing large groups of victims to sue polluters collectively (Johnson, 2004). Clearly this offers an important advantage over both the generally individual-focused criminal justice system and the administrative compensation systems discussed above, because it accommodates the 'mass victimization' that is often present in environmental cases. Nevertheless, class actions too have been criticized from the perspective of environmental harm, principally because 'these legal rules were not designed with environmental actions specifically in mind and have been noted to be notoriously difficult to get certified in environmental cases' (Skinnider, 2011: p. 75). In addition, Lin (2005) has noted the alleged misuse of the class action system in a number of (US) cases of environmental damage:

> [C]lass actions have been sharply criticized. The criticisms include charges that some actions are frivolous, that some enrich attorneys rather than benefit plaintiffs, and that some result in unfair or improper settlements. The incentive problems in class actions may be especially great in cases involving mass tort litigation, considering the multiplicity of parties and the potentially high financial stakes.
>
> (p. 1516)

In considering the relationship between criminal actions against environmental offenders and associated actions in tort on the part of victims of environmental harm, the UK House of Commons Environmental Audit Committee (2004) received evidence from the Law Society to the effect that, while victims of environmental crime may pursue offenders through the civil courts, in reality

> It frequently takes some time for an environmental crime to be brought before the court and for any appeals to be completed. Until a case has been concluded, an individual cannot obtain the documents relating to the case to assist with their civil action. On occasions the length of time for the criminal case can bring the limitation period for a personal injury claim into play.
>
> (p. 107)

The Law Society added that this state of affairs was 'clearly unacceptable' and that

> Given the relationship between environmental offences and human health and living conditions, it might be appropriate for consideration to be given to providing some mechanism whereby indirect compensation can be awarded to those who have suffered the injury.
>
> (p. 107)

This returns us to the argument that the criminal courts themselves, in sentencing environmental offenders, must be prepared to address compensation or restitution to victims much more readily. On this point, the Sentencing Council of England and Wales is at present in the process of formulating more detailed guidelines for courts to follow concerning the resolution of cases of environmental offending.[31] This will be a welcome addition to what at present is an underdeveloped expertise among judges and magistrates.

The question of what courts, and specifically judges, are prepared to do in relation to environmental harm is also of course particularly relevant to civil actions. If judicial cultures are hesitant to award significant damages from polluting corporations, or if they seek to prioritize the industrial and economic needs of the state over restitution to victims, this will obviously have a significant detrimental effect on such claims. Ebeku (2003), for example, has discussed concerns that, well into the new century, Nigerian judges were prioritizing the country's economic reliance on the oil industry over the protection and restitution of the environment or the ordering of compensation or restitution to individual victims or to communities for the massive environmental harms caused by that industry on the Nigerian Delta. The difference in attitude toward environmental governance on the part of judiciaries across different jurisdictions has also been highlighted by Kotzé and Paterson (2009).

For now, pursuing civil damages is often the 'default' position many victims of environmental harms must take, assuming they have the funds or sufficient backing, to acquire compensation (or rather 'damages') in many jurisdictions. Given what has already been shown in this volume concerning the circumstances of those disproportionately affected by environmental harm (poor, and lacking power and political influence in society) it is clear that civil litigation cannot remain the primary means of pursuing such claims as our understanding of the scope and impact of environmental harms increases. Examples such as the economically impoverished and displaced peoples of the Nigerian Delta and those affected by the Bhopal gas leak are testament to the failure of civil-law suits to adequately compensate these peoples many years after the events, as noted by Van Tassel (2011) in relation to Bhopal:

> it is widely claimed that the law has failed the victims, as over 6,000 gas-affected patients visit hospitals in Bhopal every day, and according to a *Times of India* report, massive amounts of human suffering continues with little compensations over 25 years after the event.
>
> (unpaginated)

Nor does it appear to be the case that the civil standard of proof makes such cases easier to prove. At the same time, the degree of compensation available will be heavily dictated by judicial attitudes and, while this is the same for restitution paid as part of criminal sentencing, civil litigation may lack many of the symbolic recognitions offered by a criminal conviction along with, in some countries, ever stronger requirements for judges to award restitution as part of the sentence.

5.3 International influences on compensation and restitution for victims of environmental harm

Some commentators have argued that, given the global nature of climate change, and the capacity for other environmental degradations to (sometimes literally) spill beyond borders, compensation mechanisms for the victims of environmental harm need to be conceived at the international level (see Mason, 2003). Indeed, a recent draft of a potential UN Convention on Justice and Support for Victims of Crime and Abuse of Power put forward by a consortium of the World Society of Victimology, the International Victimology Institute of Tilburg University (INTERVICT) and the Tokiwa International Victimology Institute (TIVI) contained the following provision:

> In cases of environmental crime, States Parties shall legislate to include restitution to restore the environment, reconstruction of the infrastructure, replacement of community facilities and reimbursement of the expenses of relocation, whenever such harm results in the dislocation of the community.
>
> (Article 10)

The inclusion of environmental victims in such a document is an important step forward for victimology's engagement with this issue in general.[32] Although the Draft Convention itself has not yet received sufficient government backing, the compensation of environmental victims are in fact already found in several of the international and European instruments discussed in Chapters 3 and 4. For example, following a similar requirement in the 1972 Stockholm Declaration, Principle 13 of the 1992 Rio Declaration provides:

> States shall develop national law regarding liability and compensation for the victims of pollution and other environmental damage. States shall also cooperate in an expeditious and more determined manner to develop further international law regarding liability and *compensation for adverse effects of environmental damage caused by activities within their jurisdiction or control to areas beyond their jurisdiction.*
>
> (emphasis added)

It was noted in Chapter 3 that when the UN Commission on Crime Prevention and Criminal Justice addressed environmental crime in 1994 its consequent resolution (1994/15 of 25 July 1994) urged member states to consider 'facilitation of redress and monetary compensation, by removing legal barriers such as standing to sue, participation in proceedings and actions by citizens, including class action suits and citizen suits'.[33] In addition, the United National Environment Programme (2009) has produced Draft Guidelines for the Development of Domestic Legislation on Liability, Response Action and Compensation for Damage Caused by Activities Dangerous to the Environment, which include the following requirement:

> It should be ensured that the laws relating to enforcement of decisions in environmental matters provide the appropriate mechanisms for the successful party to seek timely and effective enforcement. The laws should be adequate and sufficiently effective to remedy any harm caused to the

environment, to provide full compensation for such harm and to protect the environment from suffering similar harm in the future.

(UNEP, 2009: p. 6)

As noted above, the International Law Commission has responded to the issue of compensation with draft principles on the allocation of loss in the case of transboundary harm arising out of hazardous activities. In particular the principles call for states to 'take all necessary measures to ensure that prompt and adequate compensation is available for victims of transboundary damage caused by hazardous activities located within its territory or otherwise under its jurisdiction or control'.[34] While it is generally envisioned that such compensation should come from the 'operator' in command or control of the relevant activity at the time of the incident leading to transboundary damage, as previously noted, the ILC draft principles also maintain that states themselves must supplement funds in the event that operators are unable to provide full compensation to victims.[35]

It is notable that these international statements seem to encompass a wide variety of the options discussed previously in this chapter, including criminal, administrative and civil compensation and restitution. It is also notable that these documents seem to envisage compensation being made available not just in a restrictive sense for individuals' suffering and health expenses, but also to 'restore'[36] the environment, 'remedying' harm and protecting the environment for the future. In this sense, and somewhat unusually given the state-orientated nature of the field discussed in previous chapters, the international legal order may in fact be pushing for more extensive systems of restitution and compensation than have yet been seen at the national level, although of course none of the examples mentioned above are in fact binding legal instruments, and they remain 'soft law' at best.[37]

A slightly more 'hard law' example can be seen in the 1989 Basel Convention on the Control of Transboundary Movements of Hazardous Wastes and their Disposal, specifically in its Protocol on Liability and Compensation for Damage Resulting from Transboundary Movements of Hazardous Wastes and their Disposal. Although this instrument does not make states directly liable to provide such compensations, the protocol does mention in its preamble the obligation of states to 'develop international and national legal instruments regarding liability and compensation for the victims of pollution and other environmental damage' and compels states to 'provide for a comprehensive regime for liability and for adequate and prompt compensation for damage resulting from the transboundary movement of hazardous wastes and other wastes and their disposal including illegal traffic in those wastes' (Article 1). Such compensation provision would be civil in nature, but still represents an interesting consideration of individual victims, and their need for compensation, at the international level (albeit not linked to the responsibility of the state for environmental degradation caused by the export of hazardous waste). From a victimological perspective, mention should also be made of Article 9 of the Protocol, headed 'Contributory Fault':

> Compensation may be reduced or disallowed if the person who suffered the damage, or a person for whom he is responsible under the domestic law, by his own fault, has caused or contributed to the damage having regard to all circumstances.

Similar provisos are found in most state-based compensation schemes for victims of (traditional) violent crimes and reflect a particular interest in compensating 'ideal', blameless victims. As has been noted before in this volume, however, the victimological literature has consistently shown that 'real' victims are often far from blameless (Farrall and Maltby, 2003; Dignan, 2004). The extent to which the same applies to environmental victims would be an interesting topic for future research. Question might include, for example, to what extent are those working for or with polluting companies subject to the impacts discussed in Chapter 2? Of course, although it is attached to a fairly major international convention, in fact the Protocol is not is force, having only attracted 10 of the 20 ratifying parties it requires, compared to the 179 parties to the Convention itself. This indicates a reticence to step beyond the *rhetoric* of compensation to accept genuine liability and commit funds, especially given that the Protocol does not in fact set any theoretical maximum level of liability for states that become a party to it.

Of course, international courts and tribunals have already taken to granting, or at least advocating, compensation to environmental victims. Indeed, the first arbitration in the pivotal *Trail Smelter Case* discussed in Chapters 3 and 4 very much revolved around the degree of reparation that would be paid from the Canadian Consolidated Mining and Smelting Company to the US farmers of Washington State for damage to their crops. The company had initially offered the farmers a total sum of $350,000, which most had rejected. It was subsequent lobbying by the farmers that prompted the US government to intervene on their behalf, and the eventual outcome was an extra $78,000 worth of compensation (Wirth, 1996). Much of the existing attention paid to the Trail Smelter case has focused on the broader principles of international law it seems to establish (that is, that states are responsible for damage caused to other states by air pollution); however, from a victimological perspective, the fact that the case resulted in a state paying compensation for the benefit of individual victims in another jurisdiction is highly significant, although it also demonstrates the inability of individual victims to mount such a case themselves without effectively turning the dispute over to state actors. Another worrying point mentioned by Wirth (1996) is that the relatively modest size of the increase in compensation following the first arbitration was actually a result of a very poor presentation of the farmers' case by the US.

Compensation was also an important theme in the judgment of the African Commission on Human and Peoples' Rights in the Ogoniland case,[38] with an appeal made by the Commission to the Nigerian government to '[ensure] adequate compensation to victims of the human rights violations, including relief and resettlement assistance to victims of government sponsored raids, and undertaking a comprehensive clean-up of lands and rivers damaged by oil operations'. Of course, in this instance the ruling of the African Commission failed to bring an end to the matter, with (mainly civil) compensation claims being filed against the polluting oil companies at regular intervals ever since, the most recent occurring during the time of writing (BBC, 2012b).

It is worth mentioning one further potential avenue of compensation or restitution for victims of environmental harm at the international level: if, as was discussed in Chapter 3, an international crime against the environment ('ecocide') were adopted into the Rome Statute of the International Criminal Court. This would make relevant victims (individually or collectively) eligible to receive compensation from the ICC Victims Trust Fund. The ICC could also make orders for forfeiture and restitution or orders for compensation and rehabilitation to help victims recover from the environmental damage they and their community have suffered (Skinnider, 2011). Indeed, Wyatt (2010) has noted that the precedent of the Iraq United Nations Compensation Commission[39] and its use for environmental crime is one such source of jurisprudence covering the causation of environmental damage to which international environmental lawyers would refer the ICC.

International influences: an appraisal

In sum, it seems that many of the developments at the international level with regard to compensation and restitution to victims of environmental harm (and the environment itself) are, at least on paper, quite progressive. The difficulty seems to arise when aspirations are transposed into something more concrete (and costly), as demonstrated by the low take-up of the Basel Protocol. Once again, there are clear parallels to be drawn here with the development of the victim rights movement more generally, where for the longest time the vast majority of measures at the national and international levels were in fact purely aspiration, with little enforcement provisions to compel governments into action. We have seen this previously in such instruments as the Aarhus convention, which in this context gives its Compliance Committee the power to *recommend* that states provide compensation to environmental victims, but it cannot compel them to do so (or indeed to do anything at all). One of the fundamental difficulties is that not only does there appear to be a certain reluctance among states to make such commitments to environmental victims (if only on economic grounds), but also in practice the operation of any compensation system would be very difficult, as noted by Wyatt (2010):

> Indeed, the practical difficulties of ex post facto compensation for environmental harm are compounded at the international level, where international dispute resolution is not as suited to dealing with problems of proof and the calculation of damages as its domestic equivalents.
>
> (p. 602)

It is perhaps principally for this reason that most international instruments discussed above favour the transposition of 'environmental compensation' within *national* laws, as noted by Dryzek and Hunter (1987): 'Unfortunately, centrally administered [i.e. internationally-based] systems are extremely clumsy when it comes to dealing with conditions of complexity, uncertainty, and variability – circumstances ubiquitous in the realm of ecological problems' (p. 88). The few exceptions at the international level, such as the rulings in the Trial Smelter case and the Ogoniland decision, are very specific to their individual situations. The difficulty here is well articulated by Dryzek and Hunter (1987) when they note 'Most international environmental problems are not site-specific, clearly-defined, or limited to a small number of actors' (p. 99). In any event, it has already been argued that the 'local' nature of this jurisprudence severely curtails the argument that it represent binding principles of (customary) international law. The other point about cases like Ogoniland and Trail Smelter is that the lines of causation between polluter and victims in each case were relatively straightforward. As reflected by the statement from Dryzek and Hunter (1987) above, establishing such lines of causation *from one jurisdiction to another* is usually very difficult, and becomes even more protracted when one is considering, for example, 'climate change' as a whole. On this point, we can see that few of the schemes noted above are geared up to facilitate compensation for victims suffering the effects of climate change, especially between countries.

Of course, the UN's Framework Convention on Climate Change does contain provisions to the effect that 'developed country Parties and other developed Parties included in Annex II shall also assist the developing country Parties that are particularly vulnerable to the adverse effects of climate change in meeting costs of adaptation to those adverse effects' (Article 4(4)). Thus, at least in principle, the United States and other signatories to the framework agreement already seems to have agreed to compensation at the international level. In practice, however, the above discussion raises significant doubts that such a *principle* is to be converted to operational and binding practice in the near future.[40] Ultimately, as with other issues relating to environmental victims at the international level discussed in this volume, the analysis of compensation provision above ultimately indicates a failure of the international legal order to provide genuine solutions to the problems already highlighted at the national level.

5.4 Restorative options

In this last section I consider briefly the possibility of applying restorative solutions to the issue of environmental victims seeking restitution or compensation. I say briefly, because in fact the full implications of this option go beyond the present focus of this volume, with its general theme of criminal justice. Nevertheless, in the light of the development of restorative justice discussions in wider criminology and victimology, it may well prove an important topic of further research in the coming years. In this instance, by 'restorative options' I refer to the *procedure* put in place to facilitate compensation or restitution as being 'restorative' (as opposed to more traditional forms of adversarial or inquisitorial formal justice) rather than the 'restorative' impact of such payments themselves.

Space is lacking here to go into the growing application of restorative justice in a number of jurisdictions, and its impact upon victims (usually of more traditional crimes), although generally speaking pilot restorative justice schemes for adult offenders, in England and Wales and elsewhere, seem to confirm that when victims of crime do become involved in restorative processes they draw benefits from doing so, as does the restorative enterprise itself (Shapland *et al.*, 2006, 2011).

Information concerning the application of restorative processes to cases of environmental harm is scant and mainly anecdotal in nature, although the growing evidence of its uses for victims of other crimes makes this an area worthy of detailed research. That said, there is a small but growing literature on what has been variously termed 'environmental mediation' and 'environmental alternative dispute resolution' (ADR) (see Edwards, 1985). As with 'mediation' as applied to restorative justice options, the term is variously defined, although one concise definition is provided by Amy (1983): 'Put most simply, environmental mediation is a process in which representatives of environmental groups, business groups and government agencies sit down together with a neutral mediator to negotiate a binding solution to a particular environmental dispute' (p. 1). Of course, this definition in fact excludes environmental victims directly, which in itself is quite telling of an article devoted to the issue of environment degradation. In fact, victims themselves feature relatively little in this literature, with much more of the discussions revolving around the role of 'environmentalists' or 'environmental groups'; the extent to which such groups represent real victims of environmental harm is a moot point. Furthermore, one of the few studies to examine environmental ADR empirically, as well as to discuss the position of the victims directly (Matsumoto, 2011), suggests that when environmental victims engage in representation, or collectively group together in an effort to increase bargaining power, this in fact complicates the process to the extent that it becomes more cumbersome: 'Far from the conventional expectation that representation hastens the resolution of environmental disputes, our empirical results suggests ADR becomes less effective when many agents are involved' (p. 665).

Generally speaking, the key advantages of mediation or ADR in environmental cases is said to be considerably lower costs compared to civil or criminal justice resolutions, as well as shorter timescales (see Mernitz, 1980), although in fact very little detailed empirical evaluation has been done to test these claims. One expectation is that of Sipe (2007), who demonstrates via quantitative analysis that environmental mediation does produce a statistically significant increase in settlement rates, when compared to civil-law actions, but no difference in rates of compliance with these agreements. Again it is notable that Sipe's analysis fails to mention directly the victims of environmental harm.

Much of the literature concerning environmental mediation is US-based, which of course is a disadvantage given that it is underdeveloped nations and their people who tend to fall victim to environmental harm. Nevertheless, in one of the first test cases, Gerald Cormick and Jane McCarthy of the University of

Washington's Environmental Mediation Project were appointed by the governor of Washington State to serve as mediators in a dispute among environmentalists, farmers, developers, and public officials over the damming of the Snoqualmie River. According to Shmueli and Kaufman (2006), 'the resulting agreement illustrated one of mediation's main assets – its capacity to generate creative solutions that satisfy the interests of all parties involved' (p. 17). Certainly the adaptability of mediation and other restorative options is a big plus, especially given the long-standing criticisms of mainstream victimology that policies aimed at victim tend to assume specific victim characteristics and needs. As noted by Shmueli and Kaufman (2006):

> Each environmental conflict has a unique cast of characters, a history unlike any other except in broad strokes, a singular pattern of resources, interrelationships among parties, a special set of issues and a unique set of moves that defies simple classification and comparison.
>
> (p. 20)

Furthermore, Matsumoto (2011) notes that mediation is a fitting solution for a situation in which, as in many environmental pollution disputes, 'the polluter and its victims are located near each other and will remain in place and maintain an on-going relationship after their dispute is resolved' (p. 660).

Positive features notwithstanding, environmental mediation does nevertheless also bring difficulties, not least of which is the fact that 'those who have the time and resources to participate in a mediation process are not necessarily representative of the interest groups affected by the decisions issuing from this process' (Shmueli and Kaufman, 2006: p. 21). This might be especially true given the economic and social standing of many victims of environmental harm, as discussed in Chapter 2, and returns us to the point made above that 'environmentalists' or 'environmental groups' may not be representing the interests or needs of real environmental victims. In fact, examples of environmental mediation in the US seem to differ from Japan in this regard, where Matsumoto (2011) cites statistics indicating that 82.44 per cent of complaints are filed by a pollution victim or by his or her family members. That said, in Japan a system of environmental mediation has been adopted by the public authorities, whereas in the US these are usually private schemes; consequently access to solid data in the former country is more forthcoming.[41] Amy (1983) has further discussed the opinion expressed in some quarters of environmentalism that mediation in fact panders to big industry and the polluters themselves. Thus, the author contends, most environmental mediation actually takes place in a context of palpable political bias, power imbalance and the illusion of voluntariness. For example, Dryzek and Hunter (1987) have suggested that in the aftermath of the Indian Bhopal disaster, Union Carbide was in fact very keen to engage in attempts by Environmental Mediation International to establish a good compensation scheme rather than going down more legalistic routes. While Amy (1983) is generally more hopeful for the overall benefit of mediation in these cases than the worst of these concerns suggests, he still injects a note of caution into his conclusion: 'There is no simple answer. As a rule, it would benefit environmentalists to have a healthy suspicion of mediation, especially when the offer to mediate comes from their opponents' (p. 19). Of course, this is a rather pessimistic interpretation of the motives of corporations wishing to enter into environmental mediation. An alternative suggestion is that mediation and ADR in fact represent the usual manner in which corporations resolve conflicts with each other, and thus it may simply be the route with which they are most familiar.[42]

Overall, the development of environmental mediation is at present severely held back by a lack of basic empirical data concerning the nature of the settlements (including much information about the compensation agreements reached), the processes used and the effectiveness and enforcement of these agreements. Without such information, it is very difficult to test the more alarmist claims of power imbalances and so on. It is also problematic that the majority of information we have comes only from developed countries, which, as noted previously, simply do not bear the brunt of environmental victimization. Even within these countries, environmental victims will tend to be marginalized groups, lacking power or social standing. The concern, then, is that such groups simply lack the political or social power to meaningfully influence a mediation exercise when on the other side of the table are large multinational corporations, and perhaps their own state. In such instances it is suggested that such victims may well need the guarantees and protections (and the enforcement power) of formalized justice systems (whether criminal or civil). There is also a further complication in that the literature that exists on environmental mediation, when it mentions victims' difficulties at all, fails to consider the possibility of multiple groups of victims with *competing* interests sitting around the table. That said, it was discussed in Chapter 3 how the recent mock-ecocide trial experiment staged at the Supreme Court of the United Kingdom has indicated the suitability of restorative justice as means of sentencing offenders for environmental crime. On this point, Rivers (2012) notes:

> The experiment proved that there is real potential for using restorative justice in conjunction with ecocide. It enables dialogue, understanding, healing and creativity to emerge. It is about making whole again rather reinforcing separation and fragmentation through punishment of perpetrators and exclusion from the process of victims.
>
> (p. 18)

The future potential for further development of the restorative approach, particularly in regard to case disposal, is therefore clear.

5.5 Conclusions and ways forward

Environmental crime and environmental harm, despite their historical pedigree,[43] are novel problems behind which scientific and sociological knowledge is still lagging. It is perhaps for this reason above others that none of the systems discussed above seem particularly well adapted to offering redress mechanisms for environmental victims. In this concluding section of the chapter I will bring together some of the key themes derived from the above analysis relating to compensation and restitution and offer a potential way forward, which essentially combines administrative and criminal resolutions while rejecting civil and (for now) mediated settlements, coupled with a strong advocacy for international law to step in as a means of correcting the apparent inequality between the redress mechanisms available to victims of different socio-economic groups and nationalities. The full implications of the issues discussed in this chapter in fact go beyond questions of redress, and can greatly inform our understanding of how justice mechanisms deal with these victims as a whole. These wider issues will be returned to in the final chapter.

One of the clearest messages emerging from this discussion is that civil law, and especially tort law, in itself is insufficient to achieve the purposes of restitution in many environmental cases, even if such 'purposes' are narrowly understood as basic financial compensation or restitution for physical injuries and/or illness. Put simply, the average profile of a victim of environmental harm does not tally with those who are able to mount long-term, expensive lawsuits against large multinational companies or the state itself. This is especially true if civil courts in some jurisdictions continue to resist class actions in environmental cases. While we have seen that a state can acquire such conflicts themselves and pursue other states for compensation at the international level, from a victimological perspective the danger is that this effectively factors the victims themselves out of the equation – for so long the key criticism levied at national criminal justice systems in their dealings with traditional victims – and there is little guarantee that any compensation paid will reach them.

Beyond a move away from reliance on civil mechanisms, however, the debate over how best to offer redress to these victims becomes more complex. This is largely due to the extremely diverse nature of environmental victimizations, even if we limited our concept of such victimization to that which flows from officially recognized environmental crimes in a given jurisdiction. Any system of redress must therefore address tensions between offering tailored solutions that work in particular (perhaps unique) circumstances, and at the same time conveying a sense of certainty, fairness and consistency between cases.

In this sense an administrative-based system utilizing a standard schedule of payments seems appealing, because such schemes can be devised to deal with a wider range of 'environmental harms' than the criminal justice system. Thus far, however, such schemes as have been constituted for the purpose of offering compensation or restitution to environmental victims have been restricted to specific events, specific countries and specific forms of harm. There is also, as we have seen, a real concern that such schemes are often constituted for reasons of political expediency, and the fear is that victims once again are being used to achieve political gain.

In addition, if payment for such schemes is to come from broad-brush levies on polluting companies, with little demonstrable culpability for specific instances of environmental victimization, then the overall fairness of the system is brought into doubt. Given that large corporations have such influence over what does and does not succeed in this regulatory sphere (see Dal Bó, 2006), this lack of perceived fairness is a genuine threat to the long-term sustainability of such an administrative system. That said, it is to be noted that corporations who foster environmental pollution have learned to internalize and accept a variety of increasing costs to their business practices as our understanding of environmental degradation has increased. What is required is a shift in cultural attitudes towards the acceptance of such costs as a normal part of doing business in this area.

Of course, in cases where a sufficient degree of causation is established, polluters might be compelled to pay restitution directly to victims through an administrative system. In this instance, however, the need to demonstrate culpability removes a key advantage of the administrative route: that it does not require so high a standard of proof as criminal or civil actions and is therefore (arguably) more efficient. One way out of this conundrum is for *states* themselves to fund payments to environmental victims, just as many fund payments to (certain categories of) victims of violent crime through existing administrative schemes. We have seen that the conceptual justification for these schemes is (perhaps purposely) vague; however, the suggestions made by some that ideal victims of violent crime are being unfairly singled out for special treatment compared to victims of other crimes, or indeed victims of social harms more generally, seem especially compelling in the environmental context, where action or inaction on the part of the *state itself* may at least contribute to the environmental victimization.[44] The state need not acknowledge any fault, just as it acknowledges no fault when it paying victims of violent crime, so long as money is paid for welfare reasons as Lee (2009) suggests, or for any other well-rehearsed reason covered by the standard victimological literature on the issue. The real barrier to the opening up of such a system to victims of environmental harm, or even to environmental crime, is economic and political: economic because of the fear of opening the floodgates of claims, and political because environmental victims do not necessarily provoke the same public empathy as (the blameless) victims of violent crime.

At this stage, we might conclude that the practical realities of this complex problem of providing redress to environmental victims seem to lean towards the use of administrative systems. Certainly it is the case that for many instances of environmental harm a suitably developed (and *extended*), standardized system of administrative compensation paid for by levies on polluting industry seems the best fit with 'real' environmental victims and the diverse range of harms they suffer. Nevertheless, it is also suggested that criminal law has a very important part to play here, both for its ability to sanction actual polluters in a fair and consistent manner and also for its ability to compel them to pay restitution straight to victims which, in keeping with the victimological literature, seems desirable on a symbolic level.

It could be argued that, given that we are often talking about rich, multinational corporations as the perpetrators of environmental harms,[45] the benefit to victims (including groups of victims) of going to the criminal courts might also be financial, as the companies are likely to have much greater funds at their disposal to pay restitution orders than administrative schemes. Such funds might contribute significantly to the remedying of the damaged environment as well as individuals' suffering. The development of restitution orders so far shows that this is possible, although at present most systems are restricted to set amounts and, probably more importantly, there is a demonstrable lack of will among judges and legislators to provide for this kind of restitution as part of the criminal process and to apply it in practice. Of course, along with an apparent need in some cases for larger restitution sums, environmental victimization also confronts criminal justice with various other problems to which it is unaccustomed, associated with large groups of victims and corporate (or even state) offenders. While obviously there are practical difficulties to changing this, the barrier is in fact more cultural than representative of any true incompatibility between criminal justice and restitution for these victims, which is a point to be addressed in some detail in Chapter 6. The other concern, of course, is that to turn such compensation or restitution measures entirely over to administrative measures is in fact a denial by the state of its duty to act on environmental harms (by recognizing them as crimes) and its duty to the victims of that harm and to reflect society's condemnation of those harms.

Redress for environmental victims: a typology

We have arrived at a position where both administrative and criminal routes appear to have a role to play in offering redress to victims of environmental harm, and the implication is therefore that governments need to examine ways to better develop both these systems. The question then becomes how to allocate different cases or instances of environmental victimization to either criminal or administrative routes. A useful way of distinguishing between the two might be to return to the (critical) criminological distinction between criminal harms and wider social harms, and to allocate 'social' harms, lying beyond the remit of criminal law, to administrative systems and 'criminal' harms to criminal justice. There is a certain logic to this notion, given that the wider the net of 'social harm' is cast the more difficult it becomes to demonstrate causation, and administrative systems require less strict rules in that regard. The key features of this dual system of redress routes would map out as in Table 5.1.

The reader might find it surprising that this typology contains no mention of mediation. This is largely because the lack of evidence on this issue makes it very difficult to predict how this option would fit with the others. In addition, Dryzek and Hunter (1987) are in all likelihood right to be wary of the power inequalities that might exist in such mediation attempts, which are potentially much starker in these cases than those found in more traditional forms of restorative justice. More research is needed, the results of which might indeed strongly favour the use of environmental mediation, in terms of giving victims what they need, but at present there is simply an absence of data on which to base such a conclusion.

Table 5.1 Characteristics of redress mechanisms for environmental victims

	Criminal justice route	*Administrative route*
Classification of harm	Criminal harm	Social harm
Standard of proof	Higher standard of proof	Lower standard of proof
Scope of victimization	Potentially many victims	Potentially many victims
Necessary degree of culpability	More direct culpability	More diverse effects
Monetary amounts available	Potentially more money (assuming corporate offenders)	Potentially less money
Nature of the redress	More symbolic?	Less symbolic?

Of course the difficulty with this conceptual model is that it to some extent reinforces the status quo, and certainly begs the question which goes to the heart of the matter: *how* does one determine the boundary between harms which are suitable for criminal justice processes and those which are not? It is impossible to provide a succinct answer to this question and, indeed, from the perspective of critical criminology there cannot and *should not* be an easy answer: because the critical school holds that we should always be willing to reassess whether harms which become attributed to the administrative column 'ought' to be criminalized and (perhaps more importantly) vice versa. Inevitably it will be true that – due to limitations of evidence, time, resources and so on – some cases which *do* constitute technical breaches of the criminal law 'get away' with being dealt with under the administrative system.

Of course, while the criminalization by governments of polluting activities that lead to environmental victimization will be the initial determiner of which column a given case is apportioned to, in practice much of the discretion would be left to the criminal justice authorities, specifically prosecutors, to make determinations as to whether there is a prima facie *criminal* case to answer in a given situation, just as they do for other kinds of crime. This again raises concerns about the impact of restrictive occupational cultures and working practices among these professionals in relation to environmental crime and environmental victimization. Indeed, the model does represent something of a 'two tier' system, but one that – under its administrative limb – may account much more fully for the long-term, diverse impacts of environmental degradation in a way criminal law (bound by criminal causation) cannot. This might be based on Lin's (2005) notion of 'risk' of harm rather than harm itself, although I would argue that the full range of possible impacts discussed in Chapter 2 cannot be as predictable as Lin suggests. It should also be noted that large groups of victims are included in both pathways because, as discussed above, there is little reason that the culture of the criminal justice system cannot be adapted such that restitution orders are applied to larger groups of victims, certainly when the offender is a very wealthy company.

Concluding comments

Perhaps most significantly, another pertinent conclusion to be drawn from this review of redress mechanisms for victims of environmental harm is that at present there is a real division between the 'haves' and the 'have nots'. Those fortunate enough to be subject to a media-friendly, publicly sympathized but geographically and temporally contained environmental victimization within a developed country have been given access to generous administrative compensation, and even criminal-based restitution and/or mediation. Those resident in poorer countries, or in poorer communities where environmental degradation is viewed as necessary for the national interest, have found themselves lacking such official channels and, of course, are often not in a financial or social position to embark upon their own civil claims.[46] It is this global inequality in the treatment of such victims which, in my view, begs the intervention of international law, perhaps in the form of the International Criminal Court discussed above or, as some have suggested, the establishment of a separate International Environmental Court (Murphy, 2000).[47] On this point we have seen several pleasing rhetorical developments at the international level, but few concrete or widespread obligations placed on states or accepted by states in this regard. This again represents a cultural barrier that echoes the slow growth of international acceptance of victims of crime more broadly.

Ultimately, all of the mechanisms discussed in this chapter, with the possible exception of civil claims, have potential to assist victims of environmental crime or harm in obtaining redress. In fact the problem is often one of cultural resistance and extending such schemes beyond their traditional ambits. This is another important reason to include the criminal law, if only to affirm that such harm is real, costly (in many divergent ways), and something to which lawmakers, legal practitioners and judges must direct their full attention. Little more progress will be made in unravelling the complexities inherent in this proposition without detailed research asking victims themselves what they want or need from any form of redress provisions. Indeed, it will be noted that no evidence is presented above concerning how victims would even communicate the full impact of the harm they have suffered to either a criminal or administrative system. Presumably this could be achieved by some form of victim impact statement, although there is no discussion of any such statements being used in these cases in the literature. The typology set out in Table 5.1 is presented here as a useful starting point for thinking about redress in these cases, but at present remains incomplete and begs a number of important questions that can only be answered in the light of further *empirical* research.

6 Mapping out a green victimology

The final chapter of this volume has two key goals. First, it will marshal the evidence and debates discussed in the previous five chapters to offer reasoned answers to the three key research questions set out in Chapter 1.[1] In doing so, this will be among the first research studies to methodically assess the suitability and adaptability of criminal justice systems to meet the challenge of environmental victimization from an interdisciplinary, comparative perspective. The second key goal of the chapter is to appraise the key themes that have emerged from all the analyses that have gone before in order to arrive at a model of what I will term 'green victimology'. As noted in Chapter 1, an in-depth conceptualization of victimology to encompass environmental victimization has been almost entirely absent from the literature up until this point, certainly from the mid-1990s onwards, and it remains the principal goal of this volume to address this shortcoming.

6.1 Is criminal justice the solution?

I will begin by considering the first of the three research questions introduced in Chapter 1. This reads:

> Can criminal justice play an effective role at the national and international levels towards providing official recognition, support and redress for victims of environmental harm?

Clearly, if criminal justice as a concept is fundamentally at odds with the supposed requirements of victims of environmental harm,[2] then there is little gain to be had from continuing to debate or pursue criminal justice solutions for the challenges posed by environmental victimization. It also follows that time and resources, as well any model of green victimology, should instead be devoted to developing civil and administrative mechanisms, as well as exploring such alternatives as environmental mediation. Certainly there is plenty of evidence, as discussed during the course of this volume, to support the conclusion that criminal justice is ill suited to dealing with environmentally destructive activities as a whole, or certainly with environmental victimization. For example, we have seen that fundamentally the majority of criminal justice systems across the world are not geared up to deal with 'mass victimizations' of the kind that are often a feature of environmental offending. Furthermore, the wide and eclectic scope of possible harms that can be associated with environmental victimization go well beyond those with which criminal justice systems are traditionally concerned, or indeed, some might argue, *can ever* be concerned, given the necessarily high standard of proof that is required to convict defendants in a criminal court.

On a related point, we may be concerned that any encouragement of a greater role for criminal justice in matters of environmental degradation might well have a net-widening effect, bringing more people and corporations within the scope of criminal justice (and state control) than ever before (McMahon, 1990). For such reasons it was noted in Chapter 1 that some authors, notably Mares (2010), dismiss the idea that criminal justice can effectively deal with environmental victims – or indeed that *law* of any kind is capable of doing so – as a misnomer, preferring instead a system based on civilizing and shaming. The situation appears even further removed from traditional criminal justice principles if one approaches the issue from a less anthropocentric perspective than that adopted by the majority of this volume to consider victimization to non-human animals, the ecosystem and so on (see Cazaux, 1999; Zimmerman, 2003).

In sum, prima facie the outlook for incorporating environmental victimization within the context of criminal justice appears somewhat bleak. Nevertheless, I propose to argue that the engagement of *criminal justice* systems with environmental harm, and with environmental victimization, is in fact vital for a number of reasons. From the outset, it is clear that a number of jurisdictions around the world are reaching the same conclusion, and are thus increasingly turning to criminal justice as a way of tackling environmental harm. The EU Directive 2008/99/EC on the protection of the environment through criminal law, discussed in Chapter 3, lists in its preamble a number of justifications for adopting the criminal justice system in this context, summarizing the main rationale as follows:

> Experience has shown that the existing systems of penalties have not been sufficient to achieve complete compliance with the laws for the protection of the environment. Such compliance can and should be strengthened by the availability of criminal penalties, which demonstrate a social disapproval of a qualitatively different nature compared to administrative penalties or a compensation mechanism under civil law.

Thus the justifications for increasing the ambit of criminal law in this area are said to be primarily to increase *compliance* with existing environmental laws as well as to demonstrate social disapproval of polluting activities. Elsewhere in the preamble the Directive mentions increasing the *effectiveness* of investigation and assistance between member states in the light of environmental offences, and the *protection* of the environment through a greater deterrent effect on would-be polluters. It will be noted that a number of these justification have been reflected in the wider discussions of the previous five chapters. For example, the notion of greater social condemnation for these activities tallies well with the suggestion from the victimological literature that victims gain greater symbolic benefits from having victimization acknowledged by a criminal court as opposed to an administrative body or even a civil court.[3] Furthermore, the suggestion that criminalizing certain environmental harms will make environmental law and regulation more effective (in terms of investigation and prosecution) was reflected by DeMerieux's (2001) argument, set out in Chapter 4, that the further incorporation of victims into the justice process in relation to environmental crimes is likely to improve the overall *enforceability* of relevant laws. Certainly victims might well assist at the investigatory stage and with the collection of relevant evidence. To this we might add the argument that greater procedural involvement of victims in environmental criminal cases at the sentencing stage may lead to more proportionate sentences that equate more closely to the true impacts of environmental crimes (Erez and Rogers, 1999).[4]

Thus, while traditional criminal law might in itself face difficulties dealing with environmental offenders, the adaptation of a criminal law *which acknowledges and incorporates victims* might in fact have less practical difficulties in this regard. Adding to this the increased symbolic benefits likely to accrue to victims themselves, and also the fact that, through court-based restitution orders made against environmental offenders, victims may in fact receive larger monetary payments from the criminal system than they would from administrative schemes (see Chapter 5), we can see that the criminal law offers a number of advantages in the area of environmental degradation. This being the case, the failure of the European Union to incorporate victims (already an important and established area of wider EU policy-making in the criminal justice sphere) within the 2008 Directive becomes all the more troubling and represents a lack of joined-up thinking.

Of course, Bell and McGillivray (2008) make the point (discussed in Chapter 3) that, in a great deal of environmental regulation at present, enforcement depends very much on the working practices and cultures of enforcement agencies. It is also subject to the complexities inherent in a high degree of informal resolution, which in some cases might amount to regulatory capture (Dal Bó, 2006). While criminalization should assist with the second difficulty, it will still of course be down to state prosecutors (or possibly other bodies) to elect to bring such criminal cases to court and, when they do so, to then involve potential victims in that process. We of course saw a similar argument in Chapter 5 concerning the allocation of cases between criminal justice and administrative processes (and redress mechanisms).

Empirical work conducted by Du Rées (2001) adds a further level of complexity to these issues. Addressing specifically the question of whether criminal law can protect the environment, Du Rées concludes that the fundamental difficulties faced by the criminal law in this area are grounded in the fact that such laws have been 'constructed as a form of legislative balancing act, which involves compromises between different interests, i.e. economic factors and environmental considerations' (p. 652). This alone is not insurmountable but, as the author goes on to argue, fundamental problems occur when this is combined with 'inadequate control mechanisms contained in environmental crime legislation' (p. 652) to effectively regulate the regulating bodies and to clearly define their roles. The overall effect, so the author goes on to argue, is that such agencies take on the opposing tasks of both helping companies to follow environmental laws but also prosecuting their breaches of that law:

> This unclear role gives rise to an uneven application of the law which expresses itself *inter alia* in large differences in the frequency of reported offences in different parts of the country.... The ambivalent attitude of the supervisory agencies also creates difficulties for the agencies and actors 'higher up' in the justice system when it comes to proving intent or negligence on the part of the offender.
>
> (p. 653)

So, for Du Rées, the problem with criminal law in this area is not that criminal justice is fundamentally incompatible with addressing environmental harm, but rather that the roles of those charged with enforcing such laws are not adequately defined, sowing difficulties which then develop all the way through the system.

Bell and McGillivray (2008) and Du Rées (2001) both therefore argue that the problems inherent in the criminal justice system's approach to environmental crime begin at the stage of investigation and prosecution. While Du Rées puts greater emphasis on the failings of criminal laws or regulations to adequately set the boundaries for the operation of relevant agencies, both authors effectively agree that the difficulty lies with the working practices of those agencies, rather than fundamental incompatibilities between environmental concerns and criminal justice per se. Indeed, in Chapter 2 it was argued that the real problem facing environmental victims as far as criminal justice systems are concerned is not so much legal or definitional, as cultural. In Chapter 5 it was concluded that the failure of judges in England and Wales to pass compensation orders (effectively restitution orders) in cases of environmental crime does not reflect any true incompatibility between criminal justice and restitution for these victims, but was rather attitudinal:[5] hence the call by the Law Society of England and Wales for change (see House of Commons Environmental Audit Committee, 2004: Appendix 6). This argument is given some weight by the apparently successful incorporation of victims of environmental crime under the Crime Victims' Rights Act 2004 in the United States, following such cases as *Re Parker; U.S.* v *U.S. District Court* and *W.R. Grace & Co.*[6] It should be noted that both of these were cases of 'mass' victimization affecting hundreds of people. Again this casts doubt on the assertion that the criminal justice system is *necessarily* defeated by force of numbers. In addition, the use of criminal law in the 1989 Exxon-Valdez oil spill almost certainly resulted in more compensation being paid than would have been forthcoming from civil or administrative mechanisms, although it is unclear how much of this money actually reached individual victims directly or indirectly.

A key potential benefit of employing criminal law in cases of environmental victimization is that doing so may begin to address the fundamental inequalities we have seen in the treatment of such victims, or the modes of redress available to them, both between jurisdictions and within them. Of course Marxist criminology has taught us that to assume that the criminal law in practice treats everyone equally irrespective of gender, race or social class is at best naïve and at worst demonstrably incorrect (see O'Malley, 1987). Indeed, as noted in Chapter 1, 'red/green' alliances were in fact a key contributor to the development of green criminology itself.[7] Nevertheless, Chapter 5 has demonstrated that, certainly as far as compensation or restitution is concerned, the alternative methods of administrative or civil mechanisms of seeking redress are generally open only to the minority of environmental victims, globally and at the national level. The barriers to victims' inclusion within these schemes are often financial (the cost of civil action or the cost of compensation schemes for governments) or politically fuelled (how 'significant' is the polluting event politically and in the media?) as compared to the *cultural* barriers that, it is argued, prevent their inclusion in criminal proceedings. Such cultural barriers may in fact be less of a hurdle (if not an insignificant one), and indeed the victimological literature is replete with examples of cultural changes being effected within criminal justice systems over time: relating to victims of domestic violence (Jordan, 2004); secondary victims of homicide (Rock, 1998); and victims of human trafficking (Munro, 2012), among others.

Finally, it can be argued that criminalization of environmental harm and the recognition of environmental victims within this process will constitute an important acknowledgement that *states* have responsibilities to address such harm and such victimization, just as they have responsibilities to address other kinds of offending and, as has now been recognized in most developed jurisdictions, other kinds of victimization. As noted in Chapter 1, this in fact is a key reason green victimologists should remain cautious about labelling polluting activities as fostering 'social harm', because this might imply that such harm is beyond the responsibility of the state to address. Such an attitude, however, is incompatible with the growing international calls for states to take responsibility for environmental degradation, as exemplified by the development and expansion of international environmental law discussed in Chapter 3. This point is especially significant given the complex overlap of *state* as well as corporate actions and interests that we have seen ultimately contribute to environmental victimization. It is also of course true that criminal courts must give effect to human rights which, as we have seen in Chapter 4, are increasingly argued to encompass environmental issues, although no internationally recognized right to a clean environment per se yet exists.

As discussed in detail in Chapter 3, the application of criminal justice mechanisms as a means of recognizing and addressing environmental victimization is not intended to exclude other forms of justice, redress or resolution. It should also again be acknowledged that criminal justice models tend to exclude non-human victims.[8] Civil and administrative claims are likely to continue to prove an important resource for many victims, especially as recognition of such victimization expands. Indeed, I agree with Farber (2007) that criminal justice is unlikely to be flexible enough to encompass the possibility of *future* victimization as a result of environmental harms occurring in the present, and that the better solution is likely to be an administrative system based on risk. I have also discussed the notion of environmental mediation that, although at present largely untested and certainly under-researched, may well prove the better long-term solution to the difficulties faced by these victims, especially those experiencing more 'obscure' or indirect harms as a result of environmental degradation. Indeed, if developments in this area of investigation continue to mirror developments in wider victimological literature, then that literature increasingly points to the benefits of restorative justice processes for victims (Shapland *et al.*, 2011), and I have discussed evidence that such processes may be especially beneficial in environmental cases (Rivers, 2012). Nevertheless, these options are either too early in their development or, at present, too selective in their application to be relied upon in meeting whatever needs environmental victims might express. Consequently, it seems clear that the criminal law (nationally and, as will be discussed below, internationally) must at least for the time being play a vital role in addressing this shortfall.

6.2 What are the limitations of current provisions for environmental victims?

It will be recalled that the second research question set out in Chapter 1 reads as follows:

> What are the limitations to current provisions for official recognition, support and redress for victims of environmental harm through criminal justice both within individual jurisdictions domestically and at the international level?

Following the discussions and analyses presented in the preceding five chapters, a broad answer to this question would be that in most criminal justice systems, the environmental victim still faces considerable barriers to recognition and even greater challenges in terms of their participation in the justice process. This is especially true at the international level where, as argued in Chapters 1 and 3, the lack of regard to human agency is all too evident. Generally speaking, the significant progress made towards the integration of more traditional victims of crime with the criminal justice systems of many jurisdictions has not extended to the point of incorporating, or in many cases even acknowledging, victims of environmental harm or even victims of established environmental crimes. Thus the environmental victim is largely absent from both the policy rhetoric surrounding victims in general and indeed from most academic discussions on the topic.

More specific answers to this research question begin with the observation that the instruments that do purport to afford rights and recognition to victims of crime in criminal justice rarely contain any direct reference to environmental issues specifically. Perhaps more tellingly, the definitions of 'victimization' employed by these instruments are often quite restrictive and as such give little scope for the inclusion of victims of environmental harm indirectly. Examples of such restrictive definitions include those used by the 2001 EU Council Framework Decision on the Standing of Victims in Criminal Proceedings,[9] its upcoming replacement Directive,[10] and most criminal injuries compensation schemes.[11] We have seen that, at least according to recent interpretations by the US courts, the US Crime Victims' Rights Act 2004 may be an exception to this rule. Another possible exception at the international level is the 1985 UN Declaration of Basic Principles of Justice for Victims of Crime and Abuse of Power, and indeed the inclusion of environmental victims under this instrument is suggested by Williams (1996). Nevertheless, it is clearly the case that the 'abuse of power' provisions found within the 1985 Declaration have received markedly less attention from both academics and policy-makers compared to the provisions covering more traditional forms of victimization. The practical application of such provisions to environmental victims in individual jurisdictions is thus somewhat conjectural.

Chapter 5 discussed a number of limitations of criminal justice redress mechanisms concerning their application to environmental victims. Much of this debate turned once again on the issue of mass victimization and the divergence of possible impacts on environmental victims leading to difficulties in establishing criminal culpability. It was also noted that, certainly in England and Wales, other sources of statutory clean-up mechanisms following pollution events might be distracting courts from the possibility of employing court-based restitution in these cases (Bell and McGillivray, 2008). Another limitation highlighted in that chapter was the statutory cap placed on restitution orders in most jurisdictions which, assuming for the moment that environmental victims are indeed interested in financial redress, mean that such orders may not be sufficient to cover the costs of long-term healthcare, clean-up, economic hardship and so on. Here we might also mention state-based criminal compensation schemes that, although administrative, involve official labelling of harms as *criminally* perpetrated. The conclusion on this point is simply that almost all such compensation schemes across the world are very restrictive in their conception of victimization, and therefore exclude environmental victims from their ambit.

Of course, given the limitations of criminal justice mechanisms and the apparent reluctance of prosecutors to pursue such cases in the courts in the first place,[12] we saw in Chapter 3 how in most states the environmental victim is left with the option of mounting a private prosecution against environmental offenders. In practice, however, this will rarely be a viable alternative for most people, although we have seen examples both in England and Wales and the US.[13] The limitations here are both financial (it costs a lot of money to collect relevant evidence, hire lawyers and so on to mount a prosecution) and practical (it is extremely difficult and time-consuming), especially given the demographics of most environmental victims.

More theoretical arguments have pointed to the International Criminal Court as a means of addressing the needs of environmental victims though criminal justice mechanisms, along with other 'less ordinary' victim groups, at an international level (Bottigliero, 2004). The fact remains, however, that at present, in the absence of a crime of ecocide (Gray, 1996; Rivers, 2012), the ICC has no jurisdiction over environmental crimes not connected with wartime atrocities. Furthermore it must be recognized that, the ICC having achieved only one conviction in the first 10 years of its operation, arguments decrying its overall utility are gaining credence (see Cassese *et al.*, 2002). In addition, van Dijk and Letschert (2011) have noted that, while in principle the Rome Statute offers some very developed mechanisms of victim recognition and involvement in the ICC's procedures, in practical reality it has been extremely difficult for the court to operationalize these provisions, with the result that victims have in fact been subject to secondary victimization, having had their expectations raised but not met (Ewards, 2004). The more traditional victimological literature confirms that disappointing victims in this way can have a disastrous impact on their views of criminal justice systems (Ashworth, 2000). It should be mentioned that some see the solution to these problems with the ICC in the creation of a completely separate international environmental court (see Murphy, 2000), but such a structure is a present entirely theoretical.

It may be easy to blame these general and specific limitations of most criminal justice systems on the same social forces that critical criminologists and victimologists have long highlighted in relation to the power interests which determine what is labelled as a 'crime' and who is labelled as a 'victim'. Nevertheless, I think there is an equal challenge to be made against the criminology and victimology mainstreams that, as predicted by McBarnet (1983), have to a large extent neglected such crimes and such victimization in favour of more officially prescribed notions of harm. It is therefore not particularly surprising that 'victims of abuse of power' have received such little attention in policy-making circles when academic victimologists themselves have rarely discussed this aspect of the 1985 Declaration. Furthermore, the victimological literature on victimization at the hands of corporations or the state itself is still markedly underdeveloped. We have seen at numerous points throughout this volume that gaining an appreciation for how corporate and state interests interact with environmental issues is often crucial to understanding environmental victimization. Perhaps as a consequence, the failure of most criminal justice systems to fully tackle both corporate and state offending (Minkes and Minkes, 2008) is another key limitation of most systems from the perspective of environmental victims in particular.

In the light of growing scientific knowledge concerning the full impacts of environmental degradation, combined with a general swing towards the social condemnation of such activities (Dunlap *et al.*, 1993; Clements, 2012), it is submitted that this state of affairs cannot continue. The marked developments made in the cause of traditional victims over the last decade (especially in the context of EU criminal justice[14]) only serve to bring into sharp relief the lack of interest in environmental victims in criminal justice circles. Combined with the answers given to the first research question above, we can conclude that the limitations now impeding the development of greater official recognition, support and redress for victims of environmental harm through criminal justice are not insurmountable. Indeed, isolated cases such as the US examples discussed above are concrete evidence of this. Nevertheless, the complexity and scope of the relevant issues are too wide for lawyers, criminologists or victimologists to fully address if working in isolation from each other. Consequently, this chapter next turns to the call for an interdisciplinary approach to addressing the limitations of criminal justice from the perspective of environmental victims.

6.3 Environmental victims: the need for an interdisciplinary approach

The third research question set out in Chapter 1 of this volume reads:

> What does an interdisciplinary approach (encompassing socio-legal analysis, criminology, victimology and international law) teach us about how to effectively address these limitations?

Of course, arguments concerning the virtues of an interdisciplinary approach are widespread across the social sciences (and beyond), to the point that many would argue that these are largely incontestable (see Matthews and Ross, 2010). Drawing from a variety of sources and perspectives almost inevitably provides a deeper understanding of any given subject of research, as well as providing the scope for transposing ideas and solutions between subject areas (see Lury and Wakeford, 2012). The virtues of interdisciplinary approaches are also well recognized by criminologists (Walsh and Ellis, 2007) and by victimologists (Dupont-Morales, 1998). Indeed, criminology has often been described as a 'rendezvous discipline' (Rock and Holdaway, 1997) which in fact relies on the input of a broad range of parent disciplines, notably law and sociology.[15] Indeed, at the time of writing, the British Society of Criminology is advertizing 'challenging disciplinary boundaries within criminological discourses'[16] as a key theme for its annual summer conference.

The goal of the present section is not to rehearse well-tested arguments concerning the benefits of interdisciplinary research per se. Rather, the goal is to argue how such an approach has *particular* contributions to make to the issue of environmental victimization, while also highlighting some of the less obvious connections to be made between disciplines. This section also suggests that, concerning this topic, an interdisciplinary approach is not just desirable, but is in fact vital if progress is to be made towards the greater recognition of environmental victimization within criminal justice and beyond it. Indeed, it is suggested that the present *lack* of an integrated approach between subject areas, both in the academic and policy spheres, is one of the key reasons why environmental harm and environmental victimization at present remain low on the academic or policy agendas in most countries.

If only one major conclusion is to be drawn from the present volume, it must surely be that environmental victimization is an extremely complicated and, above all, multifaceted issue. The wide range of impacts discussed in Chapter 2 is testament to this reality. It is to be noted from the outset that many of these impacts would be impossible to identify without the input of the physical sciences, particularly in relation to health effects, but also concerning the long-term impacts of climate change. Many authors have contributed discussions on the interface between the sciences on the one hand and public policy on the other, and indeed the Rio+20 Outcome Document refers to 'strengthen[ing] the science-policy interface'.[17] Contributions include discussion of knowledge brokering (Van Kammen *et al.*, 2006) and how policy-makers deal with scientific uncertainty (Harrison and Bryner, 2004). There have also been more specific discussions of the interface between science and law, which Houck (2003) describes as a 'tale from a troubled marriage' (p. 1926). This is indeed often a difficult relationship, given that lawyers look to scientists to provide certainty while scientists look to lawyers to provide the same, frequently with neither party being satisfied with the outcome.[18] Such interactions recall the concepts of 'policy networks' and 'policy communities' (Jordan *et al.*, 2005), which I have previously applied to the development of public policy aimed at more traditional victims both nationally (Hall, 2009) and internationally (Hall, 2010), and which essentially connote 'a cluster of actors, each of which has an interest, or "stake", in a given ... policy sector and the capacity to help determine policy success or failure' (Peterson and Bomberg, 1999: p. 8). I will return to the pervading importance of policy networks and communities in my conceptualization of a green victimology in the second half of this chapter.

Another key point of interaction between disciplines identified in Chapter 2 is that between victimologists and economists. Recent work concerning the impact of traditional victimization has already fostered important collaborations between these two sets of researchers, along with mainstream criminologists, in an effort to estimate the intangible costs of crime in monetary terms (Dolan *et al.*, 2007).[19] Indeed, many of the economic models now being experimented with to count the cost of crime and victimization actually trace their origins to the healthcare field, having been initially applied to determining the relative merits of different patient care strategies, with the results expressed in quality adjusted life years (Loomes, 2007). The link between our understanding of victimization and our understanding of healthcare provision is therefore itself a multifaceted issue.

We saw in Chapter 2 how the economic impacts of environmental crime are wide and complex, and are felt right though from the individual, to community, to national, to global levels. Economic variables are of course also integral to the amount of polluting activity that goes on and, in many cases, the motivation of corporations or states to perpetuate such activities, even if this requires the breach of environmental laws and regulations. It was also discussed in Chapter 2 how economic impacts of environmental victimization are often inherently linked, perhaps more subtly, with cultural and social factors, at which point we move into the domains of sociology and anthropology. The loss of the fishing industry in the Maldives is as much a cultural issue as it is a financial one; victimologists require the input of cultural experts in order to fully appreciate and incorporate such issues.

The above paragraph touches upon another issue of vital importance to the application of criminal law to environmental harm: the fact that this is inevitably a *political* issue as much as it is a legal one. Chapter 3 highlighted the fact that states themselves may have an interest in allowing corporations to pollute, and, more generally, we have noted critical criminologists' and Marxist criminology's arguments that the criminalization or regulation of any activity is heavily influenced by power interests in society. A key example is the traditional reluctance of courts in Nigeria to address the widespread environmental destruction occurring as a result of oil extraction that is itself vital to the economic and political stability of the country (Ebebku, 2003). Such questions are of course the preserve of political scientists: another group of scholars with much to contribute to the debate concerning environmental victimization.

Only now do we come to the important contribution of academic (and, indeed, practising) lawyers themselves, which is clearly vital if in fact we are discussing the incorporation of environmental harm within *criminal* justice. We have already noted apparent difficulties in reconciling the issue of environmental victimization with the rule of law.[20] It is in fact a difficulty that victimologists and lawyers frequently come up against when sharing their views on more traditional forms of victimization. Indeed, we have seen how in terms of criminal law this often essentially pre-empts discussions of a 'zero sum game' between victim rights (or assistance) and defendant rights (Jackson, 2004).[21] For present purposes, however, the important point is that such interactions, while sometimes fraught, have proved vital in raising the status of (traditional) victims in the justice systems of many jurisdictions in the last few decades. The tensions between lawyers and victimologists highlight the more general point that, while I am arguing strongly in favour of an interdisciplinary approach in relation to environmental victims, achieving this outcome is in fact far from straightforward. I will return to this issue in my discussion of a green victimology below.

An important argument made throughout this volume is that on the question of environmental harm, victimologists need to work together not just with lawyers generally, but with international environmental lawyers specifically. Many reasons have been put forward during the course of this volume to support this view but, looking at the matter holistically, one of the most important seems to be the present inequalities we have witnessed across jurisdictions in the burden of environmental victimization and in the treatment of or options available to such individuals and groups. This become especially apparent when examining administrative redress mechanisms for this kind of harm, where there is a clear demarcation between the availability of such schemes (however limited they may be) in rich, prosperous countries compared to poor, developing ones. Of course, the assumption that *international* law works in practice in such an egalitarian fashion is almost certainly as naïve as the assumption that national law, especially criminal law, can work in this way (see for example Charlesworth *et al.*, 2001). Nevertheless, the other key contribution of international environmental law to the question of environmental victimization is that it is slowly developing mechanisms and concepts of attributing environmental harms to *states*. Given the importance the state, and its interests, in the pantheon of environmental harm, such developments are a vital component of this field. On a practical level, of course, we have seen that environmental harm often knows no borders, which again begs the intervention of an international legal approach.

Victimologists too have increasingly examined victim issues from an international and comparative perspective, though without much interaction with international lawyers per se. Indeed the benefits of *comparative work* is, along with interdisciplinary discussion, often accepted as a given in criminology (Pakes, 2011). Nevertheless, we saw in Chapters 1 and 2 how victimologists have thus far largely failed to engage with victimization attributable to the state, and indeed with victimization across borders. While it would be quite wrong to assume that international environmental law can be straightforwardly employed to fill this gap without a great deal of further theorization (just as victimologists and domestic lawyers have considerable difficulty incorporating each other's ideas) it is submitted that international environmental law can furnish victimology with a selection of tools and concepts, including principles such as the no-harm[22] and precautionary[23] principles, which can begin this process. More fundamentally, it has been argued throughout this volume that the key exchange to be had between international environmental law and victimology can be thought of in terms of structure and agency. Victimologists have often prioritized agency at the expense of the (legal) structures prized by international environmental lawyers, while international law is usually still conceived as a system devised by states, for states. Once again, therefore, there seems real potential for these two fields to learn a great deal from each other.

It is certainly possible, when advocating the need to engage in interdisciplinary work, to overstate the case. The list of possible contributors to the debate on environmental victimization could indeed go on and on. I have not for example yet mentioned engagement with insurance agents, which might be particularly important if in fact law is thought *not* to be the best means of redress for such victims. Indeed, one wider conclusion to be drawn is that, given the breadth of possible contributors and perspectives relevant to the debates concerning environmental victimization, the idea that *law* (much less *criminal law*) can or should constitute the *sole* solution to the problems of environmental victimization is surely wrong. As I have maintained from the beginning of the volume, criminal law can only be part of the solution, although for the reasons given above it is my contention that it can and should play an important role. This does not of course necessarily imply that numerically *most* cases of environmental victimization should be brought to it, but rather that it should be made into a more viable option than at present appears to be the case in most jurisdictions.[24]

Given that, as Wersig (1993) has rightly surmised, 'everything is connected with everything somehow' (p. 239), to prolong the present discussion is unnecessary for the purposes of answering the research question above, and in any event would probably water down the essential argument. That argument is that at present the literature from both victimologists and legal fields has failed to make even limited inroads into addressing environmental harm from a truly interdisciplinary perspective, to their mutual disadvantage. The interdisciplinary approach must constitute a fundamental aspect of any 'green victimology'. It is to the formation of such a research agenda that this chapter next turns attention.

6.4 Green victimology

The goal of this section is to highlight the key themes that have emerged from the previous discussions and analyses set out in this volume and present them as a road map for the continuing development of academic study in this area. For convenience I will term this area of study 'green victimology' although, as was noted in Chapter 1, I am largely unconcerned with the semantics of whether this be counted as a 'subject', 'sub-discipline', 'research interest' or other such academic classification. Rather I am concerned with identifying the key questions, issues and complexities pertinent to the impacts of environmental crime and environmental harm on individuals and (sometimes large) groups of individuals. Of course, as we have previously seen, Halsey's (2004) criticisms of the term 'green criminology' are based on the argument that the label fails to reflect the complexities of 'the inter-subjective, inter-generational, or inter-ecosystemic costs that combine to produce scenarios of [environmental] harm' (p. 247). Halsey's essential argument is at its heart very similar to that put forwarded earlier in this chapter: that simply approaching these problems from the perspective of 'criminology' or 'law' or even the two combined is woefully insufficient. I am therefore in fact in complete agreement with Halsey's argument that 'criminology' understood in a restrictive, traditional sense is the wrong label to use, and so in this context is 'victimology'. That said, it should be recalled from the discussion in Chapter 1 that 'victimology' was in fact originally conceived as extending well beyond victims of *crime*: indeed, crime victims had no special place at all in the original venture (Cressey, 1986). It is perhaps to the earliest conceptions of victimological debate that we should be turning our attention if we are to adequately conceptualize environmental harm, and this is reflected in the themes discussed below. Certainly, it is only by fully appreciating the complexities of the issues discussed in this volume that researchers can hope to produce findings and draw conclusions which not only enhance our knowledge and understanding, but also have the potential for real impact in the world of public policy and perhaps effect real change for the better in the lives of environmental victims themselves. The latter point of course reflects another traditional characteristic of victimology: that academic and activist wings frequently overlap and that this is a feature to be embraced by academics in the field, rather than rejected.[25] Indeed, I would argue that this point of view precisely reflects the interdisciplinary (or perhaps here, inter-sectorial) approach that is needed in this area.

The themes extrapolated and discussed below are: the need for a critical approach to green victimology; the importance of culture to this study; the heterogeneous nature of environmental victims; the symbolic character of environmental harm and justice mechanisms; and the importance of the human rights perspective. Of course, this is unlikely to constitute a definitive list of crucial issues in this area. They can no doubt be adapted refined and otherwise added to, and indeed *should* be. Consequently, it is important to emphasize that the following discussion genuinely constitutes only the beginnings of a green victimology. Given the lack of literature and, as will be especially emphasized below, the lack of empirical work carried out in this area, it is clear that this green victimology still has a long way to develop.

6.4.1 The need for a critical approach to green victimology

As I argued in the opening chapter of this volume, the application of a *critical* victimology to the issue of environmental victimization seems a vital component of any further research in this area. Principally this is because critical victimology draws attention to the labelling of 'victims' and, more importantly, to those who have the power to ascribe and define this label (Miers, 1990). Dignan's (2004) view on the merits of critical victimology is worth repeating here, as the author places specific emphasis on the importance of the political context of such labelling. This political context is of particular significance in relation to environmental victimization, which we have seen is reflected in the creation of administrative compensation schemes in some states (in highly mediatized cases, for some victims) but not in other states (or for other victims):

> Critical victimology has highlighted the importance of historical and cultural contexts in shaping both victimizing practices and our sensitivities towards them. Even more importantly, perhaps, critical victimology should alert us to the fact that concepts such as 'victim' and 'victimization' are contested and, being historically and culturally specific, are both malleable and far from universal. It is also worth pointing out that, perhaps because of the sympathy that it evokes, the image of 'the victim' is capable of being invoked and sometimes even manipulated or exploited, whether to serve the interests of victims per se, particular groups of victims or even other objectives altogether.
>
> (p. 35)

This perspective also reflects the important point discussed in Chapter 3, that any extension of environmental regulation or criminalization almost certainly necessitates an expansion of the power of the state. The argument that victims are often used for political gain, and specifically to justify the rollout of punitive reform, is of course familiar to mainstream victimology (Elias, 1986). In the case of environmental victims, the point may equally apply to those who suffer environmental harm only to find themselves also defined as environmental offenders: either because their existing activities are criminalized (for example their fishing or hunting practices) or because the criminogenic nature of environmental degradation, and climate change specifically (Hall and Farrall, forthcoming), has led environmental victims to turn to more traditional forms of crime, be this in the form of food riots, theft, or insurance fraud.[26] Green victimology, like mainstream victimology, must remain alert to the possibility of victims being hijacked in the cause of extending state power over individuals, which is another classic hallmark of the critical approach (Elias, 1986).

Of course, from a practical perspective, the key drawback of the critical school has always been that it does not lend itself to easy answers, or to simple characterizations and definitions of victimhood and victims' needs. It is therefore very difficult to reconcile a critical perspective with the suggestion that environmental victims should receive greater recognition by criminal justice systems, which necessarily have to operate on more certain, pre-defined categories of harm. Nevertheless, it is equally true that the state and the criminal justice system cannot shirk their responsibilities for harms resulting from activities which in some cases are already recognized as breaches of the criminal law and in other cases are receiving stronger social condemnation than ever before (Marquart-Pyatta *et al.*, 2011).[27] Furthermore, this volume has discussed moves at the international level towards the greater employment of criminal law in this area in order to (among other things) better reflect the social stigma now applied to polluting activities.

Of course, there will be many examples of environmental harm for which the criminal justice system is ill suited, which is why an important role for administrative compensation systems was mentioned in the conclusion to Chapter 5 and in the discussions above. As noted already in this chapter, such administrative systems may be particularly suitable when thought is given to *future* victimization as a result of polluting activities occurring today. Looking further ahead, and given recent positive findings concerning restorative justice for traditional victims and (more theoretically) in cases of ecocide, it seems likely that environmental mediation will also, with further development and evidence, prove an important means of addressing environmental harm in its widest sense. The inherent difficulties in deciding what should and should not merit the attention of criminal law, which is so central to the environmental crimes debate, is the very reason why a critical approach is absolutely necessary to green victimology, because without it there is little scope for *any* extension of the criminal law beyond its more traditional borders.

A further aspect of environmental victimization that makes a critical perspective vital to this study is the likely role of the state itself in (actively or passively, directly or indirectly) facilitating at least some of this victimization. Thus, we saw in Chapter 3 the growing body of literature suggesting states themselves may be attributed blame for some forms of environmental degradation and for climate change in particular. Of course, it is possible to overstate this case, as noted by Rothe *et al.* (2009):

> Although the problem of crimes by the state is important, we have to be cognizant that perhaps the power of states is declining and that other transnational actors like multi-national corporations are becoming more powerful and less controllable. This trend became noticeable starting in World War I.
>
> (p. 5)

Particularly in relation to *environmental* crime (and wider environmental harm), this observation is distinctly accurate. Indeed, in Chapter 2 it was discussed how it is often not the state alone that fosters environmental degradation and resulting victimizations, but the interaction of state interests with powerful corporate interests. The situation on the Nigerian Delta is a prime example of the victimization that results when these interest combine and are prioritized over and above those of individuals and communities (Ebebku, 2003). This interplay of corporate and state interests of course affects not just what environmental crimes (or harms) are committed, but the very definition of such 'official crimes' in the first place. Indeed, one might argue that, in light of the relevant literature as examined throughout this volume, the most pressing need for development in this area of green victimology is in relation to examining *corporate* actions and victimization by *corporations* rather than by states, which to some extent is already being addressed by a small group of victimologists (see Kauzlarich *et al.*, 2001), and in particular by some branches of international environmental law (Crawford, 2002). Whether one prioritizes state or corporate practices, however, it is a *critical* approach that is needed to fully address these issues.

6.4.2 The importance of culture

Reference has been made at a number of points during the course of this volume to the notion of 'culture' and its relevance to the development of justice systems that incorporate victims of environmental harm. Before proceeding further, it may be useful to elaborate on this concept and wider notions of 'cultures' in more detail. In criminological writings, 'occupational culture' as a concept has been most thoroughly explored and evaluated in the context of policing. Here, the literature is fairly unanimous in the view that the work of police officers is directly affected not only by their formalized training but also (and probably more significantly) by 'a patterned set of understandings that help officers to cope with and adjust to the pressures and tensions confronting the police' (Reiner, 2000: p. 87). Holdaway (1983) refers to the 'ways in which … officers construct and preserve their idea of what constitutes routine police work' (p. 134). In other words, 'occupational culture' usually refers to often deeply ingrained (sometimes subconscious) working practices passed between professionals in a given sphere by those professionals interacting (professionally and socially) and swapping stories, ideas and strategies. In so doing, members of that profession build up a 'cultural toolkit' (Chan, 1996) of ready-made solutions to specific problems. In the police context, the biggest implication of this has been the realization that such culture may render the police 'institutionally racist' even when individual officers are not actively trying to discriminate on the grounds of race (Macpherson, 1999).

I have previously drawn upon the notion of 'occupational cultures' in relation to criminal justice professionals in the domestic system of England and Wales (barristers, solicitors, court administrators and so on) as a tool for investigating how they construct ideas of their roles within the criminal justice system, and whether such roles include considerations for traditional victims of crime (Hall, 2009). Nevertheless, 'culture' can be understood in a number of other ways. In a wider sense, we can also ask whether the recognition of victims of any type in any criminal justice system is dictated by a broader 'legal culture' shared among all advocates, judges, and criminal justice personnel. Cultures may also vary at different levels of a criminal justice system (i.e. lower courts versus higher courts). Cultural working practices may be geographically based.[28] Cultures also of course pervade policy-making bodies, as noted by Rock in Canada (1986) and the UK (1990).

As has already been noted in this chapter, the importance of culture to the debates surrounding environmental victims follows from the conclusion that there is no fundamental incompatibility between addressing environmental harm and criminal justice, public policy-making in general, or state responsibility. It is submitted that cultural reticence within all these spheres is what chiefly precludes consideration of environmental victimization. In the courts, we have seen this displayed in Chapter 5 through the reluctance of judges to consider restitution orders in environmental cases. In many instances this may derive not so much from a conscious *refusal* by the judiciary to consider environmental harm but rather, as the UK House of Commons Environmental Audit Committee (2004) have emphasized, a lack of *awareness* of the issues in the first place. In the same report, it will be recalled that the English Law Society labelled this state of affairs as 'clearly unacceptable', again indicating that the problem lay with attitudes among the legal professions rather than the law itself.

A telling example of the key role played by judicial attitudes and working cultures in relation the recognition of environmental harms is that of the Nigerian Delta where, as noted above, judges have traditionally disregarded the position of environmental victims in favour of the economic interests of the state. Although Ebebku's (2003) discussion of this issue is mainly based on civil courts, the point concerning judges as the ultimate 'gatekeepers' to the justice system is well made. Ebebku (2003) has also argued that it is the *culture* of judges in Nigeria that needs to change in this regard, and is in fact slowly doing so. Kotzé and Paterson (2009) have likewise emphasized the key significance of differing attitudes taken by judiciaries across different jurisdictions to environmental governance.

Of course, the point extends well beyond the judiciary. We have seen that Bell and McGillivray (2008) have argued that the operation and enforcement of a great deal of environmental regulation and criminal law at present depends very much on the working practices and cultures of enforcement agencies.

Indeed, the environmental victim's ability to access any form of redress mechanism or even support beyond the criminal justice system will in practice be heavily reliant on the *recognition* by relevant agencies of the harm they have endured. Again, this is an issue familiar to traditional victimologists, especially when considering, for example, rape victims or indirect victims of homicide. Of course, the lingering cultural reluctance in many criminal justice systems to accept the consideration or inclusion of *any* victims still needs to be tackled by green victimologists.

In sum, it is clear that cultural debates will form an inherent part of any green victimology. Indeed, in its widest sense, the application of cultural theory could equally extend to the restrictions we have noted in Chapter 3 concerning the unwillingness of many states to accept international oblations concerning victimization which extend beyond mere rhetoric, or even to the difficulty international lawyers and institutions often have in recognizing the individual. At its heart, the latter case is certainly at the root of the prevailing wider 'legal' culture of intentional law. Cultural study is important because it can often highlight as well as begin to *explain* the differences between law or policy in theory and its operation on the ground: in this case how it affects real victims and their interactions with justice agencies. Of course, once again, a true picture of such interactions, and with it the greater exposure of resistant cultures among the legal professions, may only be possible once researchers have approached environmental victims themselves to ask about their experiences. It is to conceptualizing environmental victims within green criminology that I will next turn attention.

6.4.3 The heterogeneous nature of environmental victims

The argument that all victims of crime are not the same, do not react in the same way (or on the same schedule) to their victimization, and require different services and support from criminal justice and other agencies is another familiar tenet of mainstream victimology (Shapland and Hall, 2007), and one which may apply to an even greater degree to environmental victims. The divergent and complex nature of environmental victimization was illustrated in Chapter 2. Not only must any system designed to address such victimization account for these varying needs, it must also find ways to resolve conflicts between different groups of victims in individual cases. For example, a given pot of restitution money available in a case may be enough to fund healthcare costs of one group of victims but not restore the damaged environment, with different victim groups advocating the case for each distribution of funds. We have seen O'Hear's (2004) suggestion that a risk-based approach be adopted to resolve some of these conflicts,[29] although this method is largely theoretical and untested and would have to rely on solid scientific evidence. Consequently, it is submitted that green victimology will be largely concerned with *balancing* competing interests, among different victims as well as between polluters and victims and in relation to the human rights context to be discussed below.

It is clear that, given the varied nature of such victimization, the present literature that touches upon the issue of environmental harm is in fact quite limited. It will not have gone unnoticed that a significant proportion of examples used throughout this volume have been drawn from the United States in particular, and from developed jurisdictions more generally. This is at odds with one of the few broad conclusions we can draw about environmental victimization: that it tends to fall disproportionately on impoverished persons at both the local and global level. We have seen that the provision of such mechanisms as administrative compensation schemes varies tremendously between developed and undeveloped counties. Likewise, the high proportion of impoverished victims represents a high percentage of victims that lack the time and resources to enter environmental mediation schemes, let alone mount civil actions or private prosecutions against the perpetrators of environmental harms. The realities of environmental victimization therefore means any green victimology must take a broad view of the problem and will almost inevitably involve comparative studies, and studies of parts of the world which have often been side-lined by western criminology and victimology (India, central Africa and southeast Asia, to give some examples).

The other chief conclusion to be drawn concerning environmental victims themselves is that, while this volume has pointed out many of the common issues and difficulties faced by traditional criminologists and victimologists compared with green victimologists and international lawyers, in fact it must not be assumed that measures designed to assist traditional victims will necessarily meet the needs of environmental victims. It has been discussed throughout this volume how environmental victimization raises a number of novel problems for criminal justice: mass victimization; corporate or state offenders; difficulties in proving causation, and so on. We have seen how more generalized victim reforms have been applied in the US to environmental victims, although elsewhere it has been argued that such laws seem too restrictive to allow for such an interpretation. Differences between environmental victims and traditional victims might well necessitate different approaches in the criminal justice and support spheres. For example, given the divergent and often hidden nature of environmental harm, courts may need to employ victim impact statements far more frequently than is envisioned under many present systems put in place for victims across jurisdictions. Of course this discussion has also revealed that, environmental degradation being criminogenic, environmental victims, like traditional victims of many crimes, may also be offenders. Green victimology, like mainstream victimology, must therefore concern itself with dispelling notions of what Christie (1986) called the ideal victim. It must also test criminal justice and other mechanisms ostensibly designed for all victims but in fact limited to the ideal variety. In effect this amounts to a continuation of the critical approach outlined above.

The final point I wish to make concerning environmental victims themselves is one that has arisen many times throughout the course of this volume: that theoretical musings, or even parallels drawn with more traditional and well-studied victims groups, are, for many of the reasons given above, insufficient as a basis for the continuing development of green victimology. As with other areas of victimization, the voices and views of these victims of environmental harm have largely remained absent from the relevant literature, and indeed from policy debates. Of course, given the heterogeneous nature of environmental victims, it will pose a considerable challenge for green victimologists to draw any broad conclusions about what *these* victims need and/or want and their views of various justice mechanisms, even following empirical studies. Nevertheless, the present state of the literature indicates that research into what environmental victims themselves actually report about environmental harm, its consequences, and possible redress mechanisms should be a top priority for green victimology.

6.4.4 Symbolic character of environmental harm and justice mechanisms

Given the point made in the preceding paragraph concerning the lack of empirical evidence of the views of environmental victims themselves, it is difficult to make any concrete assertions as to how they might react to justice mechanisms, criminal or otherwise. There is however sufficient evidence on which to conclude that the impacts of much of this harm in many cases go far beyond the material (Malsch, 1999). We have noted for example the loss of culture and social stability brought about by environmental victimizations.[30] Such disparate effects lend weight to the hypothesis that mere monetary redress in the form of restitution or compensation, or indeed punitive redress in the form of an environmental offender being convicted and sentenced in a criminal court, is unlikely to be sufficient for many environmental victims. 'Redress' for many such victims may be more cathartic in nature. Of course, this might imply once again that *criminal justice* is the wrong tool to achieve such ends. This is the principal argument of Mares (2010) in advocating a 'shift in thinking' towards a 'civilizing offensive', or 'civilizing spurt', concerning the environment.[31] On the other hand, we know that many traditional victims express particular satisfaction at the recognition *by a court* of the harm that has befallen them. As such, administrative or regulatory mechanisms may not carry the same symbolic weight. Indeed, the simple *recognition* of harm may be especially important to environmental victims given the often invisible nature of their suffering.

Of course, it has also been demonstrated by the mainstream victimological literature that traditional victims are highly concerned with notions of *procedural justice* as opposed to the instrumental outcomes of the justice system (Tyler, 1990). We have seen in Chapter 5 that such victims do value monetary payments, but more so when they come from offenders themselves in the form of restitution, even when the actual sums involved are very small and are largely symbolic (Miers, 1997). We also saw that compensation itself can serve a number of functions, including focusing attention on the moral responsibility of certain actors for the plight of environmental victims; it may also provide a way of fostering socially beneficial programmes.

Much of the above emphasis on symbolic rather than instrumental outcomes is based on analogies with studies carried out on more traditional groups of victims, which of course is precisely what the preceding section warned against. Indeed, it may be that many (or the majority) of the victims of environmental harm are much more concerned about receiving monetary compensation or redress to meet health costs, financial costs and so on. This may be particularly true given the corporate or state nature of offenders in cases of environmental crime. Indeed, tangential evidence in support of this hypothesis might be drawn from empirical work that has been carried out with victims of human rights abuses at the hands of state actors, where Parmentier (2010) has found that victims seem to be expressing far greater retributive tendencies and desires for monetary compensation than victims of most other types of crime.

Paul Rock (1990) has described in detail how the development of state-funded criminal injuries compensation in England and Wales and elsewhere was driven by a host of political factors which almost inevitably did not include any reference to what victims themselves said they wanted; in effect governments sought to 'buy off what were imagined to be the angry victims of criminal violence and their allies who could obstruct the introduction of a mass of liberal policies planned by penal reformers' (1990: p. 264). Perhaps more troubling, however, is the fact that the effect of introducing such compensation schemes without any evidence was to forestall any further development in victims' policies for nearly two decades because, as Rock continues, 'There was the difficulty posed by the tacit assumption injected into policy-making for victims from the start that the needs of victims had in effect been substantially and generously met' (2004: p. 265). A vital role of green victimology must be to steer policy-makers away from these same assumptions that for so long set back the development of academic thinking and policy developments in relation to wider groups of victims. Instead, green victimology must concern itself with establishing what different victims of environmental harm need, and in what timescale, and begin working towards the establishment of systems to cater for those needs, within or beyond criminal justice, at national and international levels.

6.4.5 The human rights perspective

I have elaborated in some detail in the conclusion to Chapter 4 on a way forward for the adoption of human rights principles by green victimologists (and indeed international environmental lawyers), and there is no cause to repeat those arguments here.[32] It is clear that, in recent decades, human rights have become a cornerstone of debates going on around traditional crime victims (as well as criminal justice in general) and, as such, will prove a vital component of green victimology as well. This is all the more certain given the transnational nature of many environmental harms and therefore the necessary involvement of the *international* legal order, under which human rights are at present one of the few ways in which *individual* victims can seek recognition.

One particular theme which this volume has returned to a number of times, but which has particular relevance in the context of human rights, is that of 'balance'. As noted by Jackson (1990), traditional victimology too has been dominated by balance rhetoric, chiefly concerning the balancing of rights between victim and offender. The same balancing exercise will need to be addressed by green victimologists as well[33] although, in this case, there are if anything more complex issues at stake. Thus, while green victimology must tackle the same concerns about (environmental) offenders being prejudiced against by more victim involvement in the justice system (the 'zero-sum game'[34]), we have seen that *environmental* crimes also raise tensions between the economic needs of the broader community and the state as a whole and smaller groups or individual citizens within those communities. Furthermore, to redress environmental harm for some victims may lead to forced changes in industrial practices putting other victims out of work. We have seen arguments to the contrary in Chapter 2[35] but, notwithstanding this, it remains clear that, much more than for many traditional crimes, the balance to be struck may actually be between one set of victims' rights and those of another group of victims, or potential victims, now or in the future.

If green victimology is to adopt the language of rights it must also address another key issue raised by more traditional branches of victimology: the *enforceability* of such rights. As noted previously in this volume, there are definite parallels to be drawn between the fledgling recognition of rights for environmental victims and those rights ascribed to more traditional victims, in that the enforcement mechanisms attached to these 'rights' remain in most cases markedly underdeveloped and lacking true compulsive authority. We saw this in relation to the Compliance Committee of the Aahrus UNECE Convention on Access to Information, Public Participation in Decision-making and Access to Justice in Environmental Matters. We have also seen, in Chapter 4, that the most progressive developments concerning rights for green victims so far have come about as a result of interpreting existing, well-established rights so as to include environmental harms, specifically by the ECtHR. Green victimology therefore needs to apply itself to understanding these developments and the ways they can be applied to wider groups of environmental victims.

The final point I wish to emphasize concerning the application of human rights in green victimology again derives from the need to work collectively with international environmental lawyers. The parallel development of 'rights discourses' in victimology and international law in recent decades offers clear potential for researchers within these two subject areas to learn from each other. I have previously expressed this in terms of an exchange of ideas grounded on structure and those grounded on human agency. For victimologists, it is clear that many international legal instruments now exist with the potential to afford victims of environmental harm some measure of rights, including rights to participate in justice mechanisms. Most of these instruments are non-binding and remain what international lawyers call 'soft law'. Nevertheless, traditional victimology for much of its history was itself characterized by grand symbolic gestures with little legal force, but which over time have resulted in significant changes occurring within jurisdictions: not just legally but, in line with the above discussion, culturally. Indeed, in conclusion to their systematic review of the impact of the 2001 EU Framework Decision on the standing of victims in criminal proceedings, Groenhuijsen and Pemberton (2009) argue: 'due to the experiences with the EU- Framework Decision, we conclude that the adoption of a hard-law instrument only leads to slightly different results than the soft-law instruments' (p. 59). Once again, therefore, it seems that international environmental lawyers may learn as much from this line of developments in victimology as victimologists can learn from those who study international environmental law.

6.5 Final conclusions

In his 2011 book Rob White calls for a degree of 'horizon scanning' in the interests of finding workable solutions to environmental problems. The goal of the present volume has been to engage in just such an exercise, and indeed it is the first to do so in relation to what at present is a surprisingly under-researched and under-theorized aspect of environmental degradation, the victims of environmental harms themselves. I say this is 'surprising' because given both the escalating development of what I have called mainstream or traditional victimology, coupled with the wider macro influences predicted by Boutellier concerning harm as the new benchmark on which we can judge a shared morality, the fact that environmental victims themselves are so removed from both academic literature and policy debate is nothing short of remarkable. Indeed, the overarching impression one is left with is of a lack of joined-up thinking in this area on many of the issues I have raised in this volume. This is exemplified in particular by the European Union, which champions victims in traditional criminal justice policy areas but apparently ignores them when considering environmental issues.

Joined-up thinking is at the heart of what I am advocating in this volume: between subject disciplines as well as between policy areas and between the academic and NGO/activist sectors. Largely out of convenience, I have termed this overall exercise 'green victimology', although, as noted at the start of this chapter, the label itself is of little importance. What is important is that the study of environmental harm and its victims tackles the key challenges facing this fledgling area. In this chapter I have mapped out some of these key (and under-researched) issues, while of course acknowledging that this list will be far from conclusive.

I have also put forward the argument that *criminal justice* remains an important tool for dealing effectively with environmental victims, and will remain so for the foreseeable future. Again, it is important to appreciate that this is not the *only way* to meet the complex needs of this extremely heterogeneous group and, indeed, in many cases may not even prove the best method available. The most pressing difficulty faced by green victimologists is, as I have repeated at a number of points throughout these discussions, the lack of input from the environmental victims themselves. Until such research is carried out, green victimology will remain largely conjectural. The objective of this volume has been to provide a platform on which this important work can be based, representing the beginning rather than the conclusion of what will necessarily be a far greater endeavour. With the growing prevalence of environmental degradation and its resulting harms, the mounting of such an endeavour is unquestionably necessary. Our goal as green victimologists is therefore ultimately to ensure that the views, needs and perspectives of those upon whom such harm falls are not ignored.

Notes

1 Victims, environmental harm and international law

1 Some feminist scholars oppose the use of the term 'victim of rape', preferring the word 'survivor' (Rock, 1998: p. 23).

2 Lynch and Stretesky (2007) have argued that the lack of development in the criminological study of environmental degradation is particularly apparent in the USA, although it is generally true of the discipline globally. They note the irony in this, as one of the first true 'green criminology' discussions came out of the USA (Lynch, 1990).

3 In some cases these may be related phenomena, in other cases not (see Bowerman *et al.*, 2011).

4 See Oreskes (2007).

5 See Redgwell (2010) at pp. 689–692.

6 For discussion concerning the choice of the word 'harm' here, see pp. 13–16 below and Chapter 2 generally.

7 Which this author accepts (see Chapters 2 and 6).

8 In an early, unpublished contribution, Groombridge (1991) proposed what he called an 'eco-criminology': mapping out its core characteristics as touching on 'ethics, religion, politics, economics and feminism' (p. 4). Gibbs *et al.* (2010) speak in terms of 'conservation criminology'. Lynch and Stretesky (2007) also contrast the predominantly European understanding of green criminology with the primarily American notion of 'eco-critical criminology'.

9 Referred to by Passas (2005) as 'Lawful but awful' (p. 771).

10 Although in fact 'ecofeminism' is often considered somewhat different from more mainstream 'feminist' considerations of environmental degradation. Essentially ecofeminism suggests that there is an underlying similarity between the domination of women and the domination of 'nature', both at an international and national level. Warren (1997) suggests that ecofeminism, or 'ecological feminism', takes the position that 'there are important connections between how one treats women, people of colour, and the underclass on one hand and how one treats the nonhuman natural environment on the other' (p. xi).

11 While the widespread criminalization of such harms is a relatively new legal phenomenon, it is not without historical antecedents. McMurray and Ramsey (1986), for example, describe how 'In fourteenth century England the Crown prescribed capital punishment for Englishmen who defied a royal proclamation on smoke abatement' (p. 113). Furthermore, Roughton (2007) notes that religious scholars have begun to rediscover and reapply environmental precepts of centuries-old Islamic (shariah) law.

12 White (2008a) is equally committed to this option.

13 Katz (2010) presents the counter-argument that this solution is somewhat impotent in the face of what she calls a 'criminogenic corporate-state'.
14 See p. 17 in this volume. Although he does not ultimately advocate this position as the primary mechanism for dealing with such cases, Mares discusses the possibility of conceptualizing environmentally destructive activities under the umbrella of 'undermining the carrying capacity of the planet' as a form of crime.
15 Although I do so here out of convenience.
16 See Pointing and Maguire (1988).
17 The role of second-wave feminism for the movement in general has been emphasized by Kearon and Godfrey (2007). It has been presented as *the* key foundation of the movement in some countries, especially in Canada (Canadian Resource Centre for Victims of Crime, 2006).
18 Evidence of this proposition in relation to environmental victims will be discussed throughout this volume, but becomes particularly relevant in Chapter 5 in the context of states' creation of administrative compensation systems.
19 The term has been described as 'a rather ugly neologism' (Newburn, 1988: p. 1).
20 For arguments against the drawing of any distinction at all between 'victimology' and 'criminology', see Farrall and Maltby (2003). The authors' point concerning the significant overlap between victims and offenders in reality will be discussed in the context of the impacts of environmental harms in Chapter 2.
21 And also a recent winner of the Stockholm Prize in Criminology.
22 It will however be argued in Chapter 3 that Christie's observations now have particular relevance to the position of environmental victims under transnational and international law.
23 Assuming for the moment – along with Farrall and Maltby (2003) – that victimology lies somewhere within its ambit.
24 Discussed below.
25 See Chapter 5.
26 Defined in this case in terms of falling within the six (now seven) protected groups overseen by the UK Equality and Human Rights Commission.
27 As with the work of Hillyard and Toombs (2003), this is not to dismiss the important contribution of modern criminology.
28 For Gibbs *et al.* (2010), 'environmental risk' is a key feature of their conception of 'conservation criminology', which they use as a method of distancing the concept from more legalistic understandings of 'environmental crime'.
29 Which is not the intention of Hillyard and Toombs.
30 Good overviews can be found in Beirne and South (2007) and White (2009).
31 Such assertions will be tested in Chapter 2.
32 The implications of this Declaration for state responsibility regarding environmental derogation, and for climate change in particular, will be discussed in detail in Chapter 3.
33 See below, and Chapter 3.
34 See Alston (2005).
35 See Chapter 4.
36 See Chapter 3.
37 With some notable exceptions, including Walklate (2007) and Rock (2007a).
38 Note that I am following an *inter*disciplinary approach rather than a *multi*disciplinary one, because I am making the argument that each of the two fields (international law and victimology) needs to adapt its existing assumptions and methodologies in light of the insights provided by the other.
39 See also Reese (2000).
40 See Table 5.1 on p. 130 in this volume.

2 Identifying and conceptualizing the victims of environmental harm

1 Defined by Chivian *et al.* (1993) as 'any effect that results in altered structure or impaired function, or represents the beginnings of a sequence of events leading to altered structure or function' (p. 15).
2 Especially if one is already largely excluding non-human victims from the equation, as is the case in this chapter.
3 More difficult, of course, is their *attribution* to specific external factors, such as the activities of a given company or industrial process; again, the reader is reminded that at this point the difficult issue of legal causation is being bypassed in favour of providing a conceptual overview of the types of harm involved in environmental victimization.
4 As opposed to, say, the negative impact on a person's 'culture' or 'sense of security'.
5 Chapter 5 covers in some detail the question of compensating environmental victims.
6 It has also been predicted that changing temperatures will have a significant effect on animal diseases, with marked effects for sheep and cattle farming in particular (see BBC, 2012c).
7 Known more generally in Europe as Waste Electrical and Electronic Equipment (WEEE), where it is the subject of a European Directive (2002/96/EC). The topic of e-waste and WEEE is discussed in more detail below; see also Gottberg *et al.* (2006).
8 In Chapter 5, the availability of ad hoc redress mechanisms for victims of *these* events will be contrasted with the relative absence of such schemes for more general, endemic environmental harms.
9 Many more examples are mentioned throughout this volume: see in particular pp. 111, 117 and 141.
10 As will be highlighted in Chapter 5, there is a marked absence of empirical data to inform us what victims of environmental harm or crime might want.
11 Discussed in greater detail below.
12 Discussed below.
13 In 1970, 1977 and 1990.
14 A non-profit association of air quality agencies in the northeastern United States.
15 This last issue will be returned to below.
16 As distinguished from 'eco-terrorism', which constitutes 'terrorist' acts in support of the environment and animal rights. Eco-terrorism itself is increasingly the subject of harsh criminal responses, under the United States Animal Enterprise Terrorism Act 2006. There is also a link here with concerns over food security (discussed below), as the US Food and Drug Administration (2007) has expressed grave concerns about the possibility of bioterrorism against food supplies (White, 2008b).
17 Attributing the phrase originally to George Bush Sr.
18 See Chapter 3.
19 In this case, via the control of crop pests.
20 See the *Daily Telegraph*, 'Egypt and Tunisia Usher In the New Era of Global Food Revolutions', 30 January 2011.
21 Article 25.
22 Elaborating on the findings of Mandalia (2005).
23 See also Article 4(8).
24 The first such study having appeared in 1983 (US General Accounting Office, 1983).
25 Intergovernmental Panel on Climate Change.
26 Terazono *et al.* (2006) note the variability in the understanding and definition of e-waste in the literature; Liu *et al.* (2006) summarize it: 'in most cases, e-waste comprises the relatively expensive and essentially durable products used for data processing, telecommunications or entertainment in private households and businesses' (p. 93). Concern with e-waste lies not just in the bulk of physical dumping itself, but

in the fact that much of this material contains environmentally toxic substances, including mercury, which many developing countries are ill-equipped to dispose of appropriately.

27 The latter being because the US has allegedly put pressure on the Vatican to declare its support for genetically modified foodstuffs, which will have considerable influence in many African nations.

28 See also Reese (2000).

29 Which again reflects debates in more mainstream victimology (Shapland *et al.*, 1985; Jackson *et al.*, 1991; Rock, 1993).

3 Environmental victims across jurisdictions: criminal law and state responsibility

1 Discussed in more detail below.

2 See Skinnider (2011).

3 To be discussed in Chapter 4.

4 Although he does acknowledge the inevitable reductions in 'standard of living', this is done in the collective sense for humankind.

5 In the text of his argument, Mares only refers specifically to 'shaming', although he cites Braithwaite's (1989) famous discussion of *reintegrative* shaming. The ethos of the piece very much reflects the latter rather than the former.

6 18 USC § 3771.

7 For a discussion of the distinction between 'service' and 'procedural' rights, see Chapter 4, and specifically pp. 75–76 in this volume.

8 18 USC § 3771(a)(4).

9 18 USC § 3771(d)(4).

10 18 USC § 2241, 2233.

11 Nos. 09–70529, 09–70533 (9th Cir.).

12 The most well-known example in recent years in England and Wales is the attempted private prosecution initiated by the family of the murdered schoolboy Stephen Lawrence in 1994. Despite considerable public attention and financial backing, this was ultimately unsuccessful.

13 *R* v *Secretary of state for the environment ex parte Kingston Upon Hull City Council, The Times*, 31 January 1996.

14 See, for example, Mitsilegas (2009) and Fletcher *et al.* (2008).

15 Modern interest in victims of crime at the EU level can be traced to a special meeting held in October 1999 in Tampere on the creation of an area of freedom, security and justice in the European Union. More recently, victims once again became a major issue towards the end of 2008, and a priority for the Swedish presidency of the Council of the European Union in the second half of 2009: victims of crime were once again put on the EU policy agenda in the Stockholm programme on justice and home affairs of 2009.

16 See European Law Monitor (2012).

17 Judgment of 21 October 2010 in Case C-205/09 *Criminal Proceedings against Emil Eredics*.

18 For further discussion on this point see Chapter 5.

19 See p. 25 in this volume.

20 OJ L 328/28 (6 December 2008).

21 In the context of the development of policies for victims of crime more broadly in England and Wales, I have previously described such successive developments as 'policy chains' (Hall, 2009).

22 See Holder and Lee (2007): 'Enforcement of environmental law in the UK relies heavily on the existence of criminal law, but criminal law is rarely the first resort of

regulators; negotiation is usually the starting point, and administrative rather than criminal sanctions have real attractions' (p. 382).

23 It is interesting to note here the parallels with the development of EU interest in victims of crime more generally. The 2001 Framework Decision followed Council of Europe measures in the area, notably its 1983 Convention on the Compensation of Victims of Violent Crime, Recommendation (R (83) 7) calling for member states to develop policies to provide assistance to victims, and to take account of the public's view in forming policies; and Recommendation (R (85) 11) on the position of the victim in the framework of criminal law and procedure.

24 Judgment of 13 September 2005: *Commission of the European Communities* v *Council of the European Union* (Case C-176/03), paras 47–48.

25 Article 3.

26 ECOSOC Resolution 1994/15 (25 July 1994).

27 [P]ersons who, individually or collectively, have suffered harm, including physical or mental injury, emotional suffering, economic loss or substantial impairment of their fundamental rights, through acts or omissions that do not yet constitute violations of national criminal laws but of internationally recognized norms relating to human rights.

28 Article 1.

29 Principle 2(f).

30 Principle 2(a). See Chapter 2.

31 Although we may have more success in other areas of the 1985 Declaration.

32 Cheng (1965) has gone so far as to suggest that an appropriately worded UN resolution can create *instant* customary law.

33 A significant case in point being the UN Universal Declaration of Human Rights of 1948, enshrined in 1966 in the International Covenant on Civil and Political Rights.

34 With the possible expectations of the 2001 EU Council Framework Decision on the Standing of Victims in Criminal Proceedings (discussed below) and the US Crime Victims' Rights Act of 2004 (discussed above).

35 Other prominent examples include the Nuremburg and Tokyo tribunals set up after the Second World War, the International Criminal Tribunal for the Former Yugoslavia established in 1993 and the International Criminal Tribunal for Rwanda set up in 1994.

36 Following a provision originally found in Protocol I of the Geneva Convention.

37 It is wrong to suggest that the Rome Statute *created* these crimes; rather, it represents one of the clearest and most widely accepted codifications of crimes which already existed under customary international law (see Cryer, 2010).

38 At the time of drafting a Code of Crimes Against the Peace and Security of Mankind in 1996, available at: http://untreaty.un.org/ilc/texts/instruments/english/draft%20articles/7_4_1996.pdf [accessed 2 July 2012].

39 See Chapter 4.

40 See below.

41 Statute of the International Court of Justice, Article 38 1(b). See also Thirlway (2010).

42 Constituted by the 1936 Convention of Ottawa between the Canada and the US.

43 *Trail Smelter Arbitration Tribunal* (*US* v *Canada*), 33 AJIL 182 (1939) and 35 AJIL 684 (1941).

44 *Trail Smelter Arbitration Tribunal* (*US* v *Canada*), 33 AJIL 182 (1939) and 35 AJIL 684 (1941), Article XII, citing Eagleton (1928: p. 80).

45 *Corfu Channel Case* 1949 ICJ Reports 4 at 22.

46 The author cites the 1982 United Nations Convention on the Law of the Sea and the 1959 Antarctic Treaty as arguably containing rare examples of positive obligations to protect the environment.

47 Although there is judicial precedent to support the counter-argument, notably by Judge Weeramantry in his dissenting opinion in *Legality of the Threat or Use of Nuclear Weapons,* Advisory Opinion 1 of 1996, ICJ Reports 226 at Part 3 sec 4:1(b).
48 Principle 15.
49 Particular mention might be made here of the Basel Convention on the Control of Transboundary Movements of Hazardous Wastes and Their Disposal, and its Protocol on Liability and Compensation for Damage Resulting from Transboundary Movements of Hazardous Wastes and their Disposal. These will be discussed in Chapter 5.
50 Which the US has signed but not ratified.
51 Here we should once again acknowledge the definition of victims adopted in the International Law Commission's (2006) draft principles on the allocation of loss in the case of transboundary harm arising out of hazardous activities (Principle 2(f)). See p. 61 in this volume.
52 This being one of only three references to 'justice' in the 283-paragraph document.
53 Following the 2002 World Summit on Sustainable Development.
54 Following the 2000 Millennium Summit of the United Nations.
55 See Chapter 5.
56 Despite the provisions of the ILC draft principles.

4 Human rights, victim rights, and environmental rights?

1 Building upon the various recommendations previously made by the Council of Europe on this matter, including Recommendation (R (83) 7) calling for member states to develop policies to provide assistance to victims, and to take account of the public's view in forming policies, and Recommendation (R (85) 11) on the position of the victim in the framework of criminal law and procedure.
2 See Chapter 3.
3 For wider discussions of victim rights more broadly, see Fenwick (1995); Ashworth (2000); Cape (2004); Doak (2005); and Hall (2009), on which this section builds.
4 The assumption that these are in fact entirely 'separate' groups of individuals is not borne out by the empirical evidence (see Farrall and Maltby, 2003).
5 In view of this, the present volume must be wary of perpetuating the widespread rejection of human agency by basing its analysis on the assumption that what environmental victims 'need' is the same as what non-environmental victims 'need'.
6 United Nations Economic Commission for Europe.
7 Paragraph 99.
8 See also JUSTICE (1998).
9 Erez maintains that exposure to victim impact statements will give practitioners a more realistic impression of 'normal' levels of impact (Erez and Rogers, 1999; Erez, 1999).
10 [2004] O.J. No. 5199 (Ont. S.C.).
11 For a discussion of this issue, see Bunderson (2001).
12 Article 4.
13 Article 6(e).
14 Article 6(a).
15 Article 12.
16 Article 6(e).
17 Where the example of the US Crime Victims' Rights Act 2004 was especially significant.
18 See Chapter 1.
19 The suggestion is sometimes referred to as a 'third generation right', along with the rights to peace, development and democratic governance (DeMerieux, 2001).
20 The latter option is sometimes referred to as the 'greening' of human rights.

21 And in fact the concept has been specifically rejected by the European Court of Human Rights in *Tatar* v *Romania*, Application no. 67021/01.
22 *The Social and Economic Rights Action Center and the Center for Economic and Social Rights* v *Nigeria*, ACHPR, No 155/ 96.
23 The Social and Economic Rights Action Center (SERAC), based in Nigeria, and the Center for Economic and Social Rights (CESR), based in New York.
24 *The Social and Economic Rights Action Center and the Center for Economic and Social Rights* v *Nigeria*, ACHPR, No 155/ 96 paras 52–53.
25 That said, DeMerieux (2001) makes the important point that it is a 'great oversimplification' to assume that the presence of effective first generation rights – which are often overlooked in discussion of environmental harm – do not equally contribute to overall human wellbeing.
26 Note, however, the opinion of Coomans (2003) that 'In addition, it should be noted that the collective rights in the present case (Articles 21, 22 and 24) are facilitative of the enjoyment of individual rights but are also capable of being claimed by a group (the Ogoni)' (p. 757).
27 The Commission's ruling that the Nigerian state should pay compensation to said victims will be discussed in Chapter 5.
28 Man has the fundamental right to freedom, equality and adequate conditions of life, in an environment of a quality that permits a life of dignity and well-being, and he bears a solemn responsibility to protect and improve the environment for present and future generations.
29 Series A no 327-B (1995) 77.
30 Reports of Judgments and Decisions 1996-II, [1996] 23 EHRR 330.
31 Convention for the Protection of Human Rights and Fundamental Freedoms, Rome, 4.XI.1950.
32 (2004) 39 EHRR 13.
33 [2005] UKHL 4.
34 (2005) EWHC 2583 (Admin).
35 *Öneryildiz* v *Turkey*, 48939/99 [2004] ECHR 657 (30 November 2004).
36 Application no. 16798/90.
37 European Court of Human Rights, 27 January 2009.
38 European Court of Human Rights, 20 May 2010. Notably this was purely a case of 'noise' pollution.
39 European Court of Human Rights, 1 July 2008.
40 European Court of Human Rights, 21 July 2009. For further information on relevant ECHR case law, see www.ila-hq.org/en/committees/index.cfm/cid/1017 [accessed 4 July 2012].
41 See *Öneryildiz* v *Turkey*, 48939/99 30 November 2004 and *L.C.B.* v *The United Kingdom*, 14/1997/798/1001 9 June 1998.
42 15339/02, 21166/02, 20058/02, 11673/02 and 15343/02 20 March 2008.
43 I.C.J. Report-1 999 (1).
44 UNHRC Decision 67/1980.
45 On this point, Westra (2009) has written specifically on the lack of rights for those who are displaced by environmental changes or catastrophes and thus become environmental refugees in other states.
46 See also *Mossville Environmental Action Now* v *United States* (Inter-American Commission on Human Rights, 17 March 2010) for a discussion of the concept of 'environmental racism'.
47 Some commentators, however, speak of a prior 'golden age' of victim involvement in criminal justice (see Schafer, 1968). Certainly a focus by authorities on victims of crime can be traced back to antiquity. The draft Jamaican victims' charter of 2006 cites the Babylonian Code of Hammurabi of 1700 BC as prescribing restitution to the victim (the 'wronged man'; see Roth, 2002) in property offence cases, and the Roman

Law of the Twelve Tables of 449 BC as requiring convicted theft offenders to pay back to victims a multiple of the value of the goods stolen, depending on whether they were recovered (Jamaican Ministry of Justice, 2006).

48 [1993] IIHRL 103 (25 November 1993).
49 More specifically, their inability to obtain judicial review of a decision made by the government to reject their appeal against the original granting of the license.
50 Available at: www.unece.org/env/pp/pubcom.html [accessed 6 June 2012].
51 See p. 125 in this volume.
52 Directive 2004/35/EC OJ L 143/56 (30.4.2004).
53 See www.naaec.gc.ca/eng/index_e.htm [accessed 4 July 2012].
54 Article 14.
55 Although the UN Declaration is of course non-binding.
56 Albeit, in the case of the Aarhus convention, these administrative proceedings take place at the international level.

5 Responding to environmental victimization: compensation, restitution and redress

1 See Miers (1997).
2 Not to be confused with the term 'environmental compensation', which is usually employed in the literature to describe the possibility of compensating for environmental damage by creating commensurate environmental benefits (Cowell, 2010).
3 Which may in any case be impossible when one considers, for example, the permanent destruction of a way of life.
4 Such limitations are now found under the Oil Pollution Act 1990; although these are less stringent than those that existed at the time of the Exxon case, they still restrict civil awards to relatively small sums. Further discussion on this point will follow in the section devoted to civil law.
5 See p. 87 in this volume.
6 Which, somewhat confusingly, is the name for a criminal-court-based restitution order in England and Wales.
7 The Legal Aid and Sentencing Bill at present going through the UK Parliament places greater emphasis on courts to grant compensation orders by imposing a duty to consider making a compensation order in any case where it has power to do so.
8 This is sometimes referred to in the literature as 'corrective justice' (see Lin, 2005; Goldberg and Zipersky, 2011).
9 And, as such, will be considered below alongside examples of more ad hoc, administrative compensation schemes set up in the light of various natural and other disasters.
10 See below.
11 Further discussion of the theoretical grounding for state-based compensation will be covered below, along with other administrative schemes.
12 Following New Zealand the year before.
13 Such singling out of crime victims has a very long history. Cavanagh (1984) notes that

> [t]he idea that a society should assist those of its citizens victimized by crime has been traced back to the ancient Babylonian Code of Hammurabi (*c.*2038 BC), which provided that when a man was robbed or murdered the City in which the crime occurred should compensate the victim or his heirs for their losses.
>
> (p. 1)

14 See Chapters 1 and 2.
15 In New Zealand this dilemma is actually circumvented (although only rhetorically) by including criminal victimization under the definition of an accident. Hence victims fall within the scope of the wider Accident Compensation Scheme set out in the

Prevention, Rehabilitation and Compensation Act 2001. The scheme can be applied to cases for environmental harm, but is restrictive in the sense that it excludes disease and environmental illness.

16 O'Hear goes on to suggest that an administrative system would reduce transaction costs by making more efficient decisions. It might also be easier for an agency to produce standardized protocols and payment schedules, which would simplify the adjudicatory process.
17 As was the case following the 1989 Exxon oil spill off the coast of Alaska.
18 See p. 30 in this volume.
19 Although he does present considerable evidence in favour of this hypothesis.
20 With particular obsessions, it seems, over the speed at which applications are processed on a day-to-day basis (see, for example, nola.com, 2012).
21 By contrast, a year after France introduced legislation to compensate people suffering health effects from the country's nuclear tests carried out between 1960 and 1996, it has been reported that only one victim received compensation in the first year (Deutsche Welle, 2011).
22 And here we might also note that within a month of the 2011 Tōhoku earthquake and tsunami and the resulting meltdowns at the Fukushima Daiichi nuclear plant, the Japanese government had ordered the operator of the plant to pay compensation of one million yen ($12,000 or £7,331) per family to affected families who lived within 18 miles (BBC, 2011).
23 Broadly speaking, the purpose of the Act (often known as 'Superfund') is to compel polluters to clean up and restore environmental damage caused by spills and leaks of hazardous contaminants.
24 s.101(16).
25 42 USC § 9607(16).
26 The possible deterrent effects of compensation schemes will be returned to below.
27 A question that also relates to the other avenues of redress for environmental harm.
28 (1862) 3 B&S 66, 122 ER 27.
29 See p. 68 in this volume.
30 (1868) LR 3 HL 330.
31 Sentencing Council Minutes, 24 February 2012. Available at: http://sentencingcouncil.judiciary.gov.uk/docs/web_24–02–2012.pdf [accessed 26 July 2012].
32 Albeit informal discussions with victimologists involved in the drafting of the proposed convention at the 14th Annual Symposium of the World Society of Victimology at The Hague in May 2012 suggest this provision was transplanted from existing environmental legislation at the international level, without any especially in-depth discussion.
33 Quoted by Skinnider (2011: p. 10).
34 Principle 4(1).
35 Principles 4(5) and 7(2).
36 And indeed, at the European Level, an early draft of the EU Directive 2008/99/EC on the protection of the environment through the criminal law contained, at Article 5 Para. 5, a provision that the criminal acts proscribed by the Directive might be accompanied by other sanctions or measures, in particular the obligation to reinstate the environment.
37 This need not mean that they fail to exercise significant influences at the national or international level. See p. 62 in this volume.
38 See p. 83 in this volume.
39 Discussed previously in this chapter.
40 On this point, see Davis's (2005) discussion of the Maldives.
41 When an environmental pollution problem arises, Japanese residents file complaints with their local government. If the local government decides to handle the case,

Environment Pollution Complaint Counselors hear residents' complaints and initiate the settlement process. Local governments received 93,016 environmental complaints in 2000, and pollution counselors resolved 76,931 of them (Matsumoto, 2011).

42 My thanks to Professor Joanna Shapland of the University of Sheffield for this alterative interpretation.
43 See pp. 50–51 in this volume.
44 For more on the culpability of the *state* for environmental harm, see Chapter 3.
45 Albeit the lack of in-depth empirical data on this issue means we must approach any such assumption with due caution.
46 These may be taken up by 'environmentalists'.
47 Discussed in more detail in Chapter 6.

6 Mapping out a green victimology

1 See p. 2 in this volume.
2 Recalling here, and throughout this chapter, that those requirements have yet to be established by any empirical investigation.
3 See Chapters 3 and 5.
4 For a counter-view of victim impact statements see Ashworth (2010).
5 Although, as also noted on p. 112 in this volume, the statutory limitations placed on the sums that can be awarded through such orders may make them financially less useful for environmental victims.
6 Nos. 09–70529, 09–70533 (9th Cir.). See p. 55 in this volume.
7 See p. 5 in this volume.
8 See p. 6 in this volume.
9 See p. 58 in this volume.
10 See p. 59 in this volume.
11 See p. 104 in this volume.
12 See p. 49 in this volume.
13 See p. 55 in this volume.
14 See p. 57 in this volume.
15 It is not my intention in this context to delve into the sometimes emotive arguments surrounding this classification of criminology as either a 'discipline' or 'sub-discipline'.
16 See www.britsoccrim.org/annualconference.htm [accessed 9 July 2012].
17 Paragraph 48.
18 My thanks to my colleague Marko Maver for a number of discussions in which he alerted me to these complexities and to this literature as a whole.
19 Indeed, the *International Review of Victimology* produced a special issue on this topic in 2004 (volume 14(2)).
20 It is worth noting here that the 'rule of law' in this case is often taken to mean western conceptualizations of justice. Liu (2007) has discussed how East Asian philosophies are far readier to incorporate such notions as community, apology and honor – which may have particular relevance to environmental victims.
21 Although I and others have criticized this perspective (Hall, 2009; Walklate, 2012).
22 See p. 62 in this volume.
23 See p. 68 in this volume.
24 See the discussion of criminal versus administrative systems in Chapter 5.
25 See p. 9 in this volume.
26 See p. 40 in this volume for more discussion of these points.
27 At this point it is worth recalling Boutellier's (2000) argument that 'harm' now constitutes a common moral benchmark in an otherwise secular society; see p. 13 in this volume.

28 Hence Rock's (1993) discussion of the 'social world' of a (specific) English Crown Court.
29 See p. 108 in this volume.
30 See p. 84 in this volume.
31 The point also reflects a suggested change in *culture*, as discussed in the section above.
32 See p. 92 in this volume.
33 Relatively few rights being held up as 'unqualified', certainly within the European Convention on Human Rights (see Meron, 1986).
34 See p. 75 in this volume.
35 See p. 32 in this volume.

References

Abercrombie, N., Hill, S. and Turner, B. (2006), *The Penguin Dictionary of Sociology*, 5th edition, London: Penguin.

Adams, N. (2003), *Terrorism and Oil*, Tulsa, OK: Penn Well.

Akella, A. and Cannon, J. (2004), *Strengthening the Weakest Links: Strategies for Improving the Enforcement of Environmental Laws Globally*, Washington, DC: Center for Conservation and Government. Reprinted in R. White (ed.) (2009), *Environmental Crime: A Reader*, Cullompton: Willan Publishing, 528–567.

Alston, P. (2005), *Non-State Actors and Human Rights*, Oxford: Oxford University Press.

Alston, D. and Brown, N. (1993), 'Global Threats to People of Color', in D. Bullard (ed.), *Confronting Environmental Racism: Voices from the Grassroots*, Cambridge: South End Press, 179–194.

Amir, M. (1971), *Patterns in Forcible Rape*, Chicago: University of Chicago Press.

Amy, D. (1983), 'The Politics of Environmental Mediation', *Ecology Law Quarterly*, 11(1): 1–19.

Ashworth, A. (1993), 'Victim Impact Statements and Sentencing', *Criminal Law Review*, 40: 498–509.

Ashworth, A. (1998), *The Criminal Process: An Evaluative Study*, 2nd edition, Oxford: Oxford University Press.

Ashworth, A. (2000), 'Victims' Rights, Defendants' Rights and Criminal Procedure', in A. Crawford and J. Goodey (eds) , *Integrating a Victim Perspective Within Criminal Justice: International Debates*, Aldershot: Ashgate Dartmouth, 185–204.

Ashworth, A. (2010), *Sentencing and Criminal Justice*, 5th edition, Cambridge: Cambridge University Press.

Association of Chief Police Officers (2008), *Guidance on Investigating Domestic Abuse*, London: National Police Improvement Agency.

Barnidge, R. (2006), 'The Due Diligence Principle Under International Law', *International Community Law Review*, 8: 81–121.

Beirne, P. and South, N. (2007), *Issues in Green Criminology: Confronting Harms Against Environments, Humanity and Other Animals*, Cullompton: Willan Publishing.

Bell, S. and McGillivray, D. (2008), *Environmental Law*, 7th edition, Oxford: Oxford University Press.

Berat, L. (1993), 'Defending the Right to a Healthy Environment: Toward a Crime of Genocide in International Law', *Boston University International Law Journal*, 11: 327–348.

Berrittella, M., Bigano, A., Roson, R. and Tol, R. (2006), 'A General Equilibrium Analysis of Climate Change Impacts on Tourism', *Tourism Management*, 27(5): 913–924.

Birnie, P., Boyle, A. and Redgwell, C. (2009), *International Law and the Environment*, 3rd edition, Oxford: Oxford University Press.

Boer, J., Pastor, J., Sadd, L. and Snyder, L. (1997), 'Is there Environmental Racism? The Demographics of Hazardous Waste in Los Angeles County', *Social Science Quarterly*, 78(4): 793–810.

Bottigliero, I. (2004), *Redress for Victims of Crimes Under International Law*, Leiden: Martinus Nijhoff Publishers.

Bottoms, A. (2003), 'Some Sociological Reflections on Restorative Justice', in A. von Hirsch, J. Roberts, A. Bottoms, K. Roach and M. Schiff (eds), *Restorative Justice and Criminal Justice: Competing or Reconcilable Paradigms?*, Oxford: Hart Publishing, 79–114.

Bourdieu, P. (1990), *The Logic of Practice*, Cambridge: Polity Press.

Boutellier, H. (2000), *Crime and Morality: The Significance of Criminal Justice in Post-Modern Culture*, Dordrecht: Kluwer.

Bowerman, N., Frame, D., Huntingford, C., Lowe, J. and Allen, M. (2011), 'Cumulative Carbon Emissions, Emissions Floors and Short-term Rates of Warming: Implications for Policy', *Philosophical Transactions of the Royal Society, A: Mathematical, Physical and Engineering Sciences*, 369(1934): 45–66.

Bowman, M. (2002), 'The Definition and Valuation of Environmental Harm: An Overview', in M. Bowman and A. Boyle (eds) , *Environmental Damage in International and Comparative Law*, 1–17.

Boyle, A. (1996), 'The Role of International Human Rights Law in the Protection of the Environment', in A. Boyle, M. Anderson (eds) , *Human Rights Approaches to Environmental Protection*, Oxford: Oxford University Press, 43–65.

Boyle, A. (2006), 'Soft Law in International Law-Making', in M. Evans (ed.), *International Law*, 2nd edition, Oxford: Oxford University Press, 141–158.

BP (2010), *BP Establishes $20 Billion Claims Fund for Deepwater Horizon Spill and Outlines Dividend Decisions*, press release of June 2010. Available at: www.bp.com/genericarticle.do?categoryId=2012968&contentId=7062966 [accessed 5 July 2012].

Bradford, B. (2011), 'Voice, Neutrality and Respect: Use of Victim Support Services, Procedural Fairness and Confidence in the Criminal Justice System', *Criminology and Criminal Justice*, 11(4): 345–366.

Braithwaite, J. (1989), *Crime, Shame, and Reintegration*, Cambridge: Cambridge University Press.

Braithwaite, J. (2002), *Restorative Justice and Responsive Regulation*, New York: Oxford University Press.

Brienen, M. and Hoegen, H. (2000), *Victims of Crime in 22 European Criminal Justice Systems: The Implementation of Recommendation (85) 11 of the Council of Europe on the Position of the Victim in the Framework of Criminal Law and Procedure*, Niemegen: Wolf Legal Productions.

British Broadcasting Corporation (2006), *Extra £2.5 Million for July Bomb Victims* [online]. Available at: http://news.bbc.co.uk/1/hi/uk/5001734.stm [accessed 3 June 2012].

British Broadcasting Corporation (2007), *EU Pollution Deaths Cost Billions* [online]. Available at: http://news.bbc.co.uk/1/hi/sci/tech/4444191.stm [accessed 26 June 2012].

British Broadcasting Corporation (2011), *Tepco to Compensate Japan's Nuclear Plant Victims*. Available at: www.bbc.co.uk/news/world-asia-pacific-13090304 [accessed 12 July 2012].

British Broadcasting Corporation (2012a), *Dolphins Deserve Same Rights as Humans Say Scientists* [online]. Available at: www.bbc.co.uk/news/world-17116882 [accessed 26 June 2012].

British Broadcasting Corporation (2012b), *Shell in Court over Nigeria Oil Spill Compensation* [online]. Available at: www.bbc.co.uk/news/world-africa-17486617 [accessed 7 July 2012].

British Broadcasting Corporation (2012c), *Schmallenberg Virus: Climate 'Raising UK Disease Risk'* [online]. Available at: www.bbc.co.uk/news/science-environment-17223445 [accessed 26 June 2012].

Brody, A., Demetriades, J. and Esplen, E. (2008), *Gender and Climate Change: Mapping the Linkages – A Scoping Study on Knowledge and Gaps*, Sussex: BRIDGE Institute of Development Studies.

Bronston, D. (1983), 'Compensating Victims of Hazardous Substance Pollution in the United States and Japan: A Comparative Analysis', *Fordham International Law Journal*, 7(3): 501–534.

Brook, D. (1998), 'Environmental Genocide: Native Americans and Toxic Waste', *American Journal of Economics and Sociology*, 57(1): 105–113. Reprinted in R. White (ed.) (2009), *Environmental Crime: A Reader*, Cullompton: Willan Publishing, 392–398.

Brown, C. (2008), 'Green Tax Revolt: Britons "Will Not Foot Bill to Save Planet"', *Independent Online* [online]. Available at http://tinyurl.com/5flsml [accessed 26 May 2012].

Brown, K., Turner, R., Hameed, H. and Bateman, I. (1997), 'Environmental Carrying Capacity and Tourism Development in the Maldives and Nepal', *Environmental Conservation*, 24(4): 316–325.

Brunnée, J. (1995) 'Environmental Security in the Twenty-First Century: New Momentum for the Development of International Environmental Law?', *Fordham International Law Journal*, 18: 1742–1747.

Bryant, B. (1995), *Environmental Justice*, Boston: Island Press.

Bunderson, J. (2001), 'Normal Injustice and Morality in Complex Organizations', *Journal of Business Ethics*, 33(3): 181–190.

Burns, P. (1985), 'Private Prosecutions in Canada: The Law and a Proposal for Change', *McGill Law Journal*, 21: 269–297.

Burns, T. and Flam, H. (1987), *The Shaping of Social Organization: Social Rule System Theory with Applications*, London: Sage Publishing.

Bynoe, M. (2006), 'Citizen Participation in the Environmental Impact Assessment Process in Guyana: Reality or Fallacy?', *Law, Environment and Development Journal*, 2(1): 34–49.

Byrne, D. (1999), *Social Exclusion*, Buckingham: Open University Press.

California Department of Corrections and Rehabilitation (2009), *Restitution Responsibilities, Information for Adult Offenders* [online]. Available at: www.cdcr.ca.gov/Victim_Services/restitution_responsibilities.html [accessed 14 June 2012].

Canadian Department of Justice (2012), *Victim Surcharge, Restitution Orders and Compensation* [online]. Available at: www.justice.gc.ca/eng/contact/comm6.html [accessed 5 July 2012].

Canadian Resource Centre for Victims of Crime (2006), *Victims' Rights in Canada*, Ottawa: Canadian Resource Centre for Victims of Crime.

Cape, E. (2004), 'Overview: Is Reconciliation Possible?', in E. Cape (ed.), *Reconcilable Rights? Analysing the Tension Between Victims and Defendants*, London: Legal Action Group, 1–18.

Čapek, S. (1993), 'The Environmental Justice Frame: A Conceptual Discussion and an Application', *Social Problems*, 40(1): 5–24.

Cardwell, P., French, D. and Hall, M. (2011), 'Tackling Environmental Crime in the European Union: The Case of the Missing Victim?', *Environmental Liability*, 19(2): 35–44.

Carrabine, E., Iganski, P., Lee, M., Plummer, K. and South, N. (2004), *Criminology: A Sociological Introduction*, Abingdon: Routledge Publishing.

Cassese, A., Gaeta, P. and Jones, J. (2002), *The Rome Statute of the International Criminal Court*, Oxford: Oxford University Press.

Castle, P. (1996), *Study of Civil Liability Systems for Remedying Environmental Damage*, London: CMS Cameron McKenna.

Catton, W. (1993), 'Carrying Capacity and the Death of a Culture: A Tale of Two Autopsies', *Sociological Inquiry*, 63(2): 202–223.

Cavanagh, M. (1984), *Compensation for Crime Victims*, Issue Brief Number IB74014, Washington: The Library of Congress Congressional Research Service.

Cazaux, G. (1999), 'Beauty and the Beast: Animal Abuse from a Non-speciesist Criminological Perspective', *Crime, Law & Social Change*, 31: 105–126.

Chalecki, E. (2001), 'A New Vigilance: Identifying and Reducing the Risks of Environmental Terrorism', *Global Environmental Politics*, 2(1): 46–64.

Chan, J. (1996), 'Changing Police Culture', *British Journal of Criminology*, 36(1): 109–134.

Charlesworth, H., Chinkin, C. and Wright, S. (2001), 'Feminist Approaches to International Law', *American Journal of International Law*, 85: 613–645.

Chasteen, A. (2001), 'Constructing Rape: Feminism, Change, and Women's Everyday Understandings of Sexual Assault', *Sociological Spectrum*, 21(2): 101–139.

Cheng, B. (1965), 'United Nations resolutions on Outer Space: "Instant" Customary Law?', *Indian Journal of International Law*, 5: 23–48.

Chinese Network Television (2011), *China passes amendments to criminal law* [online]. Available at: http://english.cntv.cn/program/china24/20110226/107569.shtml [accessed 26 May 11].

Chivian, E., McGally M., Hu, H. and Haines, A. (1993), *Critical Condition: Human Health and the Environment*, Cambridge: MIT Press.

Christie, N. (1977), 'Conflicts as Property', *British Journal of Criminology*, 17: 1–15.

Christie, N. (1986), 'The Ideal Victim', in E. Fattah (ed.), *From Crime Policy to Victim Policy*, Basingstoke: Macmillan, 17–30.

Clancy, A. and Hough, M. (2001), *Crime, Policing and Justice: the Experience of Ethnic Minorities – Findings from the 2000 British Crime Survey*, Home Office Research Study 223, London: Home Office Development and Statistics Directorate.

Clements, B. (2012), 'Exploring public opinion on the issue of climate change in Britain', *British Politics,*7: 183–202.

Cole, A. (2007), *The cult of true victimhood*, Stanford: Stanford University Press.

Collin, R. (1994), 'Review of the Legal Literature on Environmental Racism, Environmental Equity and Environmental Justice', *Journal of Environmental Law and Litigation*, 9: 121–170.

Coomans, F. (2003), 'The Ogoni Case before the African Commission on Human and Peoples' Rights', *The International and Comparative Law Quarterly*, 52(3): 749–760.

Council of Europe (1998), *Convention on the Protection of the Environment through Criminal Law: Explanatory Report*, ETS n.172. Available at www.conventions.coe.int/Treaty/en/Reports/Html/172.htm [accessed 26 June 2012].

Cowell, R. (2010), 'Environmental Compensation and the Mediation of Environmental Change: Making Capital out of Cardiff Bay', *Journal of Environmental Planning and Management*, 43(5): 689–710.

Crawford, J. (2002), *The International Law Commission's Articles on State Responsibility: Introductions, Texts and Commentaries*, Cambridge: Cambridge University Press.

Cressey, D. (1986), 'Research Implications of Conflicting Conceptions of Victimology', in E. Fattah (ed.), *Towards a Critical Victimology*, London: Macmillan, 43–54.

Criminal Injuries Compensation Authority (2008), *The Criminal Injuries Compensation Scheme*, London: CICA.

Critharis, M. (1990), 'Third World Nations are Down in the Dumps: The Exportation', *Brooklyn Journal of International Law*, 16: 311–340.

Croall, H. (2007), 'Food Crime', in P. Beirne and N. South (eds) , *Issues in Green Criminology: Confronting Harms Against Environments, Humanity and Other Animals*, Cullompton: Willan, 206–229.

Croall, H. (2010), 'Economic Crime and Victimology: A Critical Appraisal', *Journal International de Victimologie*, 23. Available at: www.jidv.com/njidv/index.php/archives/150-jidv-23/425-economic-crime-and-victimology-a-critical-appraisal [accessed 26 June 2012].

Cross, F. (1989), *Environmentally Induced Cancer and the Law: Risks, Regulation, and Victim Compensation*, Santa Barbara: Greenwood Press.

Crowhurst, G. and Murphy, J. (2006), 'UK's Environmental Watchdog Brought to Heel', *European Energy and Environmental Law Review*, 15: 234–237.

Cryer, R. (2010), 'International Criminal Law', in M. Evans (ed.), *International Law*, Oxford: Oxford University Press, 3rd edition, 753–783.

Cullinan, P., Acquilla, S. and Dhara, V. (1996), 'Long Term Morbidity in Survivors of the 1984 Bhopal Gas Leak', *National Medical Journal of India*, 9(1): 5–10.

Dal Bó, E. (2006), 'Regulatory Capture: A Review', *Oxford Review of Economic Policy*, 22(2): 203–225.

D'Amato, A. (1982), 'The Concept of Human Rights in International Law', *Columbia Law Review*, 82(6): 1110–1159.

d'Aspremont, J. (2008), 'Softness in International Law: A Self-Serving Quest for New Legal Materials', *The European Journal of International Law*, 19: 1057–1093.

Davis, J.-D. (2005), *State Responsibility for Global Climate Change: The Case of the Maldives*, Medford: Tufts Fletcher School.

DeMerieux, M. (2001), 'Deriving Environmental Rights from the European Convention for the Protection of Human Rights and Fundamental Freedoms', *Oxford Journal of Legal Studies*, 21(3): 521–561.

Denton, R. (2000). 'Gendered Impacts of Climate Change – A Human Security Dimension', *Energia*, 3(3): 13–14.

Department of Health (UK) (1998), *Quantification of the Effects of Air Pollution on Health in the United Kingdom – Committee on the Medical Effects of Air Pollutants*, London: The Stationery Office.

Deschênes, O. and Greenstone, M. (2007), 'The Economic Impacts of Climate Change: Evidence from Agricultural Output and Random Fluctuations in Weather', *The American Economic Review*, 97(1): 354–385.

Deutsche Welle (2011), 'French Nuclear Test Victims Reprise Compensation Struggle'. Available at: www.dw.de/french-nuclear-test-victims-reprise-compensation-struggle/a-15293211-1 [accessed 6 November 2012].

Diamond, J. (2005), *Collapse: How Societies Choose to Fail or Succeed*, New York: Penguin Books.

Dignan, J. (2002), 'Restorative Justice and the Law: The Case for an Integrated, Systemic Approach', in L. Walgrave (ed.), *Restorative Justice and the Law*, Cullompton: Willan Publishing, 168–190.

Dignan, J. (2004), *Understanding Victims and Restorative Justice*, Maidenhead: Open University Press.

Doak, J. (2003), 'The Victim and the Criminal Process: An Analysis of Recent Trends in Regional and International Tribunals', *Legal Studies*, 23: 1–32.

Doak, J. (2005), 'Victims' Rights in Criminal Trials: Prospects for Participation', *Journal of Law and Society*, 32: 294–316.

Dobson, A. (1998), *Justice and the Environment: Conceptions of Environmental Sustainability and Dimensions of Social Justice*, Oxford: Oxford University Press.

Dolan, P. and Moore, S. (2007), 'From Preferences to Experiences: Valuing the Intangible Victim Costs of Crime', *International Review of Victimology*, 14(2): 265–280.

Dolan, P., Netten, A., Shapland, J. and Tsuchiya, A. (2007), 'Towards a Preference-Based Measure of the Impact on Well-Being Due to Victimisation and the Fear of Crime', *International Review of Victimology*, 14(2): 253–264.

Domroes, M. (2001), 'Conceptualising State-Controlled Resort Islands for an Environment-Friendly Development of Tourism: The Maldivian Experience', *Singapore Journal of Tropical Geography*, 22(2): 122–137.

Doyle, C. (2008), *Crime Victims' Rights Act*, Hauppauge: Novinka.

Dryzek, J. and Hunter, S. (1987), 'Environmental Mediation for International Problems', *International Studies Quarterly*, 31(1): 87–102.

D'Silva, T. (2006), *The Black Box of Bhopal: A Closer Look at the World's Deadliest Industrial Disaster*, Bloomington: Trafford Publishing.

Duff, P. (1998), 'The Measure of Criminal Injuries Compensation: Political Pragmatism or Dog's Dinner?', *Oxford Journal of Legal Studies*, 18(1): 105–142.

Duffy, R. (2010), *Nature Crime: How We're Getting Conservation Wrong*, New Haven: Yale University Press.

Dunlap, R., Gallup, G. and Gallup, A. (1993): 'International Public Opinion Toward the Environment', *Impact Assessment*, 11(1): 3–25.

Dupont-Morales, M. (1998), 'Constructing the Case Study in Victimology', *Journal of Criminal Justice Education*, 9(2): 293–302.

Du Rées, H. (2001), 'Can Criminal Law Protect the Environment?', *Journal of Scandinavian Studies in Criminology and Crime Prevention*, 2: 109–126. Reprinted in R. White (ed.) (2009), *Environmental Crime: A Reader*, Cullompton: Willan Publishing, 638–655.

Eagleton, C. (1928), *Responsibility of States in International Law*, New York: New York University Press.

Ebebku, K. (2003), 'Judicial Attitudes to Redress for Oil-Related Environmental Damage in Nigeria', *Review of European Community & International Environmental Law*, 12(2): 199–208.

Edwards, H. (1985), 'Alternative Dispute Resolution: Panacea or Anathema', *Harvard Law Review*, 99: 668–684.

Edwards, I. (2004), 'An Ambiguous Participant: The Crime Victim and Criminal Justice Decision-Making', *British Journal of Criminology*, 44: 967–982.

Edwards, S., Edwards, T. and Fields, C. (1996), *Environmental Crime and Criminality: Theoretical and Practical Issues*, New York: Garland Publishing.

Elias, R. (1983), *Victims of the System: Crime Victims and Compensation in American Politics and Criminal Justice*, New Brunswick: Transaction.

Elias, R. (1986), *The Politics of Victimization: Victims, Victimology and Human Rights*, New York: Oxford University Press.

Ellis, C. (2005), 'No Hammock for the Idle: The Conservative Party, "Youth" and the Welfare State in the 1960s', *20th Century British History*, 16: 441–470.

Eradicating Ecocide (2012), *The Problem* [online]. Available at: www.eradicatingecocide.com/theproblem/ [accessed 2 July 2012].

Erez, E. (1994), 'Victim Participation in Sentencing: And the Debate Goes On', *International Review of Victimology*, 3: 17–32.

Erez, E. (1999), 'Who's Afraid of the Big Bad Victim? Victim Impact Statements as Victim Empowerment and Enforcement of Justice', *Criminal Law Review*, July: 545–556.

Erez, E. (2000), 'Integrating a Victim Perspective in Criminal Justice through Victim Impact Statements', in A. Crawford and J. Goodey (eds) , *Integrating a Victim Perspective Within Criminal Justice: International Debates*, Aldershot: Ashgate Dartmouth, 165–184.

Erez, E. (2004), 'Integrating Restorative Justice Principles in Adversarial Proceedings Through Victim Impact Statements', in E. Cape (ed.), *Reconcilable Rights? Analysing the Tension between Victims and Defendants*, London: Legal Action Group, 81–96.

Erez, E. and Rogers, L. (1999), 'Victim Impact Statements and Sentencing Outcomes and Processes: The Perspective of Legal Professions', *British Journal of Criminology*, 39(2): 216–239.

Erez, E., Roeger, L. and Morgan, F. (1997), 'Victim Harm, Impact Statements and Victim Satisfaction with Justice: An Australian Experience', *International Review of Victimology*, 5: 37–60.

European Commission (2001), 'Proposal for a Directive of the European Parliament and of the Council on the Protection of the Environment through Criminal Law', Official Journal, 180 E 26/06/2001:0238–0243. Available at: http://eurlex.europa.eu/LexUriServ/LexUriServ.do?uri=CELEX:52001PC0139:EN:HTML [accessed 4 July 2012].

European Law Monitor (2012), *Parliament and Council Agree Basic Rights for Crime Victims Across the EU*. Available at: www.europeanlawmonitor.org/latest-eu-news/parliament-and-council-agree-basic-rights-for-crime-victims-across-the-eu.html [accessed 2 July 2012].

Fagan, B. (2008), *The Great Warming: Climate Change and the Rise and Fall of Civilizations*, New York: Bloomsbury Press.

Farber, D. (2007), 'Compensation for Victims of Climate Change', *University of Pennsylvania Law Review*, 155: 1605–1656.

Farrall, S. and Maltby, S. (2003), 'The Victimisation of Probationers', *Howard Journal of Criminal Justice*, 42(1): 32–54.

Faust, K. and Carlson, S. (2011), 'Devastation in the Aftermath of Hurricane Katrina as a State Crime: Social Audience Reactions', *Crime, Law and Social Change*, 55(1): 33–51.

Fattah, E. (1992), 'Victims and Victimology: The Facts and the Rhetoric', in E. Fattah (ed.), *Towards a Critical Victimology*, New York: Macmillan, 29–56.

Fenwick, H. (1995), 'Rights of Victims in the Criminal Justice System: Rhetoric or Reality?', *Criminal Law Review*, November: 843–853.

Ferguson, A. (2011), 'We're Victims, Too!: The Need for Greater Protection of Environmental Crime Victims Under the Crime Victims Rights Act', *Pennsylvania State Environmental Law Review*, 19: 287.

Fisher, C. (2001), 'The Role of Causation in Science as Law and Proposed Changes in the Current Common Law Toxic Tort System', *Buffalo Environmental Law Journal*, 9: 35–56.

Fletcher, M., Loof, R. and Gilmore, B. (2008), *EU Criminal Law and Justice*. Cheltenham: Edward Elgar Publishing.

Foster, J. (1999), 'Marx's Theory of Metabolic Rift: Classical Foundations for Environmental Sociology', *American Journal of Sociology*, 105(2): 366–405.

Freight Transport Association (2011), *Bunker Levy Passes the Buck on Tackling Climate Change* [online]. Available at: BSC www.fta.co.uk/media_and_campaigns/press_releases/20110714_bunker_levy_passes_the_buck_on_tackling_climate_change_says_bsc.html [accessed 6 July 2012].

Friedman, D. (1997). 'USA: Private Prosecution of Criminal Conduct', *Journal of Financial Crime*, 5(2): 130–137.

Fry, M. (1951), *Arms of the Law*, London: Gollancz.

Furedi, F. (1998), 'A New Britain – A Nation of Victims', *Society*, 35: 80–84.

Garkawe, S. (2004), 'Revisiting the Scope of Victimology – How Broad a Discipline Should it Be?', *International Review of Victimology*, 11: 275–294.

Garland, D. (2001), *The Culture of Control: Crime and Social Order in Contemporary Society*, Oxford: Oxford University Press.

Gibbs, C., Gore, M., McGarrell, E. and Rivers, L. (2010), 'Introducing Conservation Criminology: Towards Interdisciplinary Scholarship on Environmental Crimes and Risks', *British Journal of Criminology*, 50(1): 124–144.

Giddens, A. (1984), *The Constitution of Society*, Cambridge: Polity Press.

Giddens, A. (1990), *The Consequences of Modernity*, Cambridge: Polity Press.

Girard, A., Day, S. and Snider, L. (2010), 'Tracking Environmental Crime Through CEPa: Canada's Environment Cops or Industry's Best Friend?', *Canadian Journal of Sociology*, 35(2): 219–241.

Gold, S. (1986), 'Causation in Toxic Torts: Burdens of Proof, Standards of Persuasion, and Statistical Evidence', *The Yale Law Journal*, 96(2): 376–402.

Goldberg, J. and Zipersky, B. (2011), 'Civil Recourse Revisited', *Florida State University Law Review*, 39: 341–371.

Goodey, J. (2005), *Victims and Victimology: Research, Policy and Practice*, Edinburgh: Pearson Publishing.

Goodstein, E. (1994), *Jobs and the Environment: The Myth of a National Trade-off*, Washington, DC: Economic Policy Institute.

Gottberg, A., Morris, J., Pollard, S., Mark-Herbert, C. and Cook, M. (2006), 'Producer Responsibility, Waste Minimisation and the WEEE Directive: Case Studies in Eco-design from the European Lighting Sector', *Science of the Total Environment*, 359: 38–56.

Gray, M. (1996), 'The International Crime of Ecocide', *California Western International Law Journal*, 26: 215–272.

Green, D. (2006), *We're (Nearly) All Victims Now!*, London: CIViTAS.

Green, P. and Ward, T. (2004), *State Crime*, London: Pluto Press.

Griffin, S. (1978), *Woman and Nature: The Roaring Inside Her*, New York: Harper and Row.

Groenhuijsen, M. and Pemberton, A. (2009), 'The EU Framework Decision for Victims of Crime: Does Hard Law Make a Difference?', *European Journal of Crime, Criminal Law and Criminal Justice*, 17: 43–59.

Groombridge, N. (1991), *Corporate Crime: An Environmental View* [online]. Available at: www.criminologyinpublic.com/greencriminology.html [accessed 25 June 2012].

Hall, M. (2009), *Victims of Crime: Policy and Practice in Criminal Justice*, Cullompton: Willan Publishing.

Hall, M. (2010), *Victims and Policy Making: A Comparative Approach*, Cullompton: Willan Publishing.

Hall, M. and Farrall, S. (forthcoming), 'The Criminogenic Consequences of Climate Change: Blurring the Boundaries Between Offenders and Victims', in N. South and A. Brisman (eds) , *International Handbook of Green Criminology*, Abingdon: Routledge Publishing.

Hall, M. and Shapland, J. (forthcoming), 'International Responses to Victims in Criminal Justice: Progress and Challenges for the 21st Century', in G. Bruinsma and D. Weisburd (eds) , *Encyclopaedia of Criminology and Criminal Justice*, New York: Springer Publishing.

Halsey, M. (2004), 'Against 'Green' Criminology', *British Journal of Criminology*, 44(6): 833–853.

Hamilton, J. (1995), 'Testing for Environmental Racism: Prejudice, Profits, Political Power?', *Journal of Policy Analysis and Management*, 14(1): 107–132.

Harland, A. (1978), 'Compensating the Victim of Crime', *Criminal Law Bulletin*, 14: 203–224.

Harrison, N. and Bryner, G. (2004), *Science and Politics in the International Environment*. Lanham: Rowman & Littlefield Publishers.

Harvey, F. (2011), 'Climate Change Adviser Warns of Coming Test for Cameron's Green Credentials', *Guardian* [online]. Available at: www.guardian.co.uk/uk/2011/may/09/climate-defining-green-moment-cameron [accessed 26 June 2012].

Hayman, G. and Brack, D., *International Environmental Crime: The Nature and Control of Environmental Black Markets*, London: Royal Institute of International Affairs.

Heckler, H. (2011), *Peace and Sustainable Development Through Environmental Security*, The Hague: Institute for Environmental Security.

Helm, D. and Hepburn, C. (2009), *The Economics and Politics of Climate Change*, Oxford: Oxford University Press.

Higgins, R. (1978), 'Conceptual Thinking about the Individual in International Law', *British Journal of International Studies*, 4: 1–10.

Hillyard, P. (2006), 'Crime Obsessions: Crime Isn't the Only Harm', *Criminal Justice Matters*, 62: 26–46.

Hillyard, P. and Toombs, D. (2003), 'Introduction', in P. Hillyard, D. Toombs and C. Pantazis (eds) , *Beyond Criminology: Taking Harm Seriously*, London: Pluto Press, 1–9.

Hiskes, R. (2008), *The Human Right to a Green Future: Environmental Rights and Intergenerational Justice*, Cambridge: Cambridge University Press.

Hofrichter, R. (1993), *Toxic Struggles: The Theory and Practice of Environmental Justice*, Philadelphia: New Society Publishers.

Holdaway, S. (1983), *Inside the British Police: A Force at Work*, Oxford: Blackwell Publishing.

Holder, J. and Lee, M., *Environmental Protection, Law and Policy*, 2nd edition, Cambridge: Cambridge University Press.

Home Office (2005), *Hearing the Relatives of Murder and Manslaughter Victims: The Government's Plans to Give the Bereaved Relatives of Murder and Manslaughter Victims a Say in Criminal Proceedings: Consultation*, London: Home Office.

Homer-Dixon, T., Boutwell, J. and Rathjens, G. (2011), 'Environmental Change and Violent Conflict: Growing Scarcities of Renewable Resources can Contribute to Social Instability and Civil Strife', *Warfare Ecology*, 1: 18–25.

Houck, O. (2003), 'Tales from a Troubled Marriage: Science and Law in Environmental Policy', *Science*, 302: 1926.

Hough, M. (1986), 'Victims of Violent Crime: Findings from the First British Crime Survey', in E. Fattah (ed.), *From Crime Policy to Victim Policy*, Basingstoke: Macmillan, 117–132.

Hough, P. (2012), *Environmental Security: An Introduction*, Abingdon: Routledge Publishing.
House of Commons Environmental Audit Committee (2004), *Environmental Crime and the Courts: Sixth Report of Session 03–04*, London: The Stationery Office.
Hulsman, L. (1986), 'Critical Criminology and the Concept of Crime', in H. Bianchi and R. van Swaaningen (eds) , *Abolitionism: Towards a Non-Repressive Approach to Crime*, Amsterdam: Free University Press.
Institute of Law Research and Reform (1968), *Compensation for Victims of Crime*, Report No. 1, Edmonton: University of Alberta.
International Association for the Study of Insurance Economics (2009), *The Insurance Industry and Climate Change – Contribution to the Global Debate*, Geneva: The Geneva Association.
International Criminal Court (2002), *Rules of Procedure and Evidence*, The Hague: International Criminal Court.
International Criminal Court (2005), *Code of Judical Ethics*, The Hague: International Criminal Court.
International Law Commission (2006), *Draft Principles on the Allocation of Loss in the Case of Transboundary Harm Arising out of Hazardous Activities, with Commentaries*, report on the work of the fifty-eighth session – 1 May to 9 June and 3 July to 11 August 2006, General Assembly Official Records Sixty-first Session Supplement No. 10 (A/61/10).
Irish Criminal Injuries Compensation Tribunal (2009), *Scheme of Compensation for Personal Injuries Criminally Inflicted – As Amended from 1st April 1986*, Dublin: Irish Criminal Injuries Compensation Tribunal.
Ivanic, M. and Martin, W. (2008), *Implications of Higher Global Food Prices for Poverty in Low-Income Countries*, World Bank Policy Research Working Paper No. 4594, Washington, DC: The World Bank.
Jackson, J. (1990), 'Getting Criminal Justice Out of Balance', in S. Livingstone and J. Morison (eds) , *Law, Society and Change*, Aldershot: Dartmouth, 114–133.
Jackson, J. (2003), 'Justice for All: Putting Victims at the Heart of Criminal Justice?', *Journal of Law and Society*, 30: 309–326.
Jackson, J. (2004), 'Putting Victims at the Heart of Criminal Justice: The Gap Between Rhetoric and Reality', in E. Cape (ed.), *Reconcilable Rights? Analysing the Tension Between Victims and Defendants*, London: Legal Action Group, 65–80.
Jackson, J., Kilpatrick, R. and Harvey, C. (1991), *Called to Court: A Public Review of Criminal Justice in Northern Ireland*, Belfast: SLS Legal Publications.
Jackson, T. (2000), 'The Employment and Productivity Effects of Environmental Taxation: Additional Dividends or Added Distractions?', *Journal of Environmental Planning and Management*, 43(3): 389–406.
Jaggi, B. and Freedman, M. (2006), 'An Examination of the Impact of Pollution Performance on Economic and Market Performance: Pulp and Paper Firms', *Journal of Business Finance & Accounting*, 19(5): 673–713.
Jamaican Ministry of Justice (2006), *Towards a Victims' Charter*, Kingston: Jamaican Ministry of Justice.
Jasparro, C. and Taylor, J. (2008), 'Climate Change and Regional Vulnerability to Transnational Security Threats in Southeast Asia', *Geopolitics*, 13(2): 232–256.
Johnson, K. (2004), 'International Human Rights Class Actions: New Frontiers for Group Litigation', *Michigan State Law Review*, 643.

Jordan, A., Rüdiger, K. and Zito, A. (2005), 'The Rise of "New Policy" Instruments in Comparative Perspective: Has Governance Eclipsed Government?', *Political Studies*, 53: 477–496.

Jordan, J. (2004), 'Beyond Belief? Police, Rape and Women's Credibility, *Criminal Justice*, 4: 29–59.

JUSTICE Committee Victims in Criminal Justice (1998), *Report of the JUSTICE Committee on the Role of Victims in Criminal Justice*, London: JUSTICE.

Karstedt, S. and Farrall, S. (2006), 'The Moral Economy of Everyday Crime: Markets, Consumers and Citizens', *British Journal of Criminology*, 46(6): 1011–1036.

Katz, R. (2010), 'The Corporate Crimes of Dow Chemical and the Failure to Regulate Environmental Pollution', *Critical Criminology*, 18: 295–306.

Kauzlarich, D., Matthews, R. and Miller, W. (2001), 'Toward a Victimology of State Crime', *Critical Criminology*, 10: 173–194.

Kearon, T. and Godfrey, B. (2007), 'Setting the Scene: A Question of History', in S. Walklate (ed.), *Handbook of Victims and Victimology*, Cullompton: Willan Publishing, 17–36.

Kirchhoff, G. (1994), 'Victimology – History and Basic Concepts', in G. Kirchhoff, E. Kosovski and H. Schneider (eds) , *International Debates of Victimology*, Monchengladbach: WSV Publishing, 1–81.

Kotzé, L. and Paterson, A. (2009), *The Role of the Judiciary in Environmental Governance: Comparative Perspectives*, Amsterdam: Wolters Kluwer.

Kramer, R., Michalowski, R. and Kauzlarich, D. (2002). 'The Origins and Development of the Concept and Theory of State-corporate Crime', *Crime and Delinquency*, 48(2): 263–282.

Lauritsen, J., Sampson, R. and Laub, J. (1991), 'The Link between Offending and Victimization among Adolescents', *Criminology*, 29: 265–291.

Lawrence, R. (2006), 'Research Dissemination: Activity Bringing the Research and Policy Worlds Together', *Evidence & Policy*, 2: 373–384.

Lee, M. (2007), *Human Trafficking*, Cullompton: Willan Publishing.

Lee, M. and Blanchard, T. (2010), *Health Impacts of Deepwater Horizon Oil Disaster on Coastal Louisiana Residents*, Baton Rouge: Louisiana State University Press.

Lee, T. (2011), 'Gulf Shrimp Season Begins In Louisiana Under Oil-Black Cloud' [online], *The Huffington Post*. Available at: www.huffingtonpost.com/2011/08/22/start-of-louisianas-shrim_n_933472.html?ir=Green&ncid=edlinkusaolp00000008 [accessed 26 June 2012].

Lee, T.H-P. (2009), *A Welfare Approach to Mitigating Environmental Injustice: Exploring Needs of Pollution Victims* [online]. Available at: www.welfareacademy.org/pubs/international/epckdi/2.pdf [accessed 26 June 2012].

Lenaerts, K. and Gutiérrez-Fons, A. (2010), 'The Constitutional Allocation of Powers and General Principles of EU Law', *Common Market Law Reports*, 47(6): 1640–1644.

Lepage, H. & Partners (2007), *Study on Environmental Crime in the 27 Member States*. Available at http://ec.europa.eu/environment/legal/crime/pdf/report_environmental_crime.pdf [accessed 26 June 2012].

Levinson, A. (1996), 'Environmental Regulations and Manufacturers' Location Choices: Evidence from the Census of Manufacture', *Journal of Public Economics*, 62: 5–29.

Lidstone, K., Hogg, R. and Sutcliffe, F. (1980), *Prosecutions by Private Individuals and Non-Police Agencies*, London: Royal Commission on Criminal Procedure.

Lin, A. (2005), 'Beyond Tort: Compensating Victims of Environmental Toxic Injury', *Southern California Law Review*, 78: 1439–1528.

Liu, J. (2007) 'Principles of Restorative Justice and Confucius Philosophy in China', *European Forum for Restorative Justice*, 8(1): 2–3.
Liu, X., Tanaka, M. and Matsui, Y. (2006), 'Electrical and Electronic Waste Management in China: Progress and the Barriers to Overcome', *Waste Management & Research*, 24: 92–101.
Lobell, D., Schlenker, W. and Costa-Roberts, J. (2011), 'Climate Trends and Global Crop Production Since 1980', *Science*, 5 May: 1204531.
Lonergan, S. (1998), 'The Role of Environmental Degradation in Population Displacement', *Environmental Change and Security Project Report*, 4: 5–15.
Loomes, G. (2007), 'Valuing Reductions in the Risks of Being a Victim of Crime: The "Willingness to Pay" Approach to Valuing the "Intangible" Consequences of Crime', *International Review of Victimology*, 14(2): 237–251.
Lury, C. and Wakeford, N. (2012), *Innovative Methods: The Happening of the Social*, Abingdon: Routledge.
Lynch, M. (1990), 'The Greening of Criminology', *Critical Criminologist*, 2: 1–5.
Lynch, M. and Stretesky, P. (2001), 'Toxic Crimes: Examining Corporate Victimization of the General Public Employing Medical and Epidemiological Evidence', *Critical Criminology*, 10: 153–172.
Lynch, M. and Stretesky, P. (2003), 'The Meaning of Green: Towards a Clarification of the Term Green and its Meaning for the Development of a Green Criminology', *Theoretical Criminology*, 7: 217–238.
Lynch, M. and Stretesky, P. (2007), 'Green Criminology in the United States', in P. Beirne and N. South (eds) , *Issues in Green Criminology: Confronting Harms Against Environments, Humanity and Other Animals*, Cullompton: Willan Publishing, 248–269.
Lynch, M., Burns, R. and Stretesky, P. (2010), 'Global Warming and State-corporate Crime: The Politicalization of Global Warming under the Bush Administration', *Crime, Law and Social Change*, 54(3–4): 213–239.
Macleod, A., Pautasso, M., Jeger, M. and Haines-Young, R. (2010) 'Evolution of the International Regulation of Plant Pests and Challenges for Future Plant Health', *Food Security*, 2: 49–70.
Macpherson (1999), *The Stephen Lawrence Inquiry: Report of an Inquiry by Sir William Macpherson of Cluny*, London: HMSO.
Maginnis, J. (2002), *The 9/11 Victim Compensation Fund: Overview and Comment*, Washington, DC: The Federalist Society for Law and Public Policy Studies.
Maguire, M. (1991), 'The Needs and Rights of Victims of Crime', in M. Tonry (ed.), *Crime and Justice: A Review of Research*, Chicago: Chicago University Press, 363–433.
Malarkey, T. (2003), 'Human Health Concerns with GM Crops', *Mutation Research/Reviews in Mutation Research*, 544(2–3): 217–221.
Malsch, M. (1999), 'Victims' Wishes for Compensation: The Immaterial Aspect', *Journal of Criminal Justice*, 27: 239–247.
Mandalia, S. (2005), 'The Spice Traders' Tale', *New Statesman,* 7 March 2005: 14.
Mares, D. (2010), 'Criminalizing Ecological Harm: Crimes Against Carrying Capacity and the Criminalization of Eco-Sinners', *Critical Criminology*, 18: 279–293.
Marmo, M. and La Forgia, R. (2008), 'Inclusive National Governance and Trafficked Women in Australia: Otherness and Local Demand', *Asian Criminology*, 3: 173–191.
Marquart-Pyatta, S., Shwomb, R., Dietza, T., Dunlapc, R., Kaplowitza, S., McCrighta, A. and Zahrand, S. (2011), 'Understanding Public Opinion on Climate Change: A Call for Research', *Environment: Science and Policy for Sustainable Development*, 53(4): 38–42.

Martuzzi, F., Mitis, F., Bianchi, F., Minichilli, F., Comba, P. and Fazzo, L. (2009), 'Cancer Mortality and Congenital Anomalies in a Region of Italy with Intense Environmental Pressure due to Waste', *Occupational Environmental Medicine*, 66: 725–732.

Mason, M. (2003), 'Civil Liability for Oil Pollution Damage: Examining the Evolving Scope for Environmental Compensation in the International Regime', *Marine Policy*, 27(1): 1–12.

Matsumoto, S. (2011), 'A Duration Analysis of Environmental Alternative Dispute Resolution in Japan', *Ecological Economics*, 70: 659–666.

Matthews, B. and Ross, L. (2010), *Research Methods: A Practical Guides for the Social Sciences*, London: Longman Publishing.

Matthews, R. and Kauzlarich, D. (2007), 'State Crimes and State Harms: A Tale of Two Definitional Frameworks', *Crime, Law and Social Change*, 48: 42–55.

McBarnet, D. (1983), 'Victim in the Witness Box – Confronting Victimology's Stereotype', *Crime, Law and Social Change*, 7: 293–303.

McEldowney, J. and McEldowney, S. (2011), 'Science and Environmental Law: Collaboration Across the Double Helix', *Environmental Law Review*, 13(3): 169–197.

McMahon, M. (1990), '"NET-WIDENING" Vagaries in the Use of a Concept', *British Journal of Criminology*, 30(2): 121–149.

McMichael, A. (2006), 'Climate Change and Human Health: Present and Future Risks', *The Lancet*, 367(9513): 859–869.

McMurray, R. and Ramsey, S. (1986), 'Environmental Crime: The Use of Criminal Sanctions in Enforcing Environmental Laws', *Loyola of Los Angeles Law Review*, 19: 1133–1169.

Mendelsohn, B. (1956), 'A New Branch of Bio-psychological Science: La Victimology', *Revue Internationale de Criminologie et de Police Technique*, 2.

Mendelsohn, R., Dinar, A. and Williams, L. (2006), 'The Distributional Impact of Climate Change on Rich and Poor Countries', *Environment and Development Economics*, 11: 159–178.

Mernitz, S. (1980), *Mediation of Environmental Disputes*, New York: Praeger.

Meron, T. (1986), 'On a Hierarchy of International Human Rights', *The American Journal of International Law*, 80(1): 1–23.

Miers, D. (1980), 'Victim Compensation as a Labelling Process', *Victimology*, 5: 3–16.

Miers, D. (1990), 'Positivist Victimology: A Critique; Part 2: Critical Victimology', *International Review of Victimology*, 1(3): 219–230.

Miers, D. (1991), *Compensation for Criminal Injuries*, London: Butterworths.

Miers, D. (1997), *State Compensation for Criminal Injuries*, London: Blackstone.

Miller, K. (2008) *Empowering Victims: The Use of the Victim Impact Statement in the Case of Sexual Assault in Nova Scotia. The Perspective of Victims and Victim Services Staff*, Toronto: Centre of Criminology, University of Toronto.

Minkes, J. and Minkes, L. (2008), *Corporate and White Collar Crime*, London: Sage Publishing.

Mitsilegas, V. (2009), *EU Criminal Law*, Oxford: Hart Publishing.

Montgomery, D. (2007). *Dirt, the Erosion of Civilizations*, Berkeley: University of California Press.

Morgan, R. and Sanders, A. (1999), *The Use of Victim Statements*, London: Home Office.

Mörner, N-A., Tooley, M. and Possnert, G. (2004), 'New Perspectives for the Future of the Maldives', *Global and Planetary Change*, 40(1–2): 177–182.

Morss, E. (1996), 'Clean Air Act Implementation: An Industry Perspective', *Pace Environmental Law Review*, 14(1): 63–68.

Mouzelis, N. (2008), *Modern and Postmodern Social Theorising*, Cambridge: Cambridge University Press.

Moxon, D., Martin, J. and Hedderman, C. (1992), *Developments in the Use of Compensation Orders in Magistrates' Courts since October 1988*, Home Office Research Study 126, London: Home Office.

Mullenix, L. (2004), 'The Future of Tort Reform: Possible Lessons from the World Trade Centre Victim Compensation Fund', *Emory Law Journal*, 53: 1315–1347.

Mullier, E. (2010), 'The Emergence of Criminal Competence to Enforce EC Environmental Law: Directive 2008/99 in the Context of the Case-Law of the European Court of Justice', *Cambridge Student Law Review*, 6(1): 94–116.

Munro, V. (2012), 'Stopping Traffic? A Comparative Study of Responses to the Trafficking in Women for Prostitution', *British Journal of Criminology*, 46(2): 318–333.

Murphy, S. (2000), 'Does the World Need an International Environmental Court?', *George Washington Journal of International Law and Economics*, 32: 333–349.

Murray, S. (2006), 'Poverty and Health', *Canadian Medical Association Journal*, 174(7): 923.

Mythen, G. (2007), 'Cultural Victimology: Are We All Victims Now?', in Walklate, S. (ed.), *Handbook of Victims and Victimology*, Cullompton: Willan Publishing, 464–483.

Mythen, G. and Walklate, S. (2006), 'Criminology and Terrorism: Which Thesis? Risk Society or Governmentality?', *British Journal of Criminology*, 46(3): 379–398.

Nagin, D. and Waldfogel, J. (1998), 'The Effect of Conviction on Income Through the Life Cycle', *International Review of Law and Economics*, 18(1): 25–40.

Nash, R. (1989), *The Rights of Nature: A History of Environmental Ethics,* Madison: University of Wisconsin Press.

Nemani, R., White, M., Cayan, D., Jones, G., Running, S., Coughlan, J. and Peterson, D. (2001). 'Asymmetric Warming Over Coastal California and its Impact on the Premium Wine Industry', *Climate Research*, 19: 25–34.

Newburn, T. (1988), *The Use and Enforcement of Compensation Orders in Magistrates' Courts*, Home Office Research Study 102, London: Home Office.

New Zealand Law Commission (2008), *Compensating Crime Victims*, Issues Paper 11, Wellington: New Zealand Law Commission.

Nola.com (2012), 'BP Oil Spill Payments Speed Up Ahead of Final Settlement' [online]. Available at: www.nola.com/news/gulf-oil-spill/index.ssf/2012/04/bp_oil_spill_payments_speed_up.html [accessed 18 July 2012].

Northeast States for Coordinated Air Use Management (2011), *Economic Analysis of a Program to Promote Clean Transportation Fuels in the Northeast/Mid-Atlantic Region*, Boston: NESCAUM.

O'Hear, M. (2004), 'Sentencing the Green-Collar Offender: Punishment, Culpability, and Environmental Crime', *The Journal of Criminal Law and Criminology*, 95(1): 133–276.

O'Malley, P. (1987), 'Marxist Theory and Marxist Criminology', *Justice: Comparative and Theoretical Issues*, 29: 70–87.

Oreskes, N. (2007), 'The Scientific Consensus on Climate Change: How Do We Know We're Not Wrong?', in J. DiMento and P. Doughman (eds) , *Climate Change: What It Means for Us, Our Children, and Our Grandchildren*, Cambridge, MA: The MIT Press, 68.

Pakes, F. (2011), 'The Comparative Method in Globalised Criminology', *Australian & New Zealand Journal of Criminology*, 43(1): 117–130.

Parmentier, S. (2010), 'Epilogue: Human Trafficking Seen from the Future', *European Journal of Criminology,* 7(1): 95–100.

Passas, N. (2005), '"Lawful but Awful": Legal Corporate Crimes', *Journal of Socio-Economics*, 24: 771–786.

Patrick, D., Bush, J. and Chen, M. (1973), 'Toward an Operational Definition of Health', *Journal of Health and Social Behavior*, 14(1): 6–23.

Patz, J., McGeehin, M., Bernard, S., Ebi, K., Epstein, P., Grambsch, A., Gubler, D., Reiter, P., Romieu, I., Rose, J., Samet, J. and Trtanf, J. (2000), 'The Potential Health Impacts of Climate Variability and Change for the United States: Executive Summary of the Report of the Health Sector of the U.S. National Assessment', *Environmental Health Perspectives*, 108(4): 367–376.

Paulido, L. (2000), 'Rethinking Environmental Racism: White Privilege and Urban Development in Southern Carolina', *Annals of American Geographers*, 90(1): 12–40.

Pearce, F. (2012), 'Beyond Rio's Disappointment: Finding a Path to the Future' [online], *Yale environment360*, 28 June. Available at http://e360.yale.edu/feature/beyond_rios_disappointment_finding_a_path_to_the_future/2547/ [accessed 25 July 2012].

Pearce, F. and Tombs, S. (1990) 'Ideology, Hegemony and Empiricism: Compliance Theories of Regulation', *British Journal of Criminology*, 30(4): 423–443.

Pepper, D. (1993), *Eco-Socialism: From Deep Ecology to Social Justice*, Abingdon: Routledge Publishing.

Pernetta, J. (2002), 'Impacts of Climate Change and Sea-level Rise on Small Island States: National and International Responses', *Global Environmental Change*, 2(1): 19–31.

Peterson, J. and Bomberg, E. (1999), *Decision-Making in the European Union*, New York: Palgrave.

Pinstrup-Andersen, P. (2009), 'Food Security: Definition and Measurement', *Food Security*, 1: 5–7.

Pointing, J. and Maguire, M. (1988), 'Introduction: The Rediscovery of the Crime Victim', in M. Maguire and J. Pointing (eds) , *Victims of Crime: A New Deal?*, Milton Keynes: Open University Press, 1–13.

Possnert, G., Tooley, M. and Mörner, N-A. (2004), 'New Perspectives for the Future of the Maldives', *Global and Planetary Change*, 40: 177–182.

Pulido, L. (2000), 'Rethinking Environmental Racism: White Privilege and Urban Development in Southern California', *Annals of the Association of American Geographers*, 90(1): 12–40.

Pulido, L. (2006), 'A Critical Review of the Methodology of Environmental Racism Research', *Antipode*, 28(2): 142–159.

Queensland Department of Justice and Attorney General (2009), *Victims of Crime Review Report*, Brisbane: Queensland Department of Justice and Attorney General.

Redgwell, C. (2010), 'International Environmental Law', in M. Evans (ed.), *International Law*, 3rd edition, Oxford: Oxford University Press, 687–721.

Reese, C. (2000), 'The Implementation of the UN Declaration of Basic Principles of Justice for Victims of Crime and Abuse of Power in France', *The Victimologist*, 4:1–2.

Reid, H., Sahlén, L., MacGregor, J. and Stage, J. (2007), *The Economic Impact of Climate Change in Namibia: How Climate Change will Affect the Contribution of Namibia's Natural Resources to its Economy*, London: International Institute for Environment and Development.

Reiner, R. (2000), *The Politics of the Police*, Oxford: Oxford University Press.

Richardson, N. (2010), *Deepwater Horizon and the Patchwork of Oil Spill Liability Law*, Washington DC: Resources for the Future. Available at: www.rff.org/RFF/Documents/RFF-BCK-Richardson-OilLiability_update.pdf [accessed 4 July 2012].

Risse, T. Ropp, S. and Sikkink, K. (1999), *The Power of Human Rights: International Norms and Domestic Change*, Cambridge: Cambridge University Press.
Rivers, L. (2012), 'Shareholder Return – A "Nuremberg Defence"? Ecocide and Restorative Justice', *Environmental Law & Management,* 24(1): 17–19.
Roberts, J. and Manikis, M. (2011), *Victim Personal Statements: A Review of Empirical Research*, Report for the Commissioner for Victims and Witnesses in England and Wales, London: Ministry of Justice. Available at: www.justice.gov.uk/downloads/news/press-releases/victims-com/vps-research.pdf [accessed 12 June 2012].
Rock, P. (1986), *A View from the Shadows: The Ministry of the Solicitor General of Canada and the Making of the Justice for Victims of Crime Initiative*, Oxford: Clarendon Press.
Rock, P. (1990), *Helping Victims of Crime: The Home Office and the Rise of Victim Support in England and Wales*, Oxford: Oxford University Press.
Rock, P. (1993), *The Social World of an English Crown Court: Witnesses and Professionals in the Crown Court Centre at Wood Green*, Oxford: Clarendon Press.
Rock, P. (1998), *After Homicide: Practical and Political Responses to Bereavement*, Oxford: Clarendon Press.
Rock, P. (2007), 'Theoretical Perspectives on Victimisation', in S. Walklate (ed.), *Handbook of Victims and Victimology*, Cullompton: Willan Publishing, 37–61.
Rock, P. and Holdaway, S. (1997), *Thinking About Criminology*, London: University College London Press.
Roth, M. (2002), 'Hammurabi's Wronged Man', *Journal of the American Oriental Society*, 122: 38–45.
Rothe, D., Ross, J., Mullins, C., Friedrichs, D., Michalowski, R., Barak, G., Kauzlarich, D. and Kramer, R. (2009), 'That Was Then, This Is Now, What About Tomorrow? Future Directions in State Crime Studies', *Critical Criminology*, 17(1): 3–13.
Roughton, G. (2007), 'The Ancient and the Modern: Environmental Law and Governance in Islam', *Colombia Journal of Environmental Law*, 32: 99–140.
Royal Society for the Prevention of Cruelty to Animals (2012), *Prosecution.* Available at: www.rspca.org.uk/in-action/whatwedo/prosecution [accessed 2 July 2012].
Royal Society for the Prevention of Cruelty to Animals Prosecution Department (2010), *Annual Report 2010*, London: RSPCA. Available at: www.rspca.org.uk/ImageLocator/LocateAsset?asset=document&assetId=1232725934154&mode=prd [accessed 2 July 2012].
Ruggiero, V. and South, N. (2010), 'Critical Criminology and Crimes Against the Environment', *Critical Criminology*, 18: 245–250.
Sampson, R. (2008), 'Rethinking Crime and Immigration', *Contexts*, 7(1): 28–33.
Sanders, A. (2002), 'Victim Participation in an Exclusionary Criminal Justice System', in C. Hoyle and R. Young (eds) , *New Visions of Crime Victims*, Portland: Hart Publishing, 197–222.
Sanders, A. and Young, R. (2000), *Criminal Justice*, London: Butterworths.
Sanders, A., Hoyle, C., Morgan, R. and Cape, E. (2001), 'Victim Impact Statements: Don't Work, Can't Work', *Criminal Law Review*, June: 437–458.
Schadefonds Geweldsmisdrijven (2008), *Have You Been the Victim of Violence?*, Rijswijk: Schadefonds Geweldsmisdrijven.
Schafer, S. (1968), *The Victim and His Criminal: A Study in Functional Responsibility*, New York: Random House.
Schanbacher, W. (2010), *The Politics of Food: The Global Conflict between Food Security and Food Sovereignty*, Santa Barbara: Praeger Security International.

Schneider, H. (1991), 'Restitution Instead of Punishment – Reorientation of Crime Prevention and Criminal Justice in the Context of Development', in G. Kaiser, H. Kury and H. Albrecht (eds) , *Victims and Criminal Justice*, Eigenverlag: Max-Planck Institut, 363–380.

Schofield, T. (1999), 'The Environment as an Ideological Weapon: A Proposal To Criminalize Environmental Terrorism', *Boston College Environmental Affairs Law Review*, 26(3): 619–647.

Schwartz, D. (1998), 'Environmental Terrorism: Analyzing the Concept', *Journal of Peace Research*, 35(4): 483–496.

Shapland, J. (2003). 'Bringing Victims In from the Cold: Victims' Role in Criminal Justice', in J. Jackson and K. Quinn (eds) , *Criminal Justice Reform: Looking to the Future*, Belfast: Institute of Criminology and Criminal Justice, Queens University Belfast, 48–69.

Shapland, J. and Hall, M. (2007), 'What do we Know about the Effect of Crime on Victims?', *International Review of Victimology*, 14: 175–217.

Shapland, J., Atkinson, A., Atkinson, H., Chapman, B., Colledge, E., Dignan, J., Howes, M., Johnstone, J., Robinson, G. and Sorsby, A. (2006), *Restorative Justice in Practice – Findings from the Second Phase of the Evaluation of Three Schemes*, Home Office Research Findings 274, London: Home Office.

Shapland, J., Robinson, G. and Sorsby, A. (2011), *Restorative Justice in Practice*, London: Routledge.

Shapland, J., Willmore, J. and Duff, P. (1985), *Victims and the Criminal Justice System*, Aldershot: Gower.

Shelley, L. (2007), 'Human Trafficking as a Form of Transnational Crime', in Lee, M. (ed.), *Human Trafficking*, Cullompton: Willan Publishing, 116–137.

Shmueli, D. and Kaufman, S. (2006), *Environmental Mediation*, The Center for Environmental Policy Studies Series no. 24, Jerusalem: Center for Environmental Studies.

Sieber, J. (1998), 'Planning Ethically Responsible Research', in L. Bickman and D. Rog (eds) , *Handbook of Applied Social Research Methods*, Thousand Oaks: Sage Publications, 127–156.

Sierra Club Legal Defence Fund (1993), *Human Rights and the Environment: The Legal Basis for Human Rights to the Environment, Report to the UN Sub-Commission on the prevention of Discrimination and Protection*, San Francisco: Sierra Club.

Sills, J., Glenn, J., Florescu, E. and Gordon, T. (2001), 'Environmental Crimes in Military Actions and the International Criminal Court (ICC) – UN Perspectives', in C. Glenn, T. Gordon and E. Florescu (eds) , *State of the Future*, Washington, DC: The Millennium Project. Executive summary available at: http://millennium-project.org/millennium/es-icc.html [accessed 2 July 2012].

Sipe, N. (2007), 'An Empirical Analysis of Environmental Mediation', *Journal of the American Planning Association*, 64(2): 275–285.

Skinnider, E. (2011), *Victims of Environmental Crime – Mapping the Issues*, Vancouver: The International Centre for Criminal Law Reform and Criminal Justice Policy.

Smith, P. (2007), 'Climate Change, Mass Migration and the Military Response', *Orbis*, 51(4): 617–633.

South, N. (1998), 'A Green Field for Criminology: A Proposal for a Perspective', *Theoretical Criminology*, 2(2): 211–233.

South, N. (2010), 'The Ecocidal Tendencies of Late Modernity: Transnational Crime, Social Exclusion, Victims and Rights', in R. White (ed.), *Global Environmental Harm: Criminological Perspectives*, Cullompton: Willan Publishing, 236–240.

South African Department of Justice and Constitutional Development (2008), *Service Charter for Victims of Crime in South Africa*, Pretoria: DoJCD.

Spalek, B. (2006), *Crime Victims: Theory, Policy and Practice*, New York: Palgrave Macmillan.

Spencer, M., Garratt, A., Hockman, E., Bryant, B. and Kohn-Wood, L. (2011), 'Environmental Justice and the Well-being of Poor Children of Color', *Communities, Neighborhoods and Health*, 1(3): 219–233.

Starr, J., Flack, B. and Foley, A. (2008) 'New Intersection: Environmental Crimes and Victims' Rights', *Natural Resources & Environment*, 24: 41–52.

Stebbins, K. (1992), 'Garbage Imperialism: Health Implications of Dumping Hazardous Wastes in Third World Countries', *Medical Anthropology*, 15(1): 81–102.

Steinberg, T. (2008), *Down to Earth: Nature's Role in American History*, Oxford: Oxford University Press.

Stern, N. (2007), *The Economics of Climate Change: The Stern Review*, Cambridge: Cambridge University Press

Stern, N. (2009), *A Blueprint for a Safer Planet: How to Manage Climate Change and Create a New Era of Progress and Prosperity*, London: Bodley Head.

Stewart, R. (1993), 'Environmental Regulation and International Competitiveness', *Yale Law Journal*, 102(8): 2039–2106.

Takemura, N. (2007), *'Criticality of Environmental Crises' and Prospect of 'Complexity Green Criminology'*, Toxin University of Yokohama Research Bulletin 17, Yokohama: Toxin University of Yokohama.

Terazono, A., Murakami, S., Abe, N., Inanc, B., Moriguchi, Y., Sakai, S., Kojima, M., Yoshida, A., Li, J., Yang, J., Wong, M.H., Jain, A., Kim, I., Peralta, G.I., Lin, C., Mungcharoen, T. and Williams, E. (2006), 'Current Status and Research on E-waste Issues in Asia', *Journal of Material Cycles and Waste Management*, 8(1): 1–12.

Thirlway, H. (2010), 'The Sources of International Law', in M. Evans (ed.), *International Law*, 3rd edition, Oxford: Oxford University Press, 95–121.

Thompson, E. (1991), *Customs in Common*, Penguin Books: London.

Tobey, J. and Smets, H. (1996), 'The Polluter-Pays Principle in the Context of Agriculture and the Environment', *The World Economy*, 19: 63–87.

Tombs, S. and Whyte, D. (2010), 'Crime, Harm and Corporate Power', in J. Muncie, D. Talbot and R. Walters (eds) , *Crime: Local and Global*, Cullompton: Willan Publishing, 137–172.

Tyler, T. (1990), *Why People Obey the Law*, New Haven: Yale University Press.

Tyler, T. and Huo, Y. (2002), *Trust in the Law: Encouraging Public Cooperation With the Police and Courts*, New York: Russell-Sage Publishing.

Ullman, R. (1983), 'Redefining Security', *International Security*, 8(1): 129–153.

United Nations Development Programme (2010), *Millennium Development Goals and Climate Change Adaptation*, NewYork: UNDP-GEF.

United National Environment Programme (2009), *Commentary to the Guidelines for the Development of National Legislation on Access to Information, Public Participation and Access to Justice in Environmental Matters* [online]. Available at: www.unep.org/civil-society/Portals/59/Documents/Resources/Commentary-to-the-guidelines-for-the-development-of-national-legislation.pdf [accessed 6 July 2012].

United Nations Environment Programme (2011), *UNEP Ogoniland Oil Assessment Reveals Extent of Environmental Contamination and Threats to Human Health* [online]. Available at: www.unep.org/newscentre/Default.aspx?DocumentID=2649&ArticleID=8827&l=en [accessed 26 June 2012].

United Nations Food and Agriculture Organization (2010), *Special Programme for Food Security* [online]. Available at: www.fao.org/spfs [accessed 25 May 2012].

United Nations Office for Disaster Reduction (2007), *International Strategy for Disaster Reduction* [online]. Available at www.unisdr.org/we/advocate/drr-champions [accessed 26 July 2012].

United Nations Office for Environmental Risk Reduction (2007), *Terminology* [online]. Available at: www.unisdr.org/we/inform/terminology#letter-e [accessed 25 June 2012].

United States Food and Drug Administration (2007), *Building a Stronger Defense Against Bioterrorism*, Silver Spring: FDA.

United States General Accounting Office (1983), *Siting of Hazardous Waste Landfills and their Correlation with Racial and Economic Status of Surrounding Communities*, Washington, DC: General Accounting Office.

van Dijk, J. (1988), 'Introduction: The Rediscovery of the Crime Victim', in M. Maguire and J. Pointing (eds) , *Victims of Crime: A New Deal?*, Milton Keynes: Open University Press, 1–13.

van Dijk, J. (1998), 'A New Society of Victimology? A Letter from the President', *The Victimologist*, 1: 2–3.

van Dijk, J. and Letschert, R. (2011). 'Reconstructing Victim-centered Justice on a Global Scale', in R. Letschert and J. van Dijk (eds) , *The New Faces of Victimhood*, Dordrecht: Springer, 303–317.

Van Kammen, J., de Savigny, D. and Sewankambo, N. (2006), 'Using Knowledge Brokering to Promote Evidence-based Policy-making: The Need for Support Structures', *Bulletin of the World Health Organisation*, 84(8): 608–612.

Van Tassell, K. (2011), *Compensating Victims of Environmental Disasters* [online]. Available at: http://lawprofessors.typepad.com/healthlawprof_blog/2011/01/compensating-victims-of-environmental-disasters.html [accessed 6 July 2012].

Verkaik, R. (2001), 'Britain Now the World's Compensation Capital, with Payouts Set to Keep Rising' [online], *Independent*, 26 March. Available at: www.independent.co.uk/news/uk/crime/britain-now-the-worlds-compensation-capital-with-payouts-set-to-keep-rising-689105.html [accessed 3 May 2012].

Victim Support (2009), *2009–12 ... Building Our Future*, London: Victim Support.

Victim Support Europe (2009), *Projects Victims in Europe*, Utrecht: Victim Support Europe.

Vogel, D. (2003), 'The Hare and the Tortoise Revisited: The New Politics of Consumer and Environmental Regulation in Europe', *British Journal of Political Science*, 33: 557–580.

von Hentig, H. (1948), *The Criminal and His Victim*, New Haven: Yale University Press.

Wachholz, S. (2007), '"At Risk": Climate Change and its Bearing on Women's Vulnerability to Male Violence', in P. Beirne and N. South (eds) , *Issues in Green Criminology: Confronting Harms Against Environments, Humanity and Other Animals*, Cullompton; Willan, 161–185.

Walklate, S. (1994), 'Can There Be a Progressive Victimology?', *International Review of Victimology*, 3: 1–15.

Walklate, S. (2007a), 'Conclusions', in S. Walklate (ed.), *Handbook of Victims and Victimology*, Cullompton: Willan Publishing, 484–494.

Walklate, S. (2007b), *Imagining the Victim of Crime*, Maidenhead: Open University Press.

Walklate, S. (2012), 'Courting Compassion: Victims, Policy, and the Question of Justice', *Howard Journal of Criminal Justice*, 51(2): 109–121.

Walsh, A. and Ellis, L. (2007), *Criminology: An Interdisciplinary Approach*, Thousand Oaks: Sage.

Walters, R. (2006), 'Crime, Bio-agriculture and the Exploitation of Hunger', *British Journal of Criminology*, 46(1): 26–45.

Walters, R. (2010), 'Toxic Atmospheres: Air Pollution and the Politics of Regulation', *Critical Criminology*,18(4): 307–323.

Warner, K., Afifi, T., Dun, O., Stal, M. and Schmidl, S. (2008), *Human Security, Climate Change and Environmentally Induced Migration*, Bonn: United Nations University – Institute for Environment and Human Security.

Warren, K. (1997), *Ecofeminism: Women; Culture; Nature*, Bloomington: Indiana University Press.

Watts, H. (2008), 'The Health Benefits of Tackling Climate Change', *The Lancet Series on Climate Change*. Available at: www.wellcome.ac.uk/stellent/groups/corporatesite/@policy_communications/documents/web_document/wtx057673.pdf [accessed 26 June 2012].

Watts, J. (2010), 'In China's "Cancer Villages", Residents Pay the Price for a Dirty Revolution' [online], *Guardian*, 8 June, 21.

Weiss, E. (1995), 'Understanding Compliance with International Environmental Agreements: The Baker's Dozen Myths', *University of Richmond Law Review*, 32: 1555–1572.

Wemmers, J.-A. (1996), *Victims in the Criminal Justice System*, Amsterdam: Kugler Publications.

Wersig, G. (1993), 'Information Science: The Study of Postmodern Knowledge Usage', *Information Processing & Management*, 29(2): 229–239.

Wertham, F. (1949), *The Show of Violence*, New York: Doubleday Press.

Westra, L. (2009), *Environmental Justice and the Rights of Ecological Refugees*, Abingdon: Routledge Publishing.

Wheatley, M. (1997), 'Social and Cultural Impacts of Mercury Pollution on Aboriginal Peoples in Canada', *Water, Air & Soil Pollution*, 97(1–2): 85–90.

White, R. (2008a), *Crimes Against Nature: Environmental Criminology and Ecological Justice*, Cullompton: Willan Publishing.

White, R. (2008b), 'Depleted Uranium, State Crime and the Politics of Knowing', *Theoretical Criminology*, 12(1): 31–54.

White, R. (2009), *Environmental Crime: A Reader*, Cullompton: Willan Publishing.

White, R., ed. (2010), *Global Environmental Harm: Criminological Perspectives*, Cullompton: Willan Publishing.

White, R. (2011), *Transnational Environmental Crime: Towards an Eco-global Criminology*, Abingdon: Routledge Publishing.

Whitehead, R. and Block, W. (2003), 'Taking the Assets of Criminals to Compensate Victims of Violence: A Legal and Philosophical Approach', *Journal of Law and Society*, 5: 229–253.

Widmer, R., Oswald-Krapf, H., Sinha-Khetrwal, D., Schnellmann, M. and Boni, H. (2005), 'Global Perspectives on E-waste', *Environmental Impact Assessment Review*, 25(5): 436–458.

Williams, B. (1999), 'The Victims' Charter: Citizens as Consumers of Criminal Justice Services', *Howard Journal of Criminal Justice*, 38: 384–396.

Williams, C. (1996), 'An Environmental Victimology', *Social Science*, 23(1): 16–40. Reprinted in R. White (ed.) (2009), *Environmental Crime: A Reader*, Cullompton: Willan Publishing, 200–222.

Wilson, G. (2011), *Human Rights and Environment: The Case Law of the European Court of Human Rights in Environmental Cases*, Brno: Justice and Environment.

Wirth, J. (1996), 'The Trail Smelter Dispute: Canadians and Americans Confront Transboundary Pollution', *Environmental History*, 1(2): 34–51.

Wolfgang, M. (1958), *Patterns in Criminal Homicide*, New York: New York University Press.

Women's News Network (2010), *Climate Change, Poverty and Tourists put Maasai Daughters at Risk* [online]. Available at: http://womennewsnetwork.net/2010/04/16/kenya-climatechange-trafficking-892/ [accessed 25 May 2012].

World Health Organisation (2006), *Health Effects of the Chernobyl Accident: An Overview*. Available at: www.who.int/ionizing_radiation/chernobyl/backgrounder/en/index.html [accessed 26 June 2012].

World Health Organisation (2008a), *Air Quality and Health*, Fact Sheet no. 313. Available at: www.who.int/mediacentre/factsheets/fs313/en/index.html [accessed 26 June 2012].

World Health Organisation (2008b), *Quantification of the Health Effects of Exposure to Air Pollution Report of a WHO Working Group*, Bilthoven: WHO Regional Office for Europe.

Wright, P. (1998), '"Victims' Rights" as a Stalkinghorse for State Repression', *Journal of Prisoners on Prisons*, 9: 1–4.

Wyatt, J. (2010), 'Law-making at the Intersection of International Environmental, Humanitarian and Criminal Law: The Issue of Damage to the Environment in International Armed Conflict', *International Review of the Red Cross*, 92(879): 593–646.

Wybe, D. (1997), *The Precautionary Principle*, The Hague: T.M.C. Asser Institute.

Young, M. (1997), 'Ideological Trends Within the Victims' Movement: An International Perspective', in R. Davis, A. Lurigio and W. Skogan (eds) , *Victims of Crime*, 2nd edition, Thousand Oaks: Sage Publications, 115–126.

Yun, K., Lurie, M. and Hyde, P. (2010), 'Moving Mental Health into the Disaster-Preparedness Spotlight', *The New England Journal of Medicine*, 263:1193–1195.

Zhang, T. (2008), *Costs of Crime in Canada, 2008*, Ontario: Canadian Department of Justice.

Zimmerman, M. (2003), 'The Black Market for Wildlife: Combating Transnational Organized Crime in the Illegal Wildlife Trade', *Vanderbilt Journal of Transnational Law*, 36: 1657–1689.

Index